Mexico and the United States

Mexico and the United States

Managing the Relationship

EDITED BY

Riordan Roett

Westview Press
BOULDER & LONDON

The research for this book was sponsored by
The William and Flora Hewlett Foundation

Westview Special Studies on Latin America and the Caribbean

Copyright © 1988 by Westview Press, Inc.

Published in 1988 in the United States of America by Westview Press, Inc., 5500 Central Avenue, Boulder, Colorado 80301, and in the United Kingdom by Westview Press, Inc., 13 Brunswick Centre, London WC1N 1AF, England

Library of Congress Cataloging-in-Publication Data
Mexico and the United States: managing the relationship/edited by
  Riordan Roett.
    p.   cm.—(Westview special studies on Latin America and the
  Caribbean)
  Includes index.
  ISBN 0-8133-7658-0
  1. United States—Relations—Mexico. 2. Mexico—Relations—United
States. I. Roett, Riordan, 1938–   . II. Series.
F.183.8.M6M464 1988
303.4′8273′073—dc19

88-23644
CIP

Printed and bound in the United States of America

∞ The paper used in this publication meets the requirements of the American National
   Standard for Permanence of Paper for Printed Library Materials Z39.48-1984.

10   9   8   7   6   5   4   3   2   1

Contents

PART ONE
INTRODUCTION: MANAGING THE RELATIONSHIP

PART TWO
THE ECONOMIC AGENDA

PART THREE
KEY BILATERAL ISSUES

PART FOUR
CONCLUSION

Foreword

It has been said that the border between Mexico and the United States is more than just a dividing line between two countries. This is certainly so. The Mexican-U.S. border also marks the limit between the two Americas—the Latin and the Anglo-Saxon. But what makes this border so outstanding without a doubt is that it constitutes the separation between two contrasting worlds: the world of the industrialized countries and the world of the less developed countries. The fundamental line between Mexico and the United States is political and cultural: the border between societies with different degrees of economic development.

The Mexican-U.S. border is not only a dividing line, however. It is at the same time a point of convergence, a point of ever growing ties between these different worlds—two worlds with concrete expression in the United States and in Mexico. Indissolubly united by geography and almost inevitably linked by economic complementarity, Mexico and the United States have developed a growing relationship that goes beyond mere diplomatic formalities. This relationship has fostered an ever increasing economic interpenetration accompanied by social and cultural interpenetration. And this interpenetration has led to a need in each country for the other and a situation in which events in one has repercussions in the other. Analysts like to call this phenomenon interdependence.

Due to the difference in their economies and the asymmetry of power between the two countries, the importance of this interdependence is not equal. The United States is the richest and most powerful country in the world; Mexico is a less developed intermediate nation. The U.S. GNP in 1984 was US$3,670 billion, in contrast to Mexico's US$158 billion; per capita income in the United States in the same year was US$15,490, in contrast to Mexico's US$2,060.

The specific weight that the economic exchange has for each of the two countries is also markedly unequal. It is well known, for example, that the United States is Mexico's principal trade partner. But the point to be made here is that the United States is *by far* Mexico's most important trade partner, absorbing around 60% of

Mexican exports and producing 65% of Mexican imports. Mexico is only the third or fourth largest trading partner of the United States, with a much lower relative position: less than 6% of U.S. imports and exports.

Further, the difference in the qualitative importance that the bilateral commercial exchange has for the two countries should also be taken into consideration. Traditionally, Mexico has imported from the United States essential products such as basic foodstuffs, capital goods, and other high priority items for the economy. Consequently, any reduction in the import of these goods means either a reduction in the general growth rate, a socio-political problem, or both.

The United States, in contrast, has traditionally imported from Mexico various raw materials and certain nonessential agricultural items—goods that are either dispensable, easily substitutable, or purchasable from other countries. Even if trading with Mexico has been profitable for the United States, it is not as imperative for the U.S. economy as trade with the United States is for the Mexican economy.

I say traditionally, because the mix of Mexican goods imported into the United States has changed significantly during the last few years. During the early 1970s, manufactures gained importance and totalled more than 50% of imports coming from Mexico. In 1979, hydrocarbons surpassed every other product and accounted for more than 50% of all North American purchases from Mexico until the oil price collapse in 1986. From that date on, manufactures regained first place. It is worth noting that Mexican manufactures exported to the United States nowadays have become more complex; such is the case with the automobile industry, for example. Thus, the importance of Mexican imports to the United States has grown in the last years, at least from a qualitative point of view.

Another example of the unequal importance of the economic exchange for the two countries is tourism. The United States is the largest buyer of Mexican tourist services. In 1985, more than 4 million North American tourists visited Mexico, 85% of all visiting foreigners. Mexican visitors to the United States in 1985 totalled a little over two and a half million—the second largest number of tourists visiting that country. However, the number of visitors from Mexico is much lower than the number coming from Canada, occupying first place with ten and a half million visitors. Something similar can be said of other items such as foreign investment, finance, and technology transfers, where the differences are obvious and do not need to be demonstrated with figures.

The only item that operates in an inverse direction is human labor. Traditionally the United States has had an insatiable demand for foreign labor. A great portion of this demand has been, and continues to be, met by Mexico. Mexican workers have traditionally been a sort of regulator of the cheap labor market in the United States, constituting a reserve army for the North American market.

Beyond this economic and social interpenetration or interdependence, other elements of common interest link the two countries independent of the explicit policies of their governments. I refer to national security and political stability.

The first element relates to the good will that should preferably exist between neighbors. It is in the U.S. national interest, independent of both its politico-ideological system and its power, to have the good will of its neighbors rather than their enmity. There is, then, an objective element that dictates the need for basic understanding between neighbors and provides a framework for an atmosphere of good will and cooperation—even though it is well known that many of the bilateral problems are structural and cannot be solved by goodwill alone.

The other element of common interest for Mexico and the United States is their mutual political and economic stability. Within a bilateral relationship that is so intense and interdependent, economic or political instability in one of the two nations has repercussions in the bordering country, affecting its own stability and security. The fact that political stability in the United States seems to be a given does not invalidate this statement. Economic stagnation in the United States has had clear and pervasive effects on Mexico.

The other side of the coin is the issue of possible repercussions. The Mexican economic crisis affects the United States in several ways. A very clear effect is the reduction in Mexican imports. Another very clear effect is the increase in undocumented Mexican migration to the United States. But there is another effect which is without a doubt more important, if less easily perceived. This is the consequence or consequences for the United States were there to be a political upheaval in Mexico triggered by the deepening of the present economic crisis. I leave it up to the reader to imagine the different scenarios regarding the repercussions that such an upheaval would have in the United States.

The chapters that follow study the subject of interdependence between Mexico and the United States in detail and constitute a first effort to focus systematically on the relations between the two countries from this point of view.

Mario Ojeda, President
El Colegio de México

Preface

Mexico has been a model of political stability and economic growth for most of the last half century. As long as that situation lasted, U.S. interest in the country and its politics was minimal. The debt crisis in late 1982, and the sense that that period had come to an end, brought Mexico to the fore of U.S. national debate. Because of the complex, interdependent relationship between the two countries, the problems of each are now the problems of the other. The two countries are bound together not only by a 2,000-mile border—one the longest between any two countries in the world—but by several issues that directly affect both societies. These include Mexico's foreign debt, drug traffic and U.S. consumption, migration issues, and foreign policy differences.

Growing concern in the United States has not been accompanied, however, by a corresponding rise in the literature offering constructive policy alternatives for the two countries in the management of their relationship.

To help fill this gap, the Latin American Studies Program at The Johns Hopkins University School of Advanced International Studies, with the support of The William and Flora Hewlett Foundation, has conducted over the last two years a research project on U.S.-Mexican interdependence. This volume is the culmination of that project.

Mexican and North American analysts agree for the most part on which are the important issues in this interdependent relationship. They differ significantly, however, in their perception, analysis, and evaluation of these issues and their policy implications. In order to portray both this convergence and this divergence, we have asked a Mexican and a North American author to offer their views on the subjects discussed. Thus, this volume provides a balanced treatment of the U.S.-Mexican relationship, presenting a diversity of ideas and possible policy implications which significantly enrich the literature on the subject. All the authors have done extensive work on Mexico and U.S.-Mexican relations, and all are experts on their particular subjects.

Presidential elections are being held in 1988 both in the United States and in Mexico. Whatever the outcome of those elections, the incoming administrations will face the issues discussed here. After analyzing the background of each topic the authors present timely policy options for consideration by the incoming administrations in both countries. Solutions to the problems will not be easy or quick, but effective and sensitive handling of them will be essential if the two countries desire to manage their interdependent relationship successfully and pave the way for broader cooperation.

Lilia Ferro-Clérico, Coordinator
Mexico–United States Project
SAIS

Acknowledgments

The successful culmination of an effort of this type is always due to the collective work of a group of individuals, and it is impossible to acknowledge their work individually. There are those, however, without whose contribution this volume would not have been possible, and I would like to express to them my most sincere appreciation: Lilia E. Ferro-Clérico, the program coordinator of the Mexico-United States project, who directed the overall effort that has resulted in this volume of essays; Frederick Holborn, whose valuable critiques of every chapter are reflected in the authors' revisions; Felicity Skidmore, whose editing improved enormously the style and readability of our essays; and Anne McKinney, who devoted long hours to the preparation of the manuscript in all its stages. Finally, my deepest gratitude goes to Clint Smith and The William and Flora Hewlett Foundation. Without their support, this research project would not have been possible.

Riordan Roett

About the Contributors

Sergio Aguayo is professor of International Relations at El Colegio de México and a Visiting Senior Fellow at The Johns Hopkins University School of Advanced International Studies. This essay was written as part of ongoing research about Mexican national security made possible by a grant from the SSRC-MacArthur Program in International Peace and Security.

Bruce Michael Bagley is an Associate Professor of the Graduate School of International Studies (GSIS), University of Miami, Coral Gables, Florida. He is currently director of the Andean Studies Project at GSIS and Codirector of the Masters Degree Program of the Facultad Latinoamericana de Ciencias Sociales (FLACSO), Quito, Ecuador.

Norman A. Bailey is a private consultant. He served as Senior Director of International Economic Affairs and Special Assistant to the President for National Security Affairs, 1981–1983, and sits on the Boards of several companies and banks.

León Bendesky is currently research economist at the Instituto de Estudios de Estados Unidos at Centro de Investigación y Docencia Económicas (CIDE). He has a Ph.D. from Cornell University.

Brian Timothy Bennett is a partner in the consulting firm of Hagans/ Keys. From 1985 through July 1988 he was the Deputy Assistant U.S. Trade Representative for Mexico in the Office of the U.S. Trade Representative, Executive Office of the President. He was also one of the chief U.S. negotiators in the Uruguay Round of GATT negotiations in Geneva.

Jorge A. Bustamante is President of El Colegio de la Frontera Norte, a research and degree granting institute located in Tijuana, Mexico. He also holds The Eugene Conley Chair of Sociology at the University of Notre Dame.

José I. Casar is currently Deputy Director of the Instituto Latinoamericano para Estudios Transnacionales (ILET), Mexico. Formerly he was Deputy Director, Economics Department, Centro de Investigación y Docencia Económicas (CIDE).

Víctor M. Godínez is professor of economics at the Universidad Autónoma Nacional de México (UNAM) and Director of the Instituto de Esudios de Estados Unidos at the Centro de Investigación y Docencia Económicas (CIDE). He has a Doctorate Degree from the University of Paris.

José Juan de Olloqui, on leave from the Central Bank, is currently the Chief Executive Officer of the third largest financial group in Mexico, as well as a member of the board of several Mexican financial institutions. He has been Mexico's Ambassador to the United States and to Great Britian.

Riordan Roett is the Sarita and Don Johnston Professor and Director, Latin American Studies Program, The Johns Hopkins University School of Advanced International Studies (SAIS). He is former president of the Latin American Studies Association.

Michael S. Teitelbaum, by discipline a demographer, is Program Officer at the Alfred P. Sloan Foundation in New York and a Commisssioner of the U.S. Commission for the Study of International Migration and Cooperative Economic Development. In the recent past he has served on the faculties of Oxford University and Princeton University and as Staff Director of the Select Committee on Population, U.S. House of Representatives.

Thomas J. Trebat is Vice-President and Senior International Economist, Bankers Trust Company, New York. He has been actively involved in the negotiations between commercial banks and various Latin American countries, including Mexico, on the rescheduling of external debt.

Gregory F. Treverton is Senior Fellow at the Council on Foreign Relations. He has served as staff member for the first Senate Select Committee on Intelligence, as staff member responsible for Western Europe on the National Security Council during the Carter Administration, and as Director of Studies for the International Institute for Strategic Studies in London.

Samuel I. del Villar is professor of Constitutional Law at El Colegio de México. He coordinated with the 1982 Presidential Task Force in drafting its anticorruption program and served until September 1985 as Advisor on Special Affairs to President de la Madrid.

William Watts is President of Potomac Associates. He has served as senior staff member of the National Security Council and as a U.S. foreign service officer.

PART ONE

Introduction:
Managing the Relationship

1

Mexico and the United States: Managing the Relationship

Riordan Roett

The essays in this volume deal with the principal issues that affect the bilateral relations between Mexico and the United States. Efforts to date to manage the complex relationship between the two neighbors have achieved limited success. On questions of trade, there has been demonstrable progress. But on topics such as security and foreign policy, debt, drugs, and immigration, the record is bleak.

In analyzing the complexities of the relationship, it is crucial to include two considerations that are often overlooked or downplayed. The first is that the bilateral ties do not exist in a vacuum. The global economic and political context is highly relevant. The second is that the decision-making styles of the two governments have little in common. Both are superficially presidential and federal; but those words hold deep and significant differences in the two societies.

In this chapter I highlight the key global elements that need to be considered in any future management of the relationship. I also comment briefly on the issues of "style and substance" in the political systems of the two countries that aggravate even good faith efforts at managing complex policy issues. Finally, in an effort to understand the cross-cutting impact of the global environment and the political management challenge, I examine the current controversy over drugs. As the *New York Times* commented in early 1988, "What was once a vexing problem in narcotics law enforcement swells steadily into a first-order geopolitical peril, not only to Latin societies but now also to our own."[1] It may well be that the drug threat will emerge as the next critical policy issue between the two countries. But the drug issue is not just bilateral. It is clearly hemispheric. It involves matters of security and foreign policy. And it is the one divisive policy area in which it is probably fair to say that as much of the culpability rests with the United States as elsewhere, if not more.

The Global Environment

A number of global factors, over which Mexico has little influence, will determine the evolution of its economy in the coming decade. Most critical, perhaps, is the state of the United States economy. While the bilateral implications are clear, Mexican leaders are well aware that United States policy, to a large degree, determines world trends and developments. Carlos Salinas de Gortari, the PRI candidate in the July 1988 presidential elections in Mexico, has highlighted that concern. In an interview with James Reston, Salinas stated that

> you [the U.S.] have lived the past eight years in financial debt. When you live on debt, sooner or later you have to foot the bill. . . . The huge deficit you're running is because you want to have everything.[2]

Elsewhere the PRI candidate has said:

> I am very worried about the perspectives of the American economy . . . the debt problem in the United States, and about the commercial deficit and the United States balance of payments. I am watching very carefully the way in which you are attacking that problem and the repercussions it will have on the Mexican economy.[3]

These are real concerns for the next president of Mexico. It is fashionable in the United States to assume that other countries need not be worried about the state of the American economy. We now know that is an obscurantist position, although one maintained during the 1980s by many in the Reagan administration. From Mexico's perspective, the United States remains its largest trading partner. For the United States, Mexico is our third largest purchaser of American goods. Mexico is also the third largest supplier of crude oil to the United States. These economic and trade realities mean that any downturn in the American economy will have an immediate impact in Mexico.

Some of the implications are obvious. The minuscule progress of the United States to turn around the trade deficit has resulted in protectionist pressures. Protection threatens Mexico's exports and its capacity to earn the foreign exchange needed to service its US$108 billion foreign debt. A surge in American protectionism could impact negatively on the *maquilas*—the American assembly plants that operate across the Mexican border. The American firms take advantage of low wage rates and inexpensive transportation costs to assemble goods that are shipped back into the United States. There are already growing complaints from American labor unions that the *maquila* process takes jobs from American workers. Manufacturers in the United States who have not gone to Mexico, but produce the same or similar goods, argue that the *maquilas* are unfair competition.

An increase in American interest rates will have a damaging impact on the relations between Mexico and its creditors. The debt is a highly political issue in Mexico. The adjustment process that began in 1982 with the onset of the debt crisis has resulted in high unemployment, low or negative growth, and a dramatic drop in real wages and living standards for millions of Mexicans. If Mexico were confronted with a surge in interest rates, due to existing vulnerabilities in the American economy, a new phase of the debt crisis would erupt. Mexico's inflation rate in 1987 reached 159%; real wages have declined 50% over the last five years. These are economic realities that have a dangerous political component for the government of Mexico.

Salinas has commented that repayment of Mexico's debt must be linked to the achievement of "sustainable economic growth." He has also commented that "Mexico will pay if it can grow, because growth is an unquestionable necessity to Mexico."[4] The PRI candidate prefers "the word negotiation, strong negotiation, to open confrontation" over the debt; but he is clearly able to imagine a shift in the country's strategy if required: "what is considered impossible today may be possible tomorrow," Salinas has stated.[5]

On these two questions alone—trade and protectionism, and interest rates and debt management—the United States drives the dialogue. There is little that Mexico can do about either the trade deficit or monetary and fiscal decision making in Washington, D.C. But it is clear that the tranquil attitude of President Miguel de la Madrid will not be a model for the conduct of Salinas de Gortari. The issues are too political and too critical to the success of his administration and the overall legitimacy of the Mexican political system. The options that Salinas may pursue range from a series of debt reduction programs, to increased insistence on better terms in future negotiations, to more assertive collective action with other hemispheric countries to seek debt relief.

World Growth in the 1990s

While American decisions, or lack thereof, in the economic and financial areas have direct implications for Mexico, it is also important to understand that overall world economic performance will influence the future performance of the Mexican economy. But there appears to be a stalemate in the industrial countries' willingness to make the difficult decisions required to generate higher rates of growth in Organization for Economic Cooperation and Development (OECD) countries. World growth has been dwindling since the 1960s. It has now fallen well below what was once a "bottom line" of 3% each year. The West German government, fearful of an outburst of inflation, refuses to stimulate its economy and increase demand for foreign imports. Japan has been reluctant to step forward and exercise a leadership role by slashing its huge trade surplus, although recent data indicate a modest response to world pressure to do so. From Latin America's viewpoint, in the 1980s,

the United States was the only expanding market in the world. The surplus countries, mainly West Germany and Japan, were taking advantage of Latin America as a cheap commodity provider, but had no interest in increasing trade in manufactures and used their formal and informal barriers to keep the Latin products out.[6]

Continued low growth in Western Europe keeps demand for petroleum low, impacting on Mexico's foreign exchange earnings. Barriers to trade force Mexico and other Latin countries back into the United States market. But the threat of protectionism is on the rise as American producers and labor unions reject purchasing more goods from Mexican and other Latin American exporters. And pressures in Western Europe reinforce governments' protectionist stands. Low growth rates preclude the creation of new jobs and unemployment rates have climbed in Western Europe. The OECD has warned recently that the total employment in member countries was expected to grow at an annual rate of 1%–1.25% in 1988. But since the growth of employment was expected to be smaller than that of the workforce, the numbers of unemployed might increase further, to 31.5 million in 1988. Overall unemployment in Europe may creep up from 11% to 11.25%, with variations across the Common Market.[7]

Lack of growth in the OECD countries is a medium-term problem of real significance for Mexico and other Latin American countries. Absence of coordination on overall growth targets and appropriate macroeconomic policy among the industrial countries is something over which Mexico has little control, but for which it suffers in terms of a continuation of the debt crisis, limited export opportunities, and a continuing need for internal belt tightening.

A challenge of a different sort will emerge in 1992 when a truly common market will emerge in the European Economic Community. That development will have an impact on both Mexico and the United States. By 1992, the Community hopes to eliminate remaining trade barriers within the 12-nation entity. The nations also hope to eliminate the differing industrial standards that raise production costs and create trade barriers.

The reduction in inefficiencies should help cut costs for companies and prices for consumers. That, in turn, should spur Europe's sluggish economy and help make European companies more competitive against American and Japanese industry. While today's problem for the hemisphere with Europe is protectionism and low growth, it may change in the mid-1990s. A more competitive Europe will be a draw, theoretically, for Mexican goods but will probably emerge as a competitor in both U.S. and other foreign markets.

Implications for Mexico

As Minister of Budget and Planning during the administration of President de la Madrid, Carlos Salinas de Gortari is viewed correctly as the architect of the government's economic program. That program has emphasized liberalization and a greater integration into the world economy; but it also has been buffeted continuously by global factors. Since Salinas' nomination in October 1987, the government has had to deal with the crisis in global financial markets. That crisis exacerbated the already fragile financial situation in Mexico which had been caused, in part, by government policies in the preceding months. When the worldwide crisis occurred, the Mexican stock market took the steepest plunge of all. The government has had to adopt two drastic Mexican *peso* devaluations. And a new sweeping austerity program has been implemented.

The global dimension to Mexico's economic dilemma is obvious. Issues such as interest rates, OECD growth, new investment, trade patterns, and commodity prices, among the most critical, are issues that are determined outside Mexico. While Mexico has made impressive progress in adjustment and liberalization since 1982—and while it is recognized that there is more to do—the global environment, the absence of leadership in the industrial countries, and the overhang of debt pose an increasing level of political risk for the Mexican government. The industrial countries should not be surprised if the Salinas regime is far less complacent about adjustment without a concomitant commitment by the industrial countries to view the dilemma of Mexico and Latin America as intimately linked to world recovery and growth in the 1990s. In his acceptance speech on October 4, 1987, Salinas vowed to devote his energies to the construction of the "new Mexican economy." He said that his objective was to build a "more competitive" economy, "stronger in relation to the outside world, with a greater capacity for savings, investment, and the generation of jobs."[8]

To accomplish these goals will require considerable support from the industrial countries, led by the United States. There are strong voices in Mexico that argue for a return to state-led policies of subsidies, protection of the internal market, and less—not more—integration with the world economy. Salinas has signalled his preference for integration, a reduction of his country's dependence on oil, and a diversification of its export base. But to the degree that inflationary pressures in Mexico remain high and real wages continue to plummet, he will face strong pressures from labor and the party to "protect" and not to "open" Mexico. The United States needs to be sensitive to those pressures and consider what policies are appropriate in the bilateral relationship to foster greater integration. But that will require aggressive global leadership also, in which the United States will need to review its own priorities and policies before it will be able to hold out the possibility of real improvement and progress for Mexico.

The Political Consequences

A critical link needs to be made between Mexico's economic performance and the stability of its political system. As Jorge G. Castañeda has commented:

> Mexico's overriding political problem stems from a simple and unalterable fact: the system, which has been traditionally clumsy in its handling of the middle classes, can no longer deliver the economic growth and prosperity that these classes now expect as a matter of course. At the same time, the political system does not feel it can grant them the additional measure of democracy which might be an acceptable alternative. Political wisdom dictates that one does not open up a political system in the midst of a severe economic crisis. Not, in any case, if one wishes to remain in power.[9]

The Mexican regime's longstanding legitimacy and stability has required better-than-average economic growth levels. The economy has been in crisis since 1982. The need to renew growth levels in the 1990s is imperative. If the global outlook is grim, and the possibilities of continued dynamic integration in the world economy are limited, Mexico will have little choice but to consider other alternatives. These might include limitations of foreign debt payments, profit remittance restrictions, and related options.

The outward migration from Mexico has traditionally reflected the absence of relative economic opportunity at home. But since the crisis, many argue that the absence of opportunity is absolute. Not only are the lower income groups emigrating; but the middle class, the country's professionals, are now leaving. And they are taking with them not only their financial resources, but most importantly, their know-how and their leadership potential. The Salinas administration will need to address this issue. Not only does low economic growth endanger the economic future of the country, it also endangers its political future.

The calls by Salinas for political modernization seek to address the issue that Castañeda raises. Can the regime afford to liberalize politically? Clearly, Salinas is seeking a way to maintain support for the system while recognizing legitimate demands for participation and representation. But those demands will be nearly impossible to deal with in the absence of economic growth. The United States needs to realize that discussions of trade and investment policies, and schemes to relieve the debt burden such as the Morgan Guaranty bond program of late 1987, are seldom viewed in Mexico in narrow economic or financial terms.[10] They are all political issues that impinge on the survival of the PRI-dominated political system. American policy makers need to be keenly aware of the linkage in Mexico between economics and politics. That linkage is strong in all societies. But in Mexico, it has been the *raison d'être* of the regime for decades. In the absence of a democratic state, the institutionalized revolutionary system has delivered the economic goods. It can no longer do so—under present conditions. Either those conditions will change or the stability of the system will be challenged:

> Mexico's famed political stability has not been destroyed by the country's current economic crisis. But that stability can no longer be taken for granted. . . . though the consequences of a breakdown in the political system would be chiefly domestic, there would be grave repercussions for the United States.[11]

That reality provides a strong imperative for the United States seeking measures that will provide "space" for the needed transitions in Mexico. Those transitions are both economic and political; and they will not take place peacefully unless Mexico receives strong support from the global system as well as the government of the United States.

Decisionmaking Styles

The global context of future relations between Mexico and the United States is a key factor in determining the capacity of each to manage its relationship with the other. But as important is a realistic understanding of how management is carried out within each other's political system. Each has a distinctive style of governance. Superficially, the institutions seem similar, even parallel. But the substance is profoundly different. Neither one will change measurably in the coming decade, although there is a dynamic in each that responds to internal pressures and new policy needs. And the differences should not be used as an excuse to forgo progress in settling outstanding issues and managing those that are ongoing irritants or new topics that emerge on the agenda. Mexico needs to understand that the U.S. policy process is far from being either predictable or coherent. The American constitution guarantees an uneasy imbalance between chief executive and the Congress. Increasingly, the 50 states of the union have defined their own policy goals as they relate to trade, investment, technology, and immigration. Pressure groups, a legitimate and time-honored institution, lobby on a daily basis in Washington, D.C. and in 50 state capitals—to modify, influence, or negate legislative and administrative options and outcomes. And all these elements are at play, and interacting, simultaneously.

American policymaking is a bureaucratic process—or morass. Bureaucrats interpret and apply the laws. They determine U.S. policy on a day-to-day basis, they are the web of continuity across, and through, administrations. Efforts to change the bureaucracy are frustrating and slow, and generally fall short of any president's goals. The difference between domestic policy and foreign policy is more and more blurred in the United States. Trade and investment questions are now matters of daily concern to American trade unions, small manufacturers, and others. The work of civil rights groups and human rights activists regarding Mexican migrants cuts across both domestic concerns and foreign policy considerations. The activities of the various church groups in the United States, while domiciled in the United States, have direct consequences for our relations with Mexico. And these are activities over which neither the president nor the Congress can exercise very much control. The pluralist passion of American political and economic life guarantees autonomy for these groups. That passion permeates the executive and legislative branches. It characterizes the work not only of bureaucrats but of legislative committees and subcommittees, autonomous agencies, and other entities. Fragmentation and the right of opposition, of defiance at times, is protected within the law.

Mexico, in sharp contrast, concentrates decision making in the hands of the President of the Republic. The legislature, either national or state-level, has little to say about the flow of decisions. Lobbying in Mexico, and throughout Latin America, is viewed with distrust at best, and is often thought to border on the illegal. The national interests of Mexico are, of course, defined by a group larger than the president; but it is a secretive process that gives undue emphasis to key actors in the Mexican revolutionary family whose membership shifts glacially from *sexenio* to *sexenio*. But the purpose is always the same—to restrict access and to husband power over events at the center of the political system. David Ronfeldt has captured the essence of the system:

> Mexico is not only the scene of multiple crises. It is also the scene of multiple *luchas* (struggles) that involve the top elites and institutions, *luchas* that would exist even if there were no sense of crisis. These *luchas* include, for example, those over power within the political elite, the definition of the "national project," the State's role in the economy, the federal government's centralized control over northern Mexico, the modernization (but probably not the democratization) of the PRI and the political party system, and Mexico's participation in the international economy.[12]

Salinas has spoken eloquently of the need for political reform in Mexico during his presidential campaign. But it is well understood that those efforts are not to be seen as undermining the basic control and legitimacy of the PRI-dominant system. Salinas also has stated that his administration will be one of "continuity in principles and institutions and change in form and methods."[13] The PRI candidate has said that "modern politics demand clean elections and I reject the old thesis of the 'clean sweep.'"[14] But few observers of the political process in Mexico believe this will result in a significant weakening of the PRI itself. It may well be the best manner of actually guaranteeing the continuation of the current system. An enlarged space for the political opposition, a lessening of the tight grip on all aspects of the electoral process, could yield high benefits in terms of popular support for Salinas and his government.

With the emergence of the complicated agenda that is addressed in this volume of essays—immigration, trade, drugs, investment, debt, foreign policy—the two decision-making systems are bound to create confusion in both capitals. Americans often assume that a Mexican president can "order" anyone to do anything. But it is precisely the complicated network of power relationships within the revolutionary family that forces presidents in Mexico to move cautiously, responding to pressures within the system that are processed personally, not institutionally.

On the other side, Mexicans assume that American presidents can "order" a policy outcome—if they really want to do so. The layers of decision making, the potential vetoes, and the constant intervention of domestic pressure groups delay and divert the efforts by the U.S. chief executive to control events. America is an institutionalized system that precludes "divine intervention" from above. It needs to be understood in Mexico that if a Senator Helms decides to hold hearings about immigration policy, there is nothing the White House can do and, indeed, the executive branch must cooperate or face a confrontation with the Congress. When the governor of a border state in the American Southwest argues for or against a particular policy, he is speaking as an independent political actor with a powerful local constituency.

As well, the United States needs to comprehend that the policy-making process in Mexico is not a simplistic one. It includes real competition between party and government. There are significant generational differences within the party. Pressures from the more "modern" sectors of society, based primarily in the Northern border states, argue for more rapid liberalization. Organized labor and its powerful leader, Fidel Velasquez, need to be included in any policy equation. All of these, and many additional, factors are part of the policy process. While it appears that the Mexican chief executive orders things to be done unencumbered by checks and balances, that assumption is far from accurate. As one commentator has noted:

> there are in fact substantial institutional limits on the powers of the president. The greatest constraint is the political heritage of the Mexican revolution, institutionalizing political succession . . . political freedoms of speech and assembly are relatively unencumbered . . . organized groups are able to participate actively in politics, and not only through the PRI . . . the leadership is centralized, but it is also institutionally routinized, and regular turnover is assured.[15]

To achieve any significant level of management of the bilateral agenda in the 1990s, both countries will need to spend a good deal more time understanding the political and economic institutional framework within which each must operate. And the issue of management is critical. It is not resolution that is the key policy goal—

although resolving issues is desirable. It is to preclude sudden flare-ups of crisis, to avoid useless posturing about key policy elements, to seek accommodation. To achieve that goal, to actually learn to manage the relationship, will require the next two administrations to overcome stereotypes, exaggerated expectations, and cultural differences. It will necessitate a steady and permanent process of consultation and negotiation. In spite of great differences on questions of trade, the November 1987 agreement between the two countries demonstrates that it can be done. That approach to problem-solving needs to be translated into other policy arenas in the coming decade to assure that the bilateral relationship, by the year 2000, has matured and policymakers have learned to recognize policy differences as natural and as susceptible to political management. As Salinas de Gortari commented to James Reston:

> we need better knowledge of each other. Two countries with such a tremendous difference in their levels of living, with one of the longest borders in the world and with 22 million crossing a year—there is always the possibility of a difficult relationship. With knowledge and openness, we need to deal with trade, finances, but also migration, drugs, and, today, the difficulties in Central American policies.[16]

Managing Drugs in the Bilateral Relationship

The issue of drug trafficking has become the most contentious bilateral issue between the United States and Mexico. As it becomes obvious that both the United States and its neighbors have become imperiled by the powerful drug mafia, the role of Mexico as a point of transit has arisen as a major bone of contention. The drug issue has a highly emotional component also, since the torture and murder of Drug Enforcement Administration agent Enrique Camarena Salazar in 1985. Mexican law enforcement officials have been directly implicated in his murder and their links to the drug mafia are widely suspected.

The Camarena murder set off a process of mutual recrimination between the two countries that continues today. In 1986, Senator Jesse Helms organized a series of hearings before the Foreign Relations subcommittee that he chaired. The U.S. Customs Commissioner and other high ranking members of the administration excoriated the Mexican government for its failure to act to control both the flow of drugs and the corruption that resulted from the billions of U.S. dollars involved in the illegal shipments to the United States.

That year, William von Raab, the Customs Commissioner, was quoted as saying that "the drug situation is a horror story, increasing logarithmically, and Mexico is doing nothing about it."[17]

In response to growing concern in the United States, the Congress passed the Omnibus Drug Enforcement, Education and Control Act of 1986. The legislation includes augmented provisions for sanctions. It mandates that various types of foreign assistance provided by the United States to countries which fall into the category of major drug producers or traffickers will be withheld from an individual country unless the president certifies that the specific country has cooperated fully with the United States and has taken "adequate steps" against illicit drugs. One-half the earmarked assistance is automatically withheld at the beginning of the fiscal year, pending presidential certification. The other half would be halted if the president fails to certify or Congress disapproves the certification.

In its 1987 annual report to Congress on the global narcotics situation, the Department of State described the situation in Mexico:

> Mexico continues to be the major single source country for the production, processing and trafficking of heroin and marijuana entering the United States. Mexico's crisis with its concomitant falling living standards, declining government revenues, growing rural poverty and scarcity of domestic credit works to the advantage of drug traffickers while undercutting efforts directed at them. Despite Mexican and U.S. remedial measures, corruption and inefficiencies in the eradication campaign still impede efforts to reduce the flow of drugs to the United States from Mexico.[18]

In spite of that dour assessment, the president certified that Mexico was making progress. The appropriate committees in Congress reviewed the White House decision carefully and accepted it with great reluctance. In 1988, the situation was similar; even though the administration was pessimistic, it decided for certification to avoid a further exacerbation of the relationship. The revelation of the widespread infiltration of drugs in Panama, Honduras, and other countries in recent months has further highlighted the need for vigorous and urgent policy initiatives.

Although the focus in the United States is on Mexico and other Latin American producers and suppliers, there is another side to the story. The crux of the drug trafficking issue is more that of consumption—demand—than it is of supply, serious students of the problem have argued (see Chapter 12 for further discussion). As long as Americans are willing to pay billions of dollars a year for "recreational" drugs, the supply will always exist. Slowly, it has become obvious that what the Mexicans have been saying is in great part true. Yes, Mexico shares the responsibility for drug trafficking. Corruption has bred contempt for the law in Mexico and high-ranking officials of the armed forces, the police, and state governments are implicated. But the question, in Mexico and elsewhere in Latin America, always returns to that of North American demand. The *New York Times*, in addressing the origins of the drug problem, has commented in a recent editorial that "it is . . . the huge American appetite for illegal narcotics. Without billions of American consumer dollars, the vast illicit enterprise could not long be sustained."[19]

As early as 1986, the chief of the Drug Enforcement Administration, John C. Lawn, had stated that "law enforcement cannot, did not, and will not solve the appetite for drugs in this country."[20] Lawn called on the federal government to reduce the demand for drugs through education and treatment programs and not rely primarily on the police and federal agents.

The DEA position was echoed in the same year by one of Mexico's specialists on the drug trade when he commented:

> consumers of illegal drugs in the United States spend some $110 billion on drugs each year—almost 3 percent of the gross national product and twice the American oil bill. . . . the international narcotics market begins with the decision to consume drugs by tens of millions of people in the United States and is fueled by countless peasants and farmers in Latin America and Asia who respond to that demand. Between them is a vast organized crime network.[21]

In spite of these warnings, by both Mexicans and North American officials, the U.S. government's "war" on drugs had all but died by 1988. As Robert M. Morgenthau recently stated:

> the Federal war on drugs, announced with great fanfare in October 1986, has failed. The rhetoric then was robust: We were promised the 'total commitment of the American people and their Government to fight the evil of drugs.' The reality has been far different. The Administration has actually reduced the Federal monies available for treatment and local law enforcement, and has failed to impose sanctions on drug exporting countries.[22]

United States policy on drug trafficking is adrift. Instead of policy, the administration has used rhetoric and moral indignity to castigate the drug-exporting countries. Of course, there is culpability on the part of Mexico and others. But the United States has refused to recognize that a major part of the problem is internal, that it begins with American consumption. To fail to understand that fact, and to confront it, makes the management of drug trafficking almost impossible.

At the February 1988 summit between the two presidents, the drug issue surfaced, inevitably. One senior official commented, at the summit, that "if you measure by the flow of drugs, and that really is the bottom line, the flow of drugs is increasing."[23] Ironically, when asked whether or not the Mexicans were correct in criticizing the United States for doing little to curb consumption, the official responded that "I think one has to say they're right."[24] President Reagan reinforced that opinion in a radio address: "the traffickers would go out of business if people quit buying illegal drugs. That's the real solution."[25]

Consumption is the crux of the matter from Mexico's perspective. Mexicans interviewed in 1986 were asked "what do you consider to be the worst thing about the United States?" The highest response group, 20%, stated "drug addiction and trafficking." When asked "how serious a problem do you think the use of illegal drugs like heroin and cocaine is in the United States?" 83% responded "very serious," with another 15% saying "serious."[26] As William Watts clearly documents in Chapter 10, this is a mirror image of how North Americans view Mexican society.

Drugs stand out as the best example of how little attention has been given to one of the most vexing bilateral issues. It combines a cynicism and moral superiority on the part of the United States that is well understood in Mexico. And it demonstrates, to Mexico at least, that the United States is unwilling to relate drug trafficking not only to internal consumption at home but to the underdevelopment of the Mexican economy. Drugs play an important role in producing jobs and income. Inexorably, the trafficking leads to corruption and influence peddling. And, increasingly, they leave a country like Mexico open to infiltration by the large drug cartels that now dominate the trade.

A final aspect of the drug issue needs careful attention. Most Mexican analysts fail to grasp the growing concern in the United States about drug trafficking. At all levels of society in the United States there is awareness, fear, and anger. And Mexico is the object of those emotions. The certification provision in the 1986 Drug Law may well be a "time bomb." Some year in the near future, the Congress will reject a president's efforts to certify Mexico in compliance and vote to decertify.

That decision, in turn, will create consternation in Mexico. The outraged reaction of the Mexican government will express the widespread perception that the United States has refused to appreciate all that Mexico has done to curb drug trafficking. And it will favor the drug dealers who will take advantage of the polarization between the two countries to increase the trade. It is imperative that Mexico's elites recognize how significant drugs are—and will be—in domestic American politics in the 1990s.

The drug issue demonstrates how emotion-laden and how difficult the management issue is—and will be. Management, in this case, as in the case of immigration, requires political leadership. Leadership needs to seek changes in attitudes and behavior in the United States. Without that component of policy, rhetoric and grandstanding will accomplish little other than to further contribute to the deterioration of the bilateral ties between the two societies.

Conclusion

With the election in 1988 of new presidents in the two countries, another opportunity becomes available to refocus the policymaking process to address the bilateral agenda. But both chief executives and their key aides will need to separate rhetoric from reality. The reality is that the two countries are confronted by a complex agenda that neither can cancel or dominate. The issue is *how* they handle that agenda—not whether they do or not. That must be the *first* pillar of any bilateral relationship.

The *second* pillar must be an understanding on the part of both parties that, issue by issue, the weight of "blame" will shift back and forth across the border. It is less relevant to engage in a spate of name calling, or placing of blame, than to recognize that neither government possesses absolute wisdom in seeking to deal with the agenda.

The *third* pillar must be a recognition on the part of both parties that the problems are increasingly interrelated and urgent. Mexico must earn foreign exchange if it is to service its debt. Migrants from Mexico are increasingly needed to supplement a dwindling American labor force. The oil reserves of Mexico are key to our strategic stockpile. American technology is crucial to Mexico's next stage of industrial development. And so it goes. Interdependence. And interdependence will require careful, continuous management. Conflicts will occur. Differences of opinion will erupt, from time to time, in peculiar ways. But if the structures of negotiation and mediation are in place, and are employed for both large and small issues, the 1990s may see the management challenge become routinized.

The immediate agenda for the two administrations must focus, *first,* on a mutual program of drug control. That will require careful coordination with Colombia and other countries in the region. It will necessitate substantial amounts of money—and leadership from the United States. *Second,* the positive record on trade negotiations must continue. Ongoing negotiations should identify a "step-ladder" approach; a positive decision by one government should lead to a reciprocal move in an area of importance to the other. *Third,* the United States must continue its fight against protectionism to guarantee access to the American market for Mexican exports. *Fourth,* alternative forms of debt management will be required in the 1990s. The United States must understand that debt relief, not necessarily forgiveness, is in our interest as much, if not more, than that of Mexico.

Fifth, technology is a new frontier to be explored by the two countries. Mexico will need increasingly sophisticated amounts and kinds of technology. The United States is a logical supplier and partner in the next step of Mexico's economic development. *Sixth,* the immigration issue needs to be depoliticized. Americans need to understand that the Mexican-American community is American—and that it is here to stay. Moreover, the United States labor market will require increasing numbers of foreign workers in the 1990s—the majority will undoubtedly be Mexican. *Finally,* foreign policy and security interests will require subtle and continuous discussion. Mexico has legitimate interests in Central America and in the Caribbean, specifically. Obviously, the United States has similar concerns. The two states need to accommodate each other's interests and explore mechanisms of collaboration that will facilitate better management of the foreign policy and national security agendas of the two countries. Moreover, it is not only the bilateral agenda that is of growing relevance. There is a wide range of multilateral issues that require attention. These include divergent views over U.S. security policy in Central America and U.S. dismay at Mexican opposition (in votes at the United Nations and its specialized organizations) to U.S. policy.

This is not an impossible set of goals as a beginning. But it will require a change in mentality in the United States. That change needs to recognize that Mexico is our neighbor, not only geographically, but in terms of security, trade, and investment. And Mexico is our partner in seeking to resolve contentious issues such as drug trafficking, illegal immigration, and other high priority policy questions. How can we ensure that Mexico will be given an appropriate place on the foreign policy agenda of the next North American president? It is not far fetched to argue that after U.S. relations with the Soviet Union, Japan, and China, Mexico is next. But this geopolitical and economic reality is not obvious to U.S. foreign policy elites. As the two countries begin to make modest but continuous progress on these and related matters, it may well be that they will begin to reduce the space and lack of understanding between what have been very "distant neighbors."[27]

Notes

1. "The Drug Flames Rise Higher," *New York Times*, March 3, 1988.

2. James Reston, "Salinas: 'Let's Be More Open,'" *New York Times*, February 13, 1988.

3. Larry Rohter, "Mexican Candidate Ties Repayment of Foreign Debt to Economic Growth," *New York Times*, January 18, 1988.

4. *Ibid.*

5. *Ibid.*

6. Clyde H. Farnsworth, "Debt of Latins Making Trade Links Tortuous," *New York Times*, December 26, 1987.

7. Ian Davidson, "OECD Issues Warning on Rate of Job Creation," *Financial Times*, October 1, 1987.

8. Larry Rohter, "Mexico's Nominee Welcomed," *New York Times*, October 12, 1987.

9. Jorge G. Castañeda, "Mexico at the Brink," *Foreign Affairs*, Winter 1985/86, Vol. 64, No. 2, p. 289.

10. In late 1987, the United States and Mexico announced an innovative scheme to retire up to US$20 billion of Mexico's US$105 billion foreign debt. It called for Washington to make a special issue of up to US$10 billion of zero coupon U.S. Treasury securities to Mexico for which Mexico would pay US$2 billion. With Morgan Guaranty Trust of New York acting as its agent, Mexico offered to repurchase at a discount from its bank creditors outstanding public sector loans which the banks had made to Mexico.

In return the banks were to receive a new 20-year security, the principal of which would be secured by the U.S. Treasury zero coupon bond. The new bond will pay interest with Mexico responsible for the interest payments.

After an initial show of interest, Mexico only bought back US$3.7 billion of its bank loans with US$2.6 billion of the new bonds. That represented a helpful, but not major, reduction of US$1.1 billion in Mexico's outstanding debt.

11. Castañeda, *op. cit.*, p. 287.

12. David Ronfeldt, "Questions and Cautions About Mexico's Future," *The Rand Corporation*, P/7321, March 1987, p. 5.

13. Larry Rohter, "Waiting Game is Over in Mexico as Presidential Choice is Named," *New York Times*, October 5, 1988.

14. David Gardiner, "Salinas Drops Election Bombshell," *Financial Times*, October 26, 1987.

15. Van R. Whiting, Jr., "State Strength and Regime Resilience: Sources of Mexico's Endurance," The University of Connecticut/Brown University, *Occasional Papers in Latin American Studies*, no date, p. 4.

16. Reston, *op. cit.*

17. Joel Brinkley, "U.S. Officials Denouncing Mexico for Huge Rise in Drug Trafficking," *New York Times*, May 12, 1986.

18. "International Narcotics Control Strategy Report," Washington, D.C., U.S. Department of State, March 1987, p. 148.

19. "A Hemisphere at Risk From Drugs," *New York Times*, February 20, 1988.

20. Peter Kerr, "Top Drug Agent Chides Congress on Border Plan," *New York Times*, September 19, 1986.

21. Samuel I. del Villar, "Cooperate Against Drugs," *New York Times*, July 1, 1986.

22. Robert M. Morgenthau, "We Are Losing the War on Drugs," *New York Times*, February 16, 1988.

23. Steven V. Roberts, "President Meets with Mexico Chief; Signs Textile Pact," *New York Times*, February 14, 1988.

24. *Ibid.*

25. *Ibid.*

26. William Stockton, "Mexicans, in Poll, View U.S. as Friend," *New York Times*, November 17, 1986.

27. A reference to the insightful volume by Alan Riding, *Distant Neighbors: A Portrait of the Mexicans* New York, Vintage Books, 1986.

PART TWO

The Economic Agenda

2

Foreign Investment in Mexico

Norman A. Bailey
with the assistance of Susan Aaronson

Mexico is uniquely placed to attract massive foreign investment. Yet the desire to maintain its own political, cultural, and economic identity independent from the colossus to the north has limited Mexican acceptance of foreign direct investment as a source of development capital.

Background

There have been four distinct periods in the history of the financing of economic growth in Mexico. During the first half century of the republic Mexico relied upon external bond issues, which were often defaulted upon and which led to frequent foreign diplomatic and military interventions. The most famous and curious example was the episode of the brief empire of the Austrian Archduke Maximilian, installed and sustained by French bayonets. Most of the money thus raised was wasted through international war, internal civil disorder, and corruption.

The second period (known as the *Porfiriato*) was dominated by General Porfirio Díaz (1876–1910). It was characterized by heavy foreign direct investment primarily in mining, petroleum, and plantation agriculture, and by borrowing for railroad and telegraph expansion. Economic development was rapid but very uneven, in terms of both geographic dispersion and income distribution.

Political, social, and economic distortions led to the Mexican revolution, in which at least a million persons died. For four decades after the final consolidation of the new political and social structure of Mexico in 1929 (accompanied externally by the Great Depression, rampant protectionism, and World War II), Mexico financed rapid and relatively balanced economic growth largely through the generation and application of domestic resources.

In recent years, due to the inadequate use of revenues from vast newly identified and exploited petroleum resources, which could and should have led to an even more effective use of internally generated resources, Mexico again resorted to extensive foreign borrowing, this time primarily from banks. A substantial portion of the resulting funds was dissipated in capital flight and corruption rather than in the modernization and rationalization of Mexico's domestically oriented and overprotected industry.

Since mid-1982 Mexico has been unable to service its external debt in a normal fashion and has been subject to periodic reschedulings and renegotiations, while adopting highly restrictive economic and financial programs. The impact of these developments on both domestic and foreign investment, except for the *Maquila* program (see Graphs 2.1 and 2.2), has been very negative and has led to extensive foreign disinvestment, as illustrated in the accompanying graphs.

Paradoxically, the same recent developments may eventually increase the level and impact of foreign investment in the Mexican economy. The government has recognized that foreign capital can be usefully directed toward development without displacing Mexican investors. As a result, Mexico is increasingly facilitating investment through eased regulatory and bureaucratic hurdles and lower administrative costs. For example, under the 1986–1987 commercial bank debt rescheduling, credits can be converted to equity. The government will buy Mexican debt acquired at a discount from private banks to encourage new investments. Furthermore, the announcement of the nomination of Carlos Salinas de Gortari as the ruling party's presidential candidate in 1988 reinforces the Mexican government's commitment to continue economic restructuring and private sector growth.

Salinas is widely credited with developing policies to decrease Mexican subsidies and import protection. These policies have forced Mexican manufacturers to improve their products to compete effectively. According to Salinas, his objective is to build "a more competitive economy, stronger in relation to the outside world, with a greater capacity for savings, investment and the generation of jobs."[1] To succeed at these priorities Salinas must aggressively attack inflation. At the same time, he must balance the benefits of a low Mexican *peso* exchange rate with its potential negative impact on inflation and consequently, political support for his program. Foreign investment, if shrewdly utilized, can be a key tool in the next administration's policy mix. Recently, the presidential candidate announced the formation of a new Foreign Affairs Commission of the governing party,

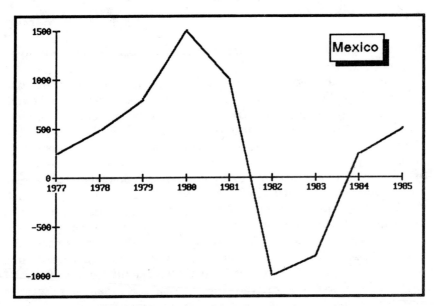

Graph 2.1 U.S. Direct Investment Abroad
Capital Outflows (inflows [-]) (millions of dollars)

Sources: U.S. Department of Commerce and Banco de México

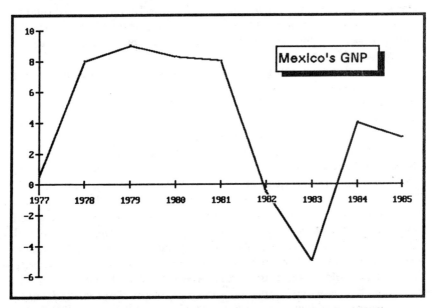

Graph 2.2 Mexico's GNP Growth Rate (based on constant pesos of 1970)

Sources: U.S. Department of Commerce and Banco de México

heavily weighted on the economic side and including representatives of the private sector.[2]

Mexico has a wide range of positive attributes in competing for investment capital. Its proximity to the world's largest market, political stability, good ports on both the Atlantic and Pacific coasts, and low-cost plentiful labor, are key incentives. The country also has a well-developed financial and physical infrastructure, as well as a domestic market with over 80 million potential consumers. Sound economic management and control of inflation would increase the real wages of Mexican workers, declining since 1983, in turn increasing their demand for locally produced goods and services. Finally the government has recently undertaken dramatic efforts to restructure the economy to play by the rules held dear by many of its major trading partners and bankers, including GATT membership, which it had resisted for years. However, the stock market crash of October 1987 and continuing high inflation and interest rates may damage Mexican and foreign investor confidence in the economy.

Foreign Direct Investment

As of year end 1987, accumulated foreign direct investment in Mexico amounted to approximately US$21.5 billion, a small figure considering the potential. The U.S. accounted for 63% of this total. Most of the investment was concentrated in the electronics, automobile, and food-stuff industries.[3]

Inward foreign investment flows have begun to inch up toward the levels attained before the Mexican debt crisis. Actual foreign direct investment increased from US$259 million in 1985 to US$357 million in 1986. Banco de México attributed most of the inflow to new investments, since the net intercompany financing was relatively low. During 1987, authorized foreign investment projects amounted to US$3.8 billion, an increase of US$1.4 billion over 1986.[4]

All foreign direct investment in Mexico is regulated under the 1973 *Law to Promote Mexican Investment and Regulate Foreign Investment.* The law delineates activities reserved to the state, based on a strategic rationale, and other activities where foreign investment is limited. Activities reserved for the Mexican government include petroleum and other hydrocarbon production, basic petrochemicals, mining, railroads, wireless communications, electricity, and the like. Thus, many of the principal industrial sectors may not have foreign equity participation. Activities reserved for Mexican public and private investors include radio and television transmission, air and maritime transportation, domestic transportation, and transportation on Federal

Highways. Finally, certain sectors are reserved for majority Mexican participation. These include exploitation and use of minerals and the manufacture of automotive components.[5]

The Mexican government believes that the remaining sectors present wide investment opportunities for non-Mexicans. From 1982–1985, the Mexican government stated that it had approved approximately 90% of the applications for majority foreign investment projects.[6] However, exactly how much foreign investment is discouraged because of the current restrictions is impossible to discern. According to the Institute of International Finance, foreign investment flow is still less than the US$2.8 billion achieved in 1981, but it is expected to increase under the most recent development plan from the very low levels of 1983–1986.[7]

When a foreign investor acquires less than 49% of a corporation, the investor need only register the activity at the National Registry of Foreign Investment. In those cases where foreign investors desire majority control, the authorization of the National Commission of Foreign Investment is required, and application is assessed for its benefits to the national economy. In scrutinizing these applications, the Commission considers a wide range of factors including:

- whether the investment will be complementary to or competitive with Mexican companies
- the potential impact of the investment on exports
- the balance of payments impact
- the extent to which the project will be financed with overseas money after it is ongoing.[8]

The Mexican government has published a list of key sectors where foreign investment is encouraged. These sectors include:

- complex activities such as aircraft, shipbuilding, textile and shoe equipment, petroleum and petrochemical industrial equipment, and turbines,
- activities with dynamic technology including biotechnology, other technology, metallurgy and electronic consumer products,
- export-oriented industries such as electronic components, in-bond industries, hotel equipment, and synthetic resins and plastics.[9]

Foreign participation is favored in these sectors because the Mexicans currently believe that such industries are central to achieving Mexican growth and development objectives. The government also believes that such investments can be made without displacing Mexican investment.[10]

In-bond Industries (*Maquilas*)

The in-bond industry or *Maquiladora* program was developed to allow manufacturers to utilize low-cost labor to assemble final products for reexport. Mexico has successfully utilized its location next to the United States to draw investment capital under this program.

Mexico's "Border Industrialization Program" was initiated in 1965 and allows Mexican factories to receive temporary duty-free entry of components and raw materials from the United States for assembly in Mexico. When reexported, duty is charged only on the value added in Mexico.

This program also allows, through the creation of a trust, 100% foreign ownership of the Mexican subsidiary as well as exemption from export taxes. In some cases firms may sell up to 20% of their production within Mexico. In-bond companies do not require authorization by the National Commission of Foreign Investment.[11] The program has benefited both the Mexican economy and the foreign firms. The in-bond industries, known as *Maquilas*, have created many new jobs, dispersed economic activity, and provided needed foreign exchange. For foreign investors the program has allowed foreign firms to match labor intensive high-tech industries with reasonably priced skilled and unskilled labor, and this has allowed the in-bond participants to remain price-competitive with non-U.S. suppliers. As a result, the number of *Maquiladora* plants has increased from approximately 450 plants employing 70,000 workers in the mid-1970s to over 1,000 plants employing approximately 300,000 in 1987.[12] These plants now represent Mexico's second largest source of foreign exchange, after oil and before tourism. Products assembled at these plants include T.V. sets, telephone switchboards, bicycles, textiles, and transportation equipment, among others.[13] Approximately 89% of the in-bond industries are located along the U.S.-Mexican border.[14] The *Maquiladora* program has consistently aroused the opposition of organized labor in the United States, which claims that U.S. jobs are exported. It is also criticized in Mexico as involving little technology transfer and being dependent on the continuation of low wage rates.

Mexico has established industrial parks to meet the infrastructure needs of these *Maquilas*. According to a survey sponsored by the Bank of America many industrial parks provide all the services normally found in similar parks throughout the United States. They have been located near ports with easy access to qualified labor and raw materials.

Additionally, several parks offer feasibility studies for assembly operations in Mexico, as well as administrative services such as hiring and training workers, payroll administration, customs requirements, utilities permits, and plant maintenance.[15]

As of 1986 there were approximately 100 industrial parks dispersed throughout Mexico. The Trust of Industrial Complexes, Parks and Cities (FIDEIN) coordinates and administers industrial cities surrounding many of the parks, and helps to facilitate their assistance to potential industrial park residents.[16]

Tourism as a Case Study of Foreign Investment in Mexico

The Mexican government has long actively encouraged foreign investment in tourism. From 1982 to 1986 employment in tourism increased from 3.7 million to 4.6 million persons and this growth has been enormously important to the health of the economy.[17]

Approximately 85% of all tourists come from the United States. In recognition of this, the government believes that foreign ownership or involvement in the tourism industry may facilitate its growth, and that foreigners may feel more comfortable in U.S.-owned or -managed hotels, such as by Hyatt or Sheraton. Thus the sector has been favored to receive investment, including the new debt-swap mechanism.

The government expects income from tourism to gradually increase through the decade. In 1987, tourism was the third largest source of foreign currency income. The sector grew 7.1% annually between 1960 through 1985. To encourage continued growth, the government has developed a special fund to finance tourism-related companies at preferential rates and to help develop new tourist sites.[18]

Portfolio Investment

Since 1983 the Mexican Stock market has risen dramatically, drawing both foreign investment and returning flight capital. The Banco de México reported that the total value of securities increased by 68% in real terms in 1986, while the volume increased by 59.8%.[19] The value of mining and construction stocks increased by 243.8% and 116.4% in real terms, respectively.[20]

According to the International Finance Corporation, an arm of the World Bank, share prices in Mexico City increased 161% over the period December 31, 1986, to October 26, 1987. This growth compares to a decline in market prices over the same period of 6% in New York and 33% in Tokyo. The Mexican market mirrored the drastic declines in share prices internationally during the week of October 19, 1987. Stocks lost approximately one-third of their previous value. This could have a strong negative impact on investors' perception of the stability of the Mexican economy and could potentially lead to fewer debt-swaps and lower foreign investment levels, especially following a similar collapse of the Mexican *peso* in November. However, in referring to the impact of the market crash on former boom markets such as Mexico's, the director of the capital markets department for the International Finance Corporation, David G. Gill, noted, "Once the dust from all this settles, the performance of these markets could help pull more capital into the countries."[21]

Debt-Equity Swaps

Debt-equity swaps include any transaction where external debt, denominated in hard currency, is prepaid in local currency. Such swaps can significantly increase the amount of foreign investment available to a debtor nation, while at the same time effectively reducing its external debt. Several nations have eagerly utilized such swaps. The Mexican program is viewed as a successful beginning, but the level of swaps has been lower than originally expected. This may stem from a wide range of reasons including the short life of the program, investor concerns regarding the health of the economy, the design of the program, or ongoing Mexican ambivalence about foreign investment.

Under the August 1985, Debt Rescheduling Agreement, debt can be traded for shares in Mexican private or public firms; such "debt rights" are available to the banks that participated in the rescheduling. Clause 5.11 of the Agreement states that foreign investors may "participate in public or private enterprise, complement investment projects, initiate business or alleviate the financial burdens of the firms they are interested in."[22]

The Mexican government states that debt-equity swaps are utilized to "cut back foreign public debt and to increase productive investment."[23] According to the General Director of the Department of Public Credit, Ministry of Finance, "Debt-equity swaps . . . complement the policy measures on money, credit, trade, taxations, etc. . . . which are collectively aimed to achieve a structural change in the productive capacity of the economy."[24]

Debt-equity swaps are not a panacea to resolve Mexico's or any other country's debt burden. But they may bring numerous advantages to the participants if properly structured. For developing countries, debt-equity swaps may stimulate new investment and growth, reduce dollar denominated debt, and thus preserve hard currency. Debt-equity swaps that allow local investors to participate may discourage capital flight, since such programs provide an incentive to indigenous investment. Debt-equity swaps allow foreign corporate investors to acquire funds at a cost lower than the official exchange rate. Finally, for creditor banks, debt-equity swaps provide a formalized mechanism to end the cycle of rescheduling and new money demands.[25]

However, there may be several significant disadvantages to debt-equity swaps. Many developing countries discourage foreign investment which displaces indigenous investment; debt swaps would lead to such displacement. Secondly, such swaps may be inflationary, since the country involved must issue local currency to repay the debt. Finally, debt-equity swaps may be limited by the regulatory requirements of the creditor countries.

Under the Mexican program, once a debt-equity swap is approved, the investor must tender the eligible debt for prepayment in local currency. The government then collects a fee for such prepayment, called a conversion fee. If such loans are acquired through the secondary market, the price can be discounted by 10% or more of the face value of the debt. Debt swaps may not be used for working capital purposes, except for payments to FICORCA (defined below), Mexican banks, or national suppliers. Debt swaps also cannot be used for foreign exchange payments to suppliers, imports, etc. The rate of exchange used is the average free U.S. dollar purchase and sale prices quoted by at least three domestic banking houses.

According to a World Bank official active in developing new mechanisms to promote investment, the Mexican debt swap program has not been as successful as the Chilean. He believes that the Mexican approach erects subtle as well as overt disincentives to such investment.[26] The Chileans allow such swaps in a broader range of sectors and charge a minimum conversion fee, approximately 10% per transaction. Under the Chilean program private debtors can buy back their own foreign debt or exchange it for internal debt which can then be swapped or sold on local capital markets. Every two weeks the Central Bank auctions US$50 million of foreign currency. Because foreign exchange is rationed by the auction's bidding process, controlled by the government, Chile's debt-swap program is not inflationary. In Mexico, swaps have been restricted to priority sectors such as tourism, steel, and autos. The conversion fee ranges from 0 to 25% and averages around 12%, depending on the sector. As of the beginning of 1988, a 30% tax was applied to debt-equity swaps. If the tax remains, it is unlikely that the program can successfully continue.[27] In any case, as of February 1988, the program was suspended pending assessment of the new anti-inflationary plan.

Recent Developments

Mexico's leaders and technocrats must still walk a fine line between the austerity measures necessary to fund the external debt and the impact of such measures on the Mexican working and middle class. Foreign investment may awaken negative political reactions, but it does not require increased debt or increased austerity.

As a result fiscal policy is now used to disperse development geographically and to encourage exports. For example, the government decreed tax credits and accelerated depreciation schedules at rates of 25% and 50% without limitation for the activity performed or its location (except office and transportation equipment). Fiscal incentives are granted through certificates of fiscal promotion (CEPROFI), consisting of a credit against many federal taxes. These certificates have a five-year duration, but may shortly be abolished.[28] Credits are also granted to companies which invest in less-developed regions of the country.

The government allows exporters to receive tax rebates for imported machinery and raw materials used to develop exportable goods. The amount returned to the firms is that of the updated tax value prevailing at the time the return was made. Exporting firms pay no value-added tax on their exports. Finally, exporting companies "with at least 30% of national content in their outputs are entitled to . . . import . . . an equivalent of 30% of the total output exported, paying either a 25% duty or the tax indicated by the *General Import Tariff Schedule.*"[29]

FICORCA, the Trust for Exchange Risk Coverage, was established in 1983 to assist companies with foreign debt. Many of these companies were caught in Mexico's devaluation with inadequate access to foreign exchange to repay their debts. This program allows the Mexican borrower to obtain dollars to cover his indebtedness.

According to the Banco de México, the original program in 1983 covered more than US$11 billion of private external liabilities, most of them to be paid in eight years, including a four-year grace period. In 1986, the program was revised when the Mexican government reached an agreement with its foreign lenders to refinance nearly US$9.3 billion of private debt covered by FICORCA. "Only the principal payments on the private debt will be included in the refinancing program. . . . If loans provided under the refinancing program are repaid before payment is due, these funds will be available for relending to other Mexican enterprises."[30] The amounts included in this program may also be converted to direct investment under similar terms to those agreed to for the restructuring of the public sector.[31]

In 1986, the Mexican government announced several new measures to attract foreign investment to Mexico. Overseas branches of BAN-COMEX (*Banco Nacional de Comercio Exterior*) were authorized to promote investment and inform the government of potential joint ventures. Under the new proposals, the international development banks would be allowed to contribute temporary risk capital to finance joint ventures in Mexico. Finally, small and medium firms will be encouraged to invest in certain export-oriented manufacturing sectors. The government did not delineate how such investment would be encouraged.[32] In sum, the period 1985 to the present (1988) brought several measures along with a new receptivity to foreign investment.

Conclusion

The role and importance of foreign direct and portfolio investment in the process of economic development is by no means simple and clear. Many examples can be found of countries which developed efficiently with high levels of foreign investment or even foreign borrowing. South Korea, for example, has one of the highest levels of per capita external debt in the world, but very little foreign direct investment. Other examples, equally successful, can be found where both foreign investment and external borrowing have been at very low levels, such as Japan and Taiwan. In fact, the actual historical record, as opposed to the voluminous literature on economic development, shows only four essential prerequisites for economic growth at an acceptable rate: a high level of domestic savings, a low level of inflation, continuity of public policy, and sufficient economic freedom so that resources thus generated can flow to their most productive uses.

This mix characterized Mexico from 1930 to 1970. Under present circumstances, foreign direct and portfolio investment is vitally important for Mexico while it struggles to reestablish its economic equilibrium. Mexico's crushing external debt burden means that if it grows at an acceptable rate with low inflation it cannot service its debt. If it fully services its debt it cannot grow without unacceptably high inflation. Foreign investment is also required to supplement the low level of domestic savings, partially caused by capital flight due to high inflation (unless counteracted by interest rates so high as to stifle investment), as well as a high, though slowly declining, rate of population growth. This is Mexico's policy dilemma, and only world economic growth and sustained demand increases in its major markets will enable it to succeed in its policy responses.

Many of the Mexican technocrats understand these policy complications and as a result Mexico has begun to change its policies. Some of the measures that have been taken have already been mentioned in this chapter, but others would be helpful:

- Clear and well-understood laws and regulations on foreign investment are important, and they must be expeditiously and fairly applied. It is inadequate to maintain counterproductive measures on the books but to tell potential investors that they will not in fact be applied.
- Debt-equity and debt-commodity swaps should be actively encouraged and used to the maximum, especially for new export-oriented investment projects, whether domestic, foreign, or mixed. There is no necessary reason why these swaps should add to inflationary pressures; the local currency issued for this purpose can easily be sterilized, a model used successfully in Chile.
- Finally, the markets in the Far East should be more extensively explored, especially Japan, Korea, Hong Kong, and Taiwan. These countries have excess investible capital and a vivid interest in possible investment opportunities in Latin America. Care should be taken, however, that not too much Far Eastern investment be directed to the *Maquiladora* program, in order to avoid a negative reaction on the part of the U.S. Congress. This is important, despite the fact that the value of the program for the U.S. producers of inputs is in no way affected, since components used must come from the United States.
- In turn, the United States and other countries must maintain their markets open to the goods produced in Mexico, whether by foreign, domestic, or mixed enterprises.

Notes

The author gratefully acknowledges the assistance of Jorge Pinto, of the Mexican Embassy in Washington, D.C., who, however, bears no responsibility for the contents of the chapter.

1. *New York Times*, October 12, 1987, p. D1.

2. *Financial Times*, February 9, 1988, p. 4.

3. *Inside U.S. Trade*, February 5, 1988, p. 4.

4. *Ibid.*, and Banco de México, *The Mexican Economy*, 1987, p. 124.

5. National Commission of Foreign Investment, *Foreign Investment, Legal Framework and Its Implications*, Mexico, 1986, pp. 13–30.

6. General Director of Foreign Investment Promotion, *An Investment Guide to Mexico*, Mexico City, Mexico, no date, p. 43.

7. Interview with Peter West, Institute for International Finance, on October 5, 1987, and Confidential Report, IIF, *Mexico: Country Report*, Washington, D.C., June 1987, pp. 2, 5, and 25.

8. Banco Mexicano Somex, *Investing in Mexico*, Mexico, 1986, p. 16.

9. *Ibid.*, p. 17.

10. General Director of Foreign Investment Promotion, *op. cit.*, p. 45.

11. Bank of America, *Mexico's In-Bond Industry Is . . .*, Mexico, 1986, p. 3.

12. *International Trade Reporter*, January 27, 1988, pp. 120–121.

13. Banco Mexicano Somex, *op. cit.*, p. 21.

14. Bank of America, *op. cit.*, Mexico, 1986, p. 28; see also Banamex, *Review of The Economic Situation of Mexico*, Vol. LXIII, No. 745, Mexico, December, 1987.

15. General Director of Foreign Investment Promotion, *op. cit.*, p. 12.

16. *Ibid.*, p. 20.

17. *Ibid.*, p. 48.

18. *Ibid.*, p. 46, and Banco Mexicano Somex *op. cit.*, p. 22.

19. *Ibid.*, p. 24.

20. Banco de México, *op. cit.*, p. 77, and Banco Mexicano Somex, *op. cit.*, p. 23.

21. Banco de México, *op. cit.*, pp. 77–78.

22. Shearson, Lehman Bros., "A Guide to Debt-Equity Conversions," New York, 1987, p. 13.

23. The Institute of International Finance, *Restoring Market Access, New Directions in Bank Lending*, Washington, D.C., 1987, pp. 16–17.

24. *Ibid.*, p. 17, and Banco de México *op. cit.*, p. 24.

25. Shearson, Lehman Bros., *op. cit.*, pp. 9 and 14.

26. Interview with Michael Bouchet, IBRD, Debt Management and Financial Advisory Services, October 8, 1987.

27. *International Trade Reporter*, January 27, 1988, pp. 120–121.

28. Ministry of Commerce and Industrial Development, *Overview of Foreign Investment in Mexico*, Mexico, 1986, pp. 9–10.

29. Banco Mexicano Somex, *op. cit.*, p. 25, and Ministry of Commerce and Industrial Development, *op. cit.*, p. 32.

30. Banco de México, *op. cit.*, p. 113.

31. Ministry of Commerce and Industrial Development, *op. cit.*, pp. 28–31.

32. Banco Mexicano Somex, *op. cit.*, p. 20.

3

An Evaluation of Mexico's Policy on Foreign Direct Investment

José I. Casar

For over a century now, economic development and foreign direct investment have been so closely intertwined that it would be difficult to find an instance dealing with the former in any depth that did not also refer to the latter. In the Mexican case, for geographical and historical reasons, foreign direct investment is frequently understood, both in Mexico and across the border, as meaning investment by U.S. firms. In the complex, often conflicted, relationship between the two countries, it is therefore hardly surprising that Mexican policy toward investment by foreign firms should be a permanent item on the bilateral agenda.

From the time of the Avila Camacho regime (1940–1946) to the present, the attitude of successive Mexican governments toward the establishment of foreign firms in the country has, in general, been one of "cautious welcome." On the one hand, foreign direct investment has been deemed desirable for its potential contribution to economic development, be it real or perceived. On the other, recognition of the economic power and at times the political influence of foreign firms, as well as the perception that their activities have certain undesirable side effects, has led to continued attempts to regulate both the sectoral pattern of expansion and the overall rate of foreign investment. No government has yet tried to impose controls so tight that they amount to a ban on foreign investment; but neither has any government relaxed controls to the extent that foreign firms are treated on the same basis as private domestic firms. Moving within these broad limits Mexican policy on foreign direct investment has never failed to be the subject of much, and usually quite heated, debate, both in Mexico and in the United States, as well as among political and economic actors on the two sides of the border.

This debate has been conducted on several planes—academic, political, and ideological—and the arguments for and against foreign direct investment have been expressed in a substantial literature on its nature and effects. Most of this literature has had the implicit—and sometimes explicit—aim of influencing policy. But it is only the exceptional case that has discussed the probable impact of Mexican foreign investment policy *per se* on the magnitude and nature of foreign investment.

Even a superficial glance at the determinants of foreign investment, however, reveals such complexity that assuming that changing Mexican policy will significantly affect it may be misleading. In spite of this, the debate has frequently overlooked evaluating policy evaluation and has proceeded as if policy were invariably effective. This chapter examines the impact of changes in Mexican policy on foreign direct investment in the past, particularly the effects of the 1973 law, and the changes in the rigor with which it has been applied. It argues that the effects of these changes have been rather limited, and that the policy objectives can be more readily achieved by other, more specific, measures of industrial policy which take into consideration the whole complex set of determinants of foreign direct investment. This last point is illustrated by reference to recent developments in the motor vehicle industry.

The 1973 Law and Its Effects
on Manufacturing Industry

Writing in the early 1960s, on the eve of the wave of investment expansion by multinational corporations, R. Vernon described the legal situation faced by a foreign investor in Mexico:

> His risks will not seem obvious from a reading of Mexican Law; in fact, on first blush, the law will seem reassuringly nondiscriminatory in most respects. . . . In practice, however, the consummation of any major foreign investment is likely to turn on the granting of a variety of licenses. . . . Therefore, the foreigner who is considering any large direct investment in Mexico is obliged to determine if the contemplated investment is acceptable to the government. . . . And at this stage . . . the foreigner is likely to discover that . . . the existence of a large Mexican equity interest . . . is indispensable to the granting of the necessary licenses.[1]

This was also the time when the two power supply companies remaining in foreign hands in Mexico and other minor concerns, were nationalized.

It is against this background that the share of foreign investment in manufacturing output in Mexico rose from around one-sixth at the beginning of the 1960s to over one quarter in 1970.[2] This was achieved, furthermore, not by individual foreign investors, but by large and powerful multinational corporations operating in several countries, whose Mexican subsidiary rarely amounted to more than 1% of global operations.[3] It is not surprising, then, that by the early 1970s pressure was mounting to further strengthen controls on foreign investment. On March 9, 1973, the Law to Promote Mexican Investment and to Regulate Foreign Investment was published in the "Diario Oficial." The law brought together a number of preexisting regulations into a new consistent framework. It defined the activities reserved exclusively for the Mexican government[4] and for Mexicans,[5] and fixed the maximum share of foreigners in the capital of firms operating in other areas: in mining the limit was set at 34% in some cases and 49% in others; in secondary petrochemicals it was 40%; in the manufacture of automotive components it was 40%; and in all other activities it was 49%—although the National Commission on Foreign Investment may decide, in other cases, to increase or reduce this limit when judged in the interest of the economy. The Commission is, however, given no less than 17 criteria to guide it in determining the advisability of authorizing foreign investment and the percentage it is allowed in each case, the most important of which seem to be (1) that the foreign investment should be complementary to Mexican investment, and (2) that it "should not enter fields that are adequately covered" by Mexican firms.

To what extent was the change in policy embodied in the 1973 law successful in promoting Mexican firms vis-à-vis foreign firms? Did the 49% limit on the capital share to be held by foreigners significantly alter the composition of foreign investment in favor of firms with a majority Mexican capital interest? Table 3.1 presents evidence on the share of manufacturing output accounted for by foreign firms in 1970, just before the law on foreign investment was passed, and in 1980, after several years of its application.

The first point to note is that, for manufacturing as a whole, the relative position of foreign firms vis-à-vis domestic firms remained practically stable over the period, at just over 25% of output. In both 1970 and 1980, six industries (food, chemicals, pharmaceutical products, basic metals, electrical equipment, and transport equipment) accounted for more than two-thirds of the output of all foreign firms. Many of these coincide with the main sectors in which the global expansion of U.S. multinational corporations occurs. At a more disaggregate level, however, several important changes seem to have

TABLE 3.1
Foreign firms in Mexican manufacturing, 1970-1980.
(Figures in %)

	1970 (a)	(b)	(c)	1980 (a)	(b)	(c)
Food	11.1	11.6	0.0	11.0	10.4	7.3
Beverages	29.5	4.9	38.7	29.8	5.8	39.9
Tobacco	96.8	4.1	34.5	78.3	2.8	0.5
Textiles	12.0	3.3	0.0	8.8	2.0	43.2
Clothes and footwear	4.9	0.7	0.0	7.9	1.3	7.6
Wood products	4.3	0.3	0.0	5.7	0.5	91.2
Furniture	3.8	0.1	0.0	11.2	0.3	45.0
Woodpulp and paper	32.9	3.4	39.2	23.1	2.5	24.7
Printing and publishing	7.9	0.6	16.4	9.7	0.6	17.5
Leather goods	2.5	0.1	30.1	11.7	0.3	59.0
Rubber products	66.9	3.2	19.2	66.6	3.3	10.4
Chemical industries	46.8	11.0	1.2	35.2	9.7	56.0
Pharmaceutical and cosmetic products	55.9	8.6	46.9	72.5	8.7	2.1
Coal and petroleum derivatives[d]	54.8	0.6	7.8	55.6	0.8	31.1
Nonmetallic minerals	17.7	2.5	46.8	12.2	2.1	79.5
Basic metals	46.6	15.6	90.2	14.1	4.3	64.8
Metallic products	20.6	3.3	47.0	19.5	3.6	39.3
Nonelectrical machinery	52.1	3.7	42.1	48.6	5.8	51.6
Electrical equipment	50.1	7.8	9.5	57.9	12.2	16.8
Transport equipment	64.0	13.6	9.3	68.9	22.4	22.6
Other manufacturing[e]	N.A.	1.1	1.3	40.0	0.3	99.5
Total	27.8	100.0	25.8	27.2	100.0	28.2

[a]Share of foreign firms (foreign capital > 15%) in output.
[b]Distribution of foreign firms' output.
[c]Share of minority owned foreign firms (foreign capital < 49%) in output produced by all foreign firms.
[d]Excludes oil refining and basic petrochemicals (PEMEX).
[e]Figures for 1970 and 1980 are not comparable due to changes in definition.

Source: Fajnzylber and Martínez Tarragó, Las Empresas Transnacionales,
          FCE, Mexico, 1976;
          J.I. Casar et. al., La Organización Industrial en México, Siglo
          XXI Editores, Mexico, forthcoming.

taken place. Substantial decreases in the relative importance of foreign firms took place in four industries: tobacco, woodpulp and paper, basic metals, and the chemical industries. This "promotion" of Mexican investment and the consequent "control" of foreign investment can hardly be said to be the result of the application of the 1973 law, however, since in all four, direct investment by state-owned firms accounts for a large proportion of the advance experienced by domestic firms.[6]

At the other extreme, increases in the market share controlled by foreign firms occurred in two groups of industries. On the one hand, multinational corporations grew at a faster pace than their domestic counterparts in three industries where they already enjoyed a dominant position in 1970: pharmaceutical products, electrical equipment and appliances, and transportation equipment. On the other hand, foreign firms increased their share of the market in several traditional industries—clothes and footwear, furniture, and leather goods—starting from very low levels in 1970 and still remaining relatively low in 1980.

The second point to note from Table 3.1, which relates to the composition of foreign investment, is that almost 75% of the output generated by foreign firms is accounted for by firms with 50% or more foreign capital. This proportion varied only marginally during the 1970s—in spite of the fact that the 1973 law intended the 49% limit to be the general rule, not the exception. It might seem at first glance then, that in practice, policy towards foreign firms was much more liberal than implied by the actual text of the law. However, this was most probably not the case. For 1970, of the 651 firms included in the figures, only 21.2% (that is 138 firms) reported a share of foreign capital under 50%. For 1980, in contrast, of the 1,054 firms included in the figures, 37.1% (that is 391 firms) reported a share under 50%. This suggests that a real attempt at reversing the trend towards majority-owned firms was made, but that the larger firms had the bargaining power required to obtain the exemptions allowed under the law.

The aggregate picture, again, is the result of offsetting changes at the sectoral level. Whereas in 1970 there was only one two-digit sector where firms with a minority foreign stake outweighed majority-owned firms, by 1980 six sectors were in this position.[7] Furthermore, in twelve sectors the position of minority-owned firms improved relative to firms that were 50% or more foreign-owned. In seven of these, however, foreign firms as a whole have a relatively weak position, never accounting for more than 12% of total output in 1980, probably because these are traditional industries where technology is not very complex and not particularly dynamic, and where local firms are well established. As for the remaining industries, at least in two of them (nonelectric machinery and transportation equipment), the rise in the relative weight of minority-owned firms is due to government promotion of joint ventures with multinational corporations—the most well-known of them being the ones undertaken with Renault and American Motors in the car industry.

Finally, in the group of six industries where foreign firms accounted for more than 50% of output both in 1970 and 1980, majority-owned firms consistently outweighed firms with less than 50% of capital in foreign hands, five of them ending up in 1980 with a below average share of minority-owned firms in the total output generated by foreign firms. Furthermore, in all these industries with the exception of tobacco (for the reasons mentioned above), foreign firms maintained or increased their share of the market. In the six sectors in which firms with a minority foreign interest outweighed majority-owned firms in 1980, in contrast, the share of output accounted for by all foreign concerns tended to be relatively small, under 15% in four of the six and almost evenly split in the other two cases—chemical industries and nonelectric machinery. As noted above, in both of them, minority-owned firms accounted for a growing share of the output of all foreign firms, as foreign firms generally lost ground to domestic firms during the decade.

In general terms, then, the relative importance of foreign firms in Mexican manufacturing did not change substantially in the period after the 1973 law was passed. Multinational corporations continued to expand, sometimes at a faster pace than local firms, in fast-growing markets in which they were already dominant. This did not, however, result in an increase in their share of manufacturing output, for reasons not directly linked to Mexico's foreign investment policy.

In terms of the relative importance of firms with a majority or minority foreign interest, foreign direct investment policy seems to have been unable to change the situation substantially. Deliberate policy in this respect seems to have only affected smaller firms in more traditional sectors. The only exception was the chemical industries, where the more noticeable change might perhaps be attributed to the application of the criteria expressed in the law. However, the specific cases of success in attaining the goals of policy were almost completely offset by developments in other industries. In this respect, then, evidence suggests that the form adopted by foreign direct investment in industry depends primarily on the actual bargaining power of multinational corporations which, in turn, depends to a large extent on the local conditions they face. In markets where local firms have a relatively smaller disadvantage—as expressed by a larger market share—bargaining power on the side of foreign firms is smaller and joint ventures or minority capital commitments are more frequent. By contrast, when local firms are marginal, multinational corporations seem to be able to impose their entry conditions, which usually involve waiving the 49% limit on the foreign capital share.

Foreign Direct Investment and Changes in FDI Policy

Besides attempting to modify the characteristics of foreign investment and the balance between foreign and domestic firms—with only limited success as we have seen—Mexico's policy on foreign direct investment has frequently been thought of as the most important instrument for regulating its overall flow. Thus, when for either short-run (generally balance of payments) or long-run (transfer of technology and structural change) reasons it is felt that foreign investment must be encouraged, controls over the activities and expansion of foreign firms is relaxed, and official pronouncements insist on the contribution of foreign investment to development. A more "open" attitude on the part of the authorities is then supposed to foster an increase in the flow of foreign investment. When, for whatever reason, the flow of investment from abroad is judged to be too large, emphasis on the strict application of controls is assumed to be the appropriate mechanism through which the flow can be checked.

We have seen, however, that the wave of investment by multinational corporations in the 1960s took place against a policy background that was not perceived as being particularly favorable to foreign investment. In the early and mid-1970s, attitudes and policy were, if not openly hostile, at least very cautious. These were the years when public opinion, particularly in the developing countries, grew conscious of the increasing power of multinational corporations, and when many governments—including Mexico's—assumed a much tougher stance on this issue. Most observers would agree that this mood started to change in the late 1970s and early 1980s and that during the present administration the attitude was decidedly positive.

This turnabout in policy can be illustrated by comparing the 1973 law with the Guidelines for Foreign Investment and Objectives for its Promotion issued by the National Commission on Foreign Investment in February 1984. Whereas the earlier document has generally been seen as a step in the direction of increased controls on foreign firms, and does not point to specific sectors where foreign investment is particularly welcome—it seeks to *promote* Mexican investment and *control* foreign investment—the 1984 guidelines (while stating that the legal framework does not require changes since it is a "flexible instrument"), openly declare that "foreign investment is welcome." Furthermore, provisions are made for speeding the decision process and a list of 42 industries is provided where, for technological and balance of payments reasons, foreign investment is to be promoted. These industries are concentrated in the capital goods sector and in high tech areas but, significantly, also include the chemical industry and metallurgy, where the foreign firms' share in total output declined throughout the 1970s.

As was mentioned earlier, deliberate policy is only one of the factors determining the actual flow of foreign investment. Local conditions—in particular the size and rate of expansion of the market in the host country and, more recently, its prospects as an export platform and

TABLE 3.2
Mexico's Share of Foreign Direct Investment to Developing Countries,
1968/1970-1983/1985
(Figures in %)

	Share of Total to All Developing Countries[a]	Share of Total to All Developing Countries (excluding Venezuela and Saudi Arabia)[a]	Share of Total to Latin America[b]
1968/1970	8.9	9.3	
1971/1973	9.3	9.0	
1974/1976	25.3	9.2	
1977/1979	8.0	8.7	
1980/1982	17.4[c]	17.4[c]	33.1
1983/1985			12.2

[a]Investment originating in Japan, Federal Republic of Germany, France, Italy, Netherlands, the United Kingdom, and the United States.
[b]Foreign investment from all sources.
[c]1980/1981.

Note: All figures correspond to the simple mean of annual shares.

Sources: IDB, "Progreso Económico y Social en América Latina, Informe 1987," Washington, D.C., Interamerican Development Bank, 1987; Peres, W. "Foreign Direct Investment and Industrial Development," Mexico, 1988.

its structural balance of payments position—are usually mentioned as key elements in a firm's decision to invest in a particular country. Global economic conditions as reflected by the overall rate of investment of multinational corporations will also, obviously, affect the magnitude of the flow of foreign investment to a particular country. One way, then, of evaluating the ability of policy to stem or enhance the flow of foreign investment is to compare the elasticity of foreign direct investment to market fluctuations in Mexico, and Mexico's share in global foreign direct investment, during periods in which the policy intent has been more or less favorable to the expansion of foreign firms.

Table 3.2 presents evidence on Mexico's share in the flow of foreign direct investment from seven major OECD countries[8] to all developing countries, and from all sources to Latin America as a whole. The periods chosen correspond to the first and second half of a Mexican presidential term. In column 2, Venezuela and Saudi Arabia have been excluded from the figures because wild fluctuations in foreign investment to these countries in the aftermath of the two oil shocks tend to distort the overall picture. The data in Table 3.2 suggest that changes in Mexico's official policy toward foreign investment have had scarcely any effect on the share in the flow of investment by foreign firms. Apparently, changes in Mexican policy toward foreign investment within the limits mentioned above, given the propensity of multinational corporations to invest abroad, have not significantly altered Mexico's relative position as a host country. From the late 1960s to the late 1970s Mexico received around 9% of all foreign investment to the developing world. The more aggressive stance of the Echeverría regime (1970–1976) on the issue, including enactment of the 1973 law, can hardly be said to have inhibited foreign investment in Mexico, relative to investment in other developing countries.

In fact, substantial changes in Mexico's position as a recipient occurred only in the 1980s. During the last two years of the oil boom, investment flows into Mexico increased significantly. The effects of this upsurge were still being felt in 1982, when Mexico's share of all foreign investment flows into Latin America was still over 27%. During the crisis years of 1983–1985, and in spite of the favorable attitude of the present administration toward foreign direct investment, the situation changed radically. The debt crisis revealed Mexico's structurally weak balance of payments position. This along with the collapse in the rate of growth of the domestic market, led to a setback in Mexico's relative standing as a host country which the shift in policy toward foreign investment was seemingly unable to check.

Furthermore, Mexico became increasingly less attractive as a location for foreign firms even in relation to other Latin American countries, most of which were also in crisis. Whereas in the early 1980s one in every three dollars flowing into the region ended up in Mexican affiliates, in 1983–1985 this proportion had fallen to less than one in eight dollars. By 1985, foreign direct investment in Argentina had gone back to its 1981 peak, and Brazil was receiving about 50% in nominal terms of its 1982 maximum flow of investment. In that same year foreign direct investment in Mexico was at 19.3% of its 1981 peak, smaller than the flow attracted by the much smaller Colombian economy for the third consecutive year.[9] Even if flows into Mexico recovered in 1986 and 1987 to around 35% of their peak value in nominal terms, it is difficult to escape the conclusion that the present administration's policy toward foreign investment has been largely ineffective in achieving its aim of capturing a larger flow.

The experience of the last two decades, then, suggests that as long as Mexico's policy toward foreign direct investment remains within the broad limits of what was earlier described as a "cautious welcome" to foreign firms, changes in policy will leave foreign investment flows largely unaffected.

The evidence with regard to Mexico's share in foreign investment flows, especially the yearly figures, indicates that, given the propensity to invest abroad by foreign firms, Mexico's overall economic growth and its balance of payments position are much more important determinants of foreign investment than explicit foreign investment policy.

In order to explore the relation between foreign investment and the overall domestic market, a relationship linking foreign direct investment in 1970 prices with the trend value for Mexico's Gross Domestic Product (GDP) and a cyclical term was estimated over the 1950–1986 period. The fit seems quite reasonable for an investment equation, and was used to forecast the value of foreign direct investment flows over the period. Forecast and actual values are shown in Graph 3.1.

The basic point to be noted from the graph is the lack of any clear relation between shifts in policy toward foreign investment and the departure of forecast values from what one would expect from the average response of investment flows to trend growth and cyclical fluctuations in Mexico's GDP. In particular, during the five years after the implementation of the 1973 law, foreign investment behaved much as one would expect from the underlying relationship. If anything, 1974 saw a larger than normal inflow of funds.

In the late 1970s, the unusual strength of the upswing associated with the oil boom, and the general optimism about Mexico's future, led to an upsurge in foreign direct investment that exceeded by far— particularly in 1980 and 1981—what one could have expected from past experience. After the onset of the debt crisis, real foreign investment fell quickly to levels that had not been observed since the 1950s, overshooting the fall that one would predict from historical experience. The change in the policy environment was unable to stop this free fall until 1985.

It might be argued that the modest recovery in foreign direct investment in 1985–1986, which in fact is the only major turning point in the period that the equation fails to predict, constitutes evidence pointing to the success of the more open attitude. It should be noted, however, that the flow of investment recorded in 1986 is still analogous in real terms to the flows observed in the 1960s when the economy was several times smaller. Furthermore, as of 1986, the figures for foreign direct investment include swap operations by foreign firms on the external debt of the Mexican government or Mexican private firms. According to reports from the National Commission

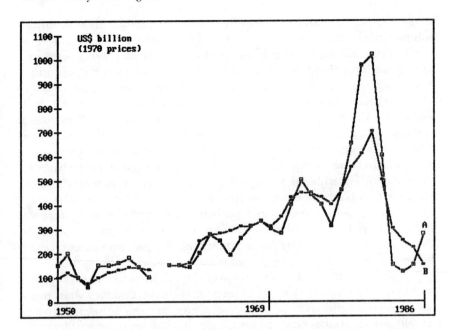

Graph 3.1 FDI in Mexico 1950-1986, Actual and Forecast Values

A = Foreign Direct Investment (Forecast)
B = Foreign Direct Investment (Actual)

Note: Forecast values were obtained from the following equation estimated by ordinary least squares corrected for first order autocorrelation:

Log FDI = -1.73 + 0.70 Log GDP (trend) + 5.43 Log GDP/GDP (trend)
$\quad\quad\quad$ (-1.08) (4.53)$\quad\quad\quad\quad\quad\quad$ (5.00)
The numbers in parentheses are t-statistics

R^2 = 0.768, F(2,31) = 55.5, D.W. = 1.37

on Foreign Investment, around two-thirds of the total amount of foreign investment authorized during 1986 correspond to these operations, which involve the exchange of a financial liability for a physical asset under very attractive conditions for the foreign investor.

The Need for an Active Industrial Policy

The evidence discussed in the previous sections suggests that, in spite of the seemingly endless debate it has generated, Mexican foreign investment policy has had only a minor impact on the nature and magnitude of foreign firms' involvement in Mexico. It should not be inferred from this, however, that the debate is sterile since not very much can be said, on the basis of the analysis of past experience, about the potential impact of the more radical changes in policy frequently advocated by those involved in the policy debate.

The arguments and evidence presented so far cannot provide a full answer to the question of what would happen if foreign firms were treated on the same basis as domestic firms. However, the preceding analysis does point to two tentative conclusions in this respect.

First, there does not seem to be any reason to expect that the abolition of controls on foreign direct investment would modify the strongly procyclical behavior of foreign investment flows. If anything, one might expect a once-and-for-all increase in the level of foreign investment, which would then resume its normal behavior. If this is the case, it is misleading to assume that foreign investment could become the engine of growth even if controls were dismantled.

Second, where would this once-and-for-all increase in foreign investment take place? We have seen that explicit policy has been particularly ineffective in those industries in which foreign firms, usually multinational corporations, face little or no competition from domestic firms. These are, furthermore, the industries in which the bulk of foreign investment in developing countries is concentrated. If foreign firms in these sectors have in fact behaved much as if there were no regulations, eliminating controls would seem unlikely to have much effect on their propensity to invest in Mexico. We are left, then, with a potential field of expansion for new foreign firms in mainly traditional industries where the firms of industrialized countries tend not to invest abroad on a large scale, and in sectors that have hitherto been considered strategic (such as energy, banking, and radio and television). It would seem, then, that only if these strategic sectors were to be open to foreign firms should we expect a massive increase in foreign investment to take place. This change in policy, however, would involve such political conflict in Mexico that it seems reasonable to discard it as hardly probable, without going into a discussion of whether its potential effects on Mexican economic development would be positive or negative.

The basic conclusions seem clear: On the one hand, as long as policy change remains within the limits observed in the past decades, its effect on foreign direct investment will be rather small. On the other hand, certain goals of foreign direct investment policy seem more readily achieved when other industrial policy measures are brought into play. Recent developments in the motor vehicle industry provide a particularly good example.

By the mid-1970s Mexico's automobile industry was a constant cause of concern for policymakers. A very large number of car makes and models produced with obsolete technology in very small numbers led to high average costs. The industry, furthermore, was perhaps the largest single contributor to the trade deficit, since its import substitution effects had almost disappeared by the early 1970s. In the second half of the 1970s, furthermore, the car industry was immersed in a process of structural change on a world scale as a result of technological change, the oil shocks, and the increasing involvement of Japan in world markets. This restructuring involved substantial investment by car manufacturers and a reassessment of the relative merits of different locations as export platforms for the different parts of the productive process.[10]

Given the opportunities created by the redefinition of corporate strategies, the challenge posed to policymakers was how to ensure that Mexico's role in the process brought about a technological upgrading of the industry and a reversal of its overall trade performance. The size of the Mexican market, its proximity to the U.S. market, and the existence of an experienced labor force were the basic elements on which the authorities based an aggressive policy designed to secure a new role for the Mexican subsidiaries of leading corporations. Through two major presidential decrees (1977 and 1983) involving specific measures in almost every relevant field, what was in principle only a potentially interesting course of action for the firms involved became a reality. Mexico has become an export platform for several firms, many of which have continued to expand in the midst of the crisis. New plants have started operations every year between 1978 and 1987 with the exception of 1979 and 1982 and a more rational industrial structure has evolved.

It must be noted that the specific policy dealing with the motor vehicle industry has been given priority over other aggregate policies potentially affecting it. Thus, for example, the recent drive towards the liberalization of foreign trade has largely bypassed the industry. Not only have import licenses been maintained, but new controls on the operations of firms in international trade have been introduced, including an annual foreign exchange budget and the granting of concessions on the domestic market depending on export performance.

Finally, the results obtained in the automobile industry could hardly have come about as a consequence of the application of a general policy dealing with all foreign firms in all sectors. The general conclusion that might reasonably be drawn from the evidence presented here is that global foreign investment policy should be seen as the overall institutional context within which specific policies for specific sectors, and even specific firms, should be framed. Given the meager results to be expected from changes in policy in this respect, and given the reactions and frictions such changes inevitably bring about, it seems more reasonable to concentrate on the specific policies mentioned, rather than attempting to influence the behavior of all firms in all sectors through changes in foreign direct investment policy.

Notes

I am indebted to Wilson Peres of CIDE, Mexico, for his helpful comments on and insights into the issue discussed in this chapter.

1. R. Vernon, *The Dilemma of Mexico's Development*, Harvard University Press, Cambridge, 1963, pp. 9–10.

2. R. Vernon, *op. cit.*, p. 22.

3. F. Fajnzylber, and T. Martínez Tarrago, *Las Empresas Transnacionales*, Mexico City, Fondo de Cultura Económica (FCE), 1976.

4. Petroleum, basic petrochemicals, nuclear energy, electricity, railroads, telegraphic communications.

5. Radio and television, urban and interurban transportation, domestic air and maritime transportation, forestry, and gas distribution.

6. The creation of Tabamex and the expansion of public firms in basic metallurgy (Las Truchas project mainly) in the chemical industries (FERTIMEX and the involvement in basic chemicals production) are the most important examples.

7. From here on, other manufacturing industries are not included in the comments on Table 3.1.

8. France, Federal Republic of Germany, Italy, Japan, the Netherlands, the United Kingdom and the United States.

9. See Banco Interamericano de Desarrollo (BID), *Progreso económico y social en América Latina, Informe 1987*, Washington, D.C., 1987.

10. See Moreno Brid, *The Motor Vehicle Industry in Mexico in the Eighties*, paper prepared for the International Labor Organization (ILO), Mexico City, 1987, mimeographed, for a full discussion of recent developments in the automobile industry.

4

The Mexican Foreign Debt: A Case of Conflictual Cooperation

León Bendesky and Víctor M. Godínez

In Mexico we know that the foreign debt has become a serious obstacle—and not the only one—to the growth and development of the economy. Servicing that debt under the conditions that have prevailed to date has caused a prolonged decline in production, higher unemployment, and increased concentration of property and income. We also know that in spite of the efforts made to comply with the payment obligations, the weight of the debt has not been reduced and the financial relations with the rest of the world have not normalized. Finally, we know that the last six years have not been years of progress and we suspect that the immediate future is not promising.

Economic Heritage of a *Sexenio*

The process of economic adjustment that was a condition for renegotiation of the foreign debt since December 1982 has sought to reduce inflationary pressures, diminish the fiscal deficit, and reduce the external imbalance. Added to the objectives of stabilization was a policy of structural change, designed to reconstruct the bases of dynamic growth through modification of relative prices and freeing of market forces in both domestic production and foreign trade. It was hoped that over three years (1983–1986) the economy would have responded to this program and regained its historic growth rate, strengthened its ability to respond to external shocks, and substantially improved its payment capacity. However, the actual behavior of the market did not proceed as expected.

Between 1983 and 1987 the rate of inflation was always greater than expected. It is true that from January 1983 to June 1985 there was significant success in reducing inflation (although, it must be noted, less than anticipated), but from June 1985 until October 1987 there was not a single month in which the annual rate of inflation was lower than the previous month. Thus, in the last trimester of 1987 Mexican inflation tended to stabilize at a much higher level than at the beginning of the six year plan.[1] The growth of real national product was, in general, below the forecasts, the only exception being in 1984 when GNP grew much more than expected (and desired). The current account surplus of the balance of payments, which at first surpassed the established goals, has gradually diminished since 1985. Finally, up to 1983 the public deficit was reduced as part of the adjustment program, but in the following years it increasingly exceeded the budgeted level until, in the last two years, it accounted for virtually the same proportion of GDP as it did in 1982.

The economic policy adopted in December 1982 had been expected to generate a new profile of the current account that would lead to a real reduction of the economic and financial weight of the foreign debt. Changing the profile of the trade balance was pursued by a combination of stabilization policies and altering relative prices between commercial and noncommercial goods. The underlying model for economic policy assumed that these measures would produce an expansion in net exports at least equal to the reduction in internal demand. These results also did not materialize. A summary examination of the basic indicators of foreign indebtedness demonstrates that it kept increasing after 1982. Today the foreign debt is greater than it was six years ago and, due to economic stagnation, the debt level at the end of each year has represented a greater portion of the GDP than in the previous year. The debt has also grown in proportion to the export of goods and nonfactor services. As for interest payments, although these fell slightly in relation to exports, they increased significantly in terms of government revenues and expenses. This suggests, on one hand, that the economy suffered a significant erosion in the maneuverability that stems from abundant oil resources and, on the other hand, that the sensitivity of public finances to external changes increased substantially.

At the start of the de la Madrid government's last year in office, Mexico faces prolonged stagflation and widespread macroeconomic imbalances. Aggravating this are indications that its potential for growth may have diminished sharply, with less capacity for absorption of the work force and an external vulnerability that appears to have worsened. In this economic climate, the confidence of domestic and international economic agents, as well as the government's credibility, do not appear today to be better than in 1982 and may even have deteriorated seriously.

The current and long term costs of securing service on a foreign debt whose economic and financial weight has increased are already, in fact, very high. Real per capita production fell slightly more than 10% in six years. Average annual real minimum wages declined to a level comparable to that of almost a quarter of a century ago. Until 1986, the accumulated decline in wages as a proportion of the GDP reached 40%. The ratio of gross domestic product to investment expenditure is today at the 1962 level, and personal consumption— due to the fall in wages and the rise in unemployment—has returned to 1974 levels. Real accumulated external transfers between 1982 and 1986 represent little more than one-fifth of the real GDP of 1981, which was a year of intense growth. And the margin of unused productive capacity for the same period shows an accumulated loss of output equivalent to almost three-quarters of the 1981 GDP.

Furthermore, Mexico's terms of trade show significant deterioration. The economy suffered an accumulated trade loss of US$21 billion between 1982 and 1986. From this amount, US$18 billion are attributable to losses in the petroleum sector. There also occurred heavy losses in real national income which, in contrast to real GDP, includes changes in the terms of trade and external factor payments. The combined effect of payment of debt service and commercial losses represented for Mexico a much higher cost than that attributable to the fall in real GDP.

The policies of adjustment and structural change do not seem to have succeeded in reducing foreign restrictions which historically weaken the economy. This situation may appear paradoxical given the recent increase in nonpetroleum exports and the reduction in imports. The paradox, nevertheless, is only apparent. Mexico's imports are made up principally of intermediate and capital goods. There is a direct relationship between the importation of these goods and investment expenditure, as well as a strong multiplier effect on manufacturing production. The procyclical behavior of total imports with respect to investment is very clear in the Mexican economy. In the present decade, perhaps as a result of commercial liberalization and partial destruction of productive capacity, this structural characteristic seems to indicate that for the same level of the capacity utilization a larger import volume is required. Exports, in contrast, are counter-cyclical with respect to GDP growth. The widely publicized increase in nonpetroleum exports in recent years is due fundamentally to the combined effects of internal recession and growth of world demand.

All this suggests that improvement in the nonpetroleum commercial balance is temporary while the foreign restrictions have indeed increased. Today only a lower level of economic activity is compatible with the current account balance required to cover the foreign debt service. Reduction in the level of economic activity is associated with a sharp fall in total investment. Gross capital formation has fallen at an average annual rate of 7% since 1982. This decline is tied to the existing financial instability in the economy. During this entire period the expected profitability from investment in financial assets (denominated in U.S. dollars) and, in 1986–87, investment in the Mexican Stock Exchange has been larger vis-à-vis productive investment. Furthermore in 1982–83 and 1986–87 the increase in prices of imported capital goods, plus the increase in the real value of the foreign debt of firms and the fall in the real value of their physical assets, caused a substantial change in the relationship between the cost of capital and the general level of prices. Finally, uncertainty persists concerning the permanence and viability of economic policy measures. This combination of factors suggests that in order to attain an increase in real GDP now, a more than proportional increase in investment is required.

The prolonged and acute recession in the Mexican economy has had adverse repercussions on both the use of resources and the level of productivity. Recovering the economic growth potential will require an even stronger process of expansion in the future. Growth beyond the historic trend will be required in order to absorb the unemployment caused by the crisis, and to reverse the deterioration in plant and equipment.

The development of the economy since 1982 is tightly linked to the strategy adopted for managing the foreign debt. Given this link it is difficult, at least from a Mexican perspective, to make a positive evaluation of the results of such negotiations.

Renegotiation of the External Debt: Limits of an Iterative Exercise

Until early 1985 Mexico was considered not only a successful case of macroeconomic adjustment but also an example of a responsible debtor. On one hand, the severity of the shock policy in 1983, plus the weak economic recovery starting in the second half of 1984, seemed to truly demonstrate (domestically as well as abroad) the viability of the economic strategy that had been adopted. On the other hand, the lukewarm participation of the Mexican government in the attempts to coordinate a Latin American position on the debt issue contributed to reducing the political importance of the extreme positions defended by some countries at the time, which appeared to have the potential to spread in the area.

This moderate position and the depth and rigor with which the policy of adjustment was originally applied contributed to the capacity for persuasion of Mexican negotiators against the creditors. From the first phase, in which the maturity profiles were modified on a basis which only deferred the short term problem, the second stage went on to consider a multiannual restructuring of amortization which extended the payment schedule until 1990. The signing of the multiyear agreement was presented by the international financial community as an authentic reward for Mexico's disciplined and responsible posture. For the Mexican government this agreement appeared in early 1985 to be the result of a successful strategy in which "all the desired results were obtained." The official evaluation of the national perspective in regard to the debt was extremely optimistic. It came to be expected that, upon consolidation—as planned—of the adjustment process and structural change undertaken in the previous two years, the restructuring signed in 1985 would in itself ensure the solution of the problem of the foreign debt and the economy's gradual reentry into the credit markets.[2] This analysis was sustained by the conviction that the Mexican economy would respond positively to the economic policy model proposed by the government and in the accord entered into with the IMF at the beginning of the de la Madrid *sexenio.*

In retrospect, nonetheless, it can be seen that the possibilities for maintaining the adjustment process were only viable as long as the economy remained in recession. As soon as the recovery began in the second half of 1984, a conflict became evident—irreconcilable within the framework of the prevailing economic policy—between growth and the need to generate a surplus to assure external payments. In accordance with the objectives established for 1984, economic activity would have had to be maintained at a level as low as the year before. However, production grew more than planned, due primarily to the combined impact of three factors: the delayed effect of the rise in exports (favored by the real devaluation of the Mexican *peso* in 1982–83), the favorable state of import demand from the United States, and the relative relaxation of fiscal policy (expressed in an increase in public employment and the granting of fiscal investment incentives). The economic recovery, which continued to mid-1985, was moderate (real GDP grew 3.7%) compared to Mexico's historic experience. Despite its relative weakness this growth led to a marked decrease in the current account surplus. This, in turn, made it impossible to reduce the fiscal deficit, while also demonstrating the existence of an inflationary floor which has proven impossible to reduce in the absence of substantial modifications of the antiinflationary policy. In this environment the speculative moves against the Mexican *peso* and the flight of capital reappeared in strength.

The nature of this growth interlude in the *sexenio* demonstrated that in spite of the macroeconomic adjustment in place in 1982 and 1983, when signs of revival appear—as moderate as these may be— the factors which have traditionally restricted growth resurface. This is shown, for example, in the reduction in the trade balance registered in 1985. That was due, on one hand, to a significant rise in imports, which generated an economic impulse led by the manufacturing sectors (which have a high import content) and, on the other hand, to the deceleration of exports made inevitable by the reduction of surplus product and the gradual appreciation of the real exchange rate of the Mexican *peso*.

Under these conditions the perception arose in international political and financial circles that Mexico was failing to meet the goals agreed upon with the IMF. This negative evaluation was reinforced by the proposal to postpone US$950 million of principal which, according to the plan of the multiyear restructuring agreement, would have had to be paid in the first months of 1985. In fact the signing of the second phase of this agreement (in August of that year) was preceded by numerous signals indicating a hardening toward Mexico by the financial community whose negative judgment was manifested in the IMF declaration that Mexico was ineligible for greater financial support. (This decision was extremely unfortunate in that it coincided with the earthquakes which devastated parts of Mexico City).

The loss of coherence in the government's economic program during 1985, the abrupt fall of international petroleum prices at the end of the same year, and the development in 1986 of an economic framework dominated by deterioration of growth prospects in the industrialized world, marked the beginning of the third phase of negotiation of Mexico's foreign debt.

This new round developed on notably different grounds from those in the 1982–84 period. One of the notable changes was the previously mentioned hardening of positions toward Mexico by their creditors. Another change, in the internal arena, was a shift in the political consensus within the government in terms of treatment of the foreign debt and evaluation of the economic strategy. As an expression of the latter point the thesis of coresponsibility between debtors and creditors gained strength in Mexico and was manifest in the conflict of two currents of thought. One of them—upheld by the Secretary of Finance and Public Credit, Silva Herzog—argued in favor of a more radical attitude toward commercial banks and of deepening the economic adjustment process. The other—upheld by the Secretary of Programming and Budgeting, Salinas de Gortari—proposed exerting greater pressure on creditors to obtain more concessions (but without reaching the point of rupture) and deepening the structural change through liberalization policies. The political dispute between these two positions was resolved by the resignation of Silva Herzog from the Cabinet.

In this context of tension with the creditors and political adjustments in the Mexican government, the third round of foreign debt negotiations was begun: a round that would prove to be prolonged and arduous. Given the dimensions and the multiplicity of financing sources of the agreement finally signed, the actual progress of negotiations was subjected to a complicated set of conditions. The financial backing requested from the IMF, as usual, required acceptance by the Mexican government of certain economic management goals, but the disbursement of the funds was not conditioned on the granting by private banks of the agreed-upon fresh credit. The credits from the World Bank (SALs), besides its own conditionality, were required by commercial banks for their own participation in the financial package. Lastly, the negotiation with official creditors at the Paris Club was conditioned on the implementation of the agreement signed with the IMF.

This third renegotiation of the Mexican foreign debt made up the greatest package for restructuring and new resources achieved to date, as well as having incorporated a series of novel characteristics (such as contingency clauses for growth goals and protection from external shocks originating in the petroleum market). All in all, it does not modify the guidelines established since 1982. The financial commitments associated with the Mexican foreign debt were not reduced and the banks were not forced to make any "sacrifice," as was implied in the coresponsibility thesis. It is true that the payment profile was again improved, especially during the politically crucial years of 1987 and 1988, but the problem will reappear in the following two years. It is also true that the rates applied to the restructured debt diminished appreciably, but their weight continues to exert strong pressures on the economy. Although the third round of debt negotiation widened the financial base for a smoother political transition in 1988, it does not ensure a resumption of growth, due to the bounds imposed on economic policy by the adjustment criteria. The virtual freezing of international reserves at the Banco de México, which reached an unprecedented level by 1987, appears to reinforce this last impression.

One can say, in summary, that in spite of its innovative aspects the last reprogramming of the Mexican foreign debt did not alter the basic strategy established since 1982. With this reprogramming it was possible to again avoid a financial rupture, but not to eliminate the need in the future—presumably under the new government—to repeat what becomes each time more arduous and prolonged negotiation. Management of the Mexican external debt has until now allowed for the preservation of the principles of a "free and open" economy, and has maintained the existing power scheme, which dominates relations between Mexico and its creditors. These two objectives were present from the beginning in the negotiating position of the banks, international organizations, and economic agencies of the United States government. From that position these actors can still make a positive evaluation of the results and continue backing the same strategic course of action.

The negotiating strategy of the Mexican government, for its part, has a central component—the desire to avoid confrontations with the financial community and to search for cooperative arrangements which can gradually lead to an effective lessening of the debt burden. The definition of this posture was heavily influenced by the nature of the economic program adopted by the government in response to imbalances inherited from the past decade. Given that the economic philosophy underlying this project is essentially compatible with that of foreign financial agents, there was more room for establishing cooperative arrangements with creditors than for an open explosion of conflicts and polarization of positions that could not be resolved. The possibility of maintaining this negotiating scheme depended in large part on the expectation of the success of the economic program outlined in December 1982.

The ambition to pay and grow has fallen far short of realization. The *sexenio* experience shows that to satisfy Mexico's payment obligations the economy must generate a commercial surplus and that this cannot be obtained except at the cost of internal recession. Keeping up payments under the present conditions means reducing domestic demand, repressing wages, sacrificing jobs, and lowering the standard of living. It is important to emphasize that this is in marked contrast to the assumption shared by the Mexican government and the financial community on the possibility to pay and grow. And even though this assumption was authenticated in the last Mexican financial arrangement, experience seems to show that, in the absence of a fundamental change in the established strategic course, the option is either to pay with a domestic recession, or pay substantially less (or not pay) and grow. Given the internal economic deterioration, the option of keeping the present direction unchanged appears hardly viable; and it is reasonable to suppose that some kind of policy alternative should be adopted by the incoming government in the face of the possibility of a rupture in the social and political order.

Several problems of a structural nature in the Mexican economy persist which affect growth possibilities. The foreign debt is not the only obstacle to overcome; others include productive stagnation and inflationary pressures. But owing to its relationship with these other problems, dealing with the foreign debt is inescapable. For this reason, and within the existing political framework, external cooperation is required. The positive flow of financing and the export markets required by Mexico constitute a close link to the United States. For the creation of a cooperative environment, there are factors which are not subject to bilateral negotiation but which respond instead to internal forces. The relationship between the two countries cannot escape, then, the scenario of conflict. In the economic terrain bilateral relations can be characterized as a situation of conflictual cooperation which will certainly mark the course of action of the next governments in both countries. In any case, confronting the conditions of a bilateral economic relationship marked by conflict demands that the foreign debt question *not* be seen as emanating from a market anomaly.

Between Cooperation and Conflict

The previous considerations imply that evaluation of strategy with respect to the external debt is essential. However, the question of how to continue paying the debt may lose its relevance in the face of global deterioration caused by the economic crisis. That is an uncertainty shared by Mexico, its creditors, and the United States. The experience of the last *sexenio* suggests that the subject of the foreign debt cannot continue to be treated as a problem the solution to which can be developed with the framework of functioning financial markets.

The credit market has become "involuntary." This in reality is a euphemism which conceals the fact that its mechanisms were modified due to Mexico's difficulty in complying with its payment commitments. Debt renegotiation (which has become a repetitive exercise) expresses this situation in the divergence that exists between the minimum funds required by Mexico to continue both servicing its debt and financing the economy, and the maximum funds which the banks and financial agencies are willing to commit beyond their actual level of exposure in the country. Under these conditions, the prices and amounts of new credits are the product of a process of negotiation which develops in a framework of conflict.

The development of secondary debt markets also allows us to glimpse the conflict-ridden character of financial relationships. The discount imposed on the nominal value of the debt is highly significant; the part of the Mexican debt which is considered in this market is discounted up to 50%. But this market value of liabilities does not extend to the total debt, only to selective amounts that differentiate some debts from the others.

Mexico has participated in two different schemes of capturing market discounts. Debt conversion brought together banks (which would decrease their unwanted portfolio), the Mexican government (which would cancel part of its debt), and foreign investors (who would obtain resources in Mexican *pesos* that could be invested productively). Part of the cost of the operation fell on the Banco de México, which had to cover a portion of the discount and issue money for the equivalent of the converted debt. Due to inflationary pressures within the economy, the conversions were limited (reaching a value of about US$2 billion) and later suspended. The other mechanism for capturing the discount was designed jointly with Morgan Guaranty Trust. In accordance with the original plan, Mexican government bonds would be issued, which would cancel a portion of the debt already negotiated in relation to these discounts. Simultaneously there would be an offering of zero coupon bonds issued by the United States Treasury. The expected discounts by Mexico for this operation were higher than the banks were inclined to accept to reduce the value of their portfolios, and the final results were far below the expectations created when this formula was announced. With respect to this experience it is worth emphasizing that the whole initiative was developed under the assumption that the market had already decreed a certain discount on the value of the debt. Nevertheless, the same market forces reduced the margin of this discount, thus showing their inability (or unwillingness) to date to solve the debt problem. Added to this are the adverse repercussions of a high discount of the value of the debt on the total liabilities of the economy, given that it would tend to raise the expected yield for foreign agents who invest in the country.

These proposals to capture market discounts are nonetheless relevant in that they explicitly endorse reduction of the stock of indebtedness, and *could* establish a precedent with respect to future negotiations on the size of the debt. This objective appears increasingly necessary for Mexico, since the current restructuring of payments affects the terms of maturity but not service on a volume of debt which continues to grow.

In effect, the principal question for Mexico since 1982 with respect to its foreign debt—how to pay—could be replaced with another question: how to stop paying. Before reaching this extreme, the questions are instead: how to pay substantially less, how to effectively reduce the obligations associated with the debt, and how to overcome the dilemma between payment and growth. This implies a reevaluation by the Mexican government of the strategy it has followed during this period, as much as in the internal order as in its relationships with banks and the United States government.

On the creditors' side there are indications that this circumstance is also incorporated in their perceptions. There is no single response among the banks. Some increase their reserves against bad loans; others promote operations in the secondary debt market; still others opt to get rid of their Mexican portfolio, accepting larger discounts in exchange for liquidity and lower risk. The heterogeneous response on the part of the banking community seems to reflect the differences within its structure between money center banks and regional banks. The former have followed a systematic approach to the debt problem since the beginning of the crisis in 1982. Regional banks, for their part, were drawn into the strategy designed to manage the Mexican external debt under that global vision. But now there are signs that the initial cohesion of the creditor banks might be losing its initial strength. For its part, the United States government could face the need for greater political intervention to avoid confrontation, from which can derive important questions regarding the course of bilateral relations.

The limitations seen so far in the administration of the debt crisis make it appear as an effort to continue operating within the framework of the market—an effort that is rigidly maintained by the banks and multilateral agencies. Those who add political considerations to strictly financial reasoning have proposed some "deviations" from the central course of action, which give rise to what could be called administrative solutions to the debt problem. The best known and most debated is the Baker plan, set out in October 1985, which posed the need to promote economic growth in the debtor nations. This would be achieved by means of a strengthening of the original measures in the strategy designed to face the debt, that is: granting of additional financing from the banking system, with joint actions on the part of IMF and the World Bank, and with continued application of measures for structural change and opening of the Mexican economy to international markets. With respect to Mexico, which was considered one of the principal objects of this plan, it meant recognizing that credit flows could not be reestablished in voluntary financial markets, and represented, in fact, a truce in the hostilities which would eventually permit a return to full operation of market forces. The banks accepted the spirit of the Baker plan in principle—even when its application turned out to be only partially materialized, as indicated by the last reprogramming of the Mexican debt—inasmuch as it did not attack the mechanisms of the marketplace and in the end did not openly imply the conflict inherent in the debt. This, perhaps, explains the slight response other proposals have had in the financial community, such as that of Senator Bradley in 1986 which called for reduction of the debt level and widening of trade flows to relieve the scarcity of foreign exchange of the debtor economies.

The limitations shown by the market solutions and their inability to eliminate the risk of an eventual rupture between Mexico and the creditor banks impose the need to find new forms of cooperation. But it also must be recognized from the beginning that this will come forward in the framework of a conflict generated by the internal deterioration in Mexico and by the inherent character of the process of debt renegotiation.

The essence of this cooperation in terms of the existing levels of indebtedness is the exercise of unequal powers. Putting the question of the debt in the perspective of the powers that are engaged, as we are proposing, means to place oneself in the conflict. It implies not thinking of it as a marketplace anomaly but rather as an exercise with different negotiating capacities. The forms of cooperation taking place during debt negotiations, and those which can arise in the future, indicate that the relationships between cooperation and conflict which come forth from this analysis do not necessarily lead to collective advantages. It is a conflictual cooperation, and as such does not constitute a useful model of voluntary cooperation. In the case of the foreign debt cooperation arises as a natural requirement of the conflict, due to the complex repercussions that the economic and political disruption will have for the United States and Mexico. The condition of indebtedness constitutes a game in which the losses on one side have been larger than those that could be counted as gains by the other side, since both sides break down into winners and losers in a fragmented fashion. It is precisely this different assessment of costs and benefits—which appears to abridge the rules of the game (or break them)—that complicates the analysis of bilateral relationships, shows the limits of political action, and also makes more difficult any attempts to define the strategic changes needed to confront the problems.

Mexico has shown moderation in its handling of the foreign debt; the strategy pursued expresses a high present discount value on the future, creating little political desire for confrontation with the creditors. The anticipated benefits of maintaining a cooperative attitude, then, have been greater than the perceived cost of a change from the present status. The creditors make similar calculations. But the development of the conflict, with the high costs involved for Mexico and with the diverse actions orchestrated by the creditors, could eventually lead to a discrepancy in the relative discount values underlying the respective positions. With that would come a weakening of the cooperative framework so far established, creating a different scenario in order to prevent a rupture.

In 1982 the banks were highly vulnerable in economic terms and assigned a high discount value to the future of their ties to Mexico. Their actions were also based on the supposition that the crisis corresponded to a lack of liquidity which could be financed. Mexico cooperated out of necessity and because of the compatibility that existed between the government program and the economic philosophy of the foreign financial agents.

One of the discernible characteristics of conflict is that it develops as a process and thus doesn't necessarily have *one* solution. What follows then is consideration of the limits for establishing and modifying the strategies in accordance with the changes registered in the conditions of the conflict itself. The considerations dealt with thus far pose an important question: can cooperation be sustained which avoids a rupture and capitalizes on the benefits to be derived from the moderate conduct that Mexico has pursued?

The financial problem has been placed at the center of the economic agenda for relations between Mexico and the United States. This is due not only to the proportion of the debt contracted with American banks and the high exposure level they have reached, but also to the great concentration of economic transactions between Mexico and the U.S. market and, of course, the global strategic content of these bilateral relations.

Both the ongoing financial negotiations and the patterns of foreign trade show increasing limitations for providing solutions to the Mexican debt problem; they also illustrate the restrictions of the current strategy. In the last six years there has been an even greater concentration of Mexico's foreign trade with the United States; more than 60% of the exports and imports take place in that market, and from it also comes the highest portion of direct foreign investment in the country.

The United States has adopted an ambivalent position concerning its trade policy. While it advocates free growth of world wide commerce, in practice one sees a tendency toward greater protectionism. This stems from the principal outlines of the 1985 legislation concerning trade and tariffs, which likewise fosters bilateral negotiations over the existing multilateral framework. The Generalized System of Preferences was renewed, expanding the application of restrictive measures (escape clauses, antidumping, and compensatory rights). A series of "new themes" has been introduced which are associated with the liberalization of trade in services and investment in high technology sectors. There is a strengthened capacity of the executive branch to impose mechanisms for negotiations of reciprocal treatment in regard to market access for North American products, and to the flow of investment to the rest of the world. In this framework Mexico negotiated the "Understanding Regarding Subsidies and Compensatory Tariffs" (April 1985) agreeing to reduce or eliminate subsidies which encourage exports to the United States in a noncompetitive manner (especially affecting energy and petrochemical products produced by the public sector) and the use of preferential financing instruments which favor exportation. Subsequently, in 1987, a new agreement was signed regarding a framework of consultation principles and procedures for trade and investment relations.

These questions make up a large part of the international economic environment in which Mexico is involved. Financial and commercial relationships between the two countries are now more intense, more complex, and probably more unequal than before the crisis. American economic policy will necessarily have adverse repercussions on global economic conditions and on the very ability to apply economic policy in Mexico. The consequences of the crisis on the productive sector and the direction of the commercial and financial negotiations are the framework for new forms of bilateral economic interaction. Upon these depends, in a substantial manner, the possibility of sustaining or the need for changing the strategy of moderation in the face of the foreign debt. While the financial aspect of the bilateral relation can be contained, the commercial side of a cooperative scheme may be harder to maintain, thus becoming a more permanent source of conflict.

In the face of these developments the United States government will need to become involved as a more active participant in the dispute surrounding the debt. But along parallel lines the next United States administration must face the resolution of the large macroeconomic imbalances inherited from the Reagan administration. The difficulties in finding easy solutions—a "soft landing"—and the changes produced in the functioning of the economy have been further compounded by the Stock Market crash of October 1987.

The adjustment of the United States economy now requires measures similar to those demanded of other countries that follow the orthodox model—that is, the need to modify the relative price structure to permit reallocation of productive resources toward the export sector, which implies the restriction of internal demand and (as a consequence) real public and private spending. Monetary policy must play a crucial role in management of the economy in the face of the dilemma implied by easing up on the money supply and inflationary pressures, or rather its restriction and the repercussion on interest rates.

Forecasts of economic growth of the United States in the next two years are not too optimistic. The possibility of encouraging expansion of production based on exports encounters the difficulties associated with the precarious dynamism of international markets. The effectiveness of this export drive requires the coordination of economic policy with other OECD countries in the fiscal and monetary arena, and it also depends on the recovery of the debtor nations' capacity to import.

The content and manner in which the adjustment policies are applied will have implications for the possible performance of the Mexican economy. The uncertain expansion of the United States economy in coming years will make it more difficult for Mexico to participate in U.S. financial and product markets. The calls for "taking advantage" of existing interdependence and pursuing greater integration with the North (United States) produce, in the present situation, great skepticism. The bilateral relations will, without doubt, be determined by the strategic need to prevent a possible rupture. For the Mexican government, sustaining moderation as a negotiating position could become an ever greater challenge. In the present situation the possibilities for the Mexican government to sustain its moderation appear very uncertain. From the creditor banks' perspective this uncertainty is now probably less relevant than in previous years, since Mexico's capacity to inflict damage on the financial system has decreased. There is an increasing need to promote economic growth and to reduce the costs associated with external indebtedness and there is also a need to pursue cooperation between the two countries. The result is a seeming paradox: keeping moderation will require the next Mexican government to become a tougher negotiator. This means the need for Mexico to "sell its moderation dear."

TABLE 4.A1
Economic Indicators
(Real % Growth)

	1982	1983	1984	1985	1986	1987
GDP	-0.5	-5.3	3.7	2.8	-3.8	1.1
Per capita GDP	-3.2	-6.6	1.0	0.0	-6.3	-1.2
Total consumption	1.2	-6.8	3.2	2.0	-4.6	0.2
Total investment	-15.9	-27.9	5.5	6.4	-11.7	-0.7
Minimum wage	-9.0	-17.4	-5.6	-1.7	-8.8	-14.9
Imports	-37.1	-41.7	19.7	11.0	-12.2	7.9
Exports	13.7	11.7	10.5	-2.6	5.2	17.0

Source: Banco de México and Secretaria de Hacienda y Crédito
Público.

TABLE 4.A2
Cost of Payment Indicators

	1982	1986[a]	1982-1986	Level in 1986 equal to the year
Real per capita GDP (% rate of growth)	-3.2	-6.0	-10.4	1978
Open unemployment rate (%)	6.7	15.5	8.8[b]	pre-1970
Real minimum wage (yearly average as % rate of growth)	11.6	-9.0	-30.3	1964
Personal per capita consumption (as % rate of growth)	1.0	-7.7	-17.3	1974
Gross fixed investment (% of GDP)	21.0	15.5	-26.0	1962

[a]Preliminary figures.
[b]Percentage points increase.

Source: Banco de México, Annual Report. National Commission on Minimum
Wages, Economía Mexicana, #8, Centro de Investigación y Docencia
Económicas (CIDE), 1987.

TABLE 4.A3
Costs, Wages, External Transfers and Unused Capacity
(Billions of Mexican Pesos -- 1970)

	Loss in wages participation[a]	Real external transfers[b]	Unused productive capacity[c]
1982	9.0	1.6	78.5
1983	73.5	50.2	160.7
1984	85.3	50.6	133.8
1985[d]	84.5	39.4	123.1
1986[d]	84.7	62.3	178.6
Total as a proportion of the product in 1981	38%	22%	74%

[a]Loss in wages participation is obtained by multiplying the difference between wage participation in the product in 1981 (37.4%) with that of each year, by the respective product value.
[b]The transfer of real resources is measured as the difference between the gross domestic product and domestic demand, and is equal to the difference between factor payment and net indebtedness.
[c]Unused productive capacity is equal to potential product minus actual product.
[d]Preliminary figures.

Source: Economía Mexicana, #8, CIDE, 1987.

TABLE 4.A4
Foreign Debt Indicators

	1982	1983	1984	1985	1986	1987
Total foreign debt (US$ billion, year end)	90.76	90.63	98.38	101.58	102.98	105.07
Interest payments (US$ billion)	12.28	9.98	11.59	9.81	8.30	8.70
Foreign debt as percentage of:						
Export goods and nonfactor services	312.0	364.1	331.3	426.5	481.0	n/a
GDP	85.5	71.1	57.5	70.1	102.1	103.0[a]
Interest payments as percentage of:						
Total exports	43.3	37.2	39.0	42.6	39.3	36.0
Petroleum exports	76.3	66.1	76.4	76.4	149.5	111.5
Payment of interest on public debt as percentage of:						
Public expenditures	11.6	11.9	14.6	12.3	14.3	n/a
Public revenues	7.0	9.5	11.5	9.5	9.2	n/a

[a]Through September.
n/a = Not available.

Source: Calculated from data from the Banco de México and Secretaría de Hacienda y Crédito Público.

Notes

1. The financial deterioration of the last quarter of 1987 demanded a drastic change in the antiinflationary policy, which was expressed in adoption of the "Economic Solidarity Pact." In its two versions (indexation, in the first, freezing of key prices in the second), this pact includes a series of heterodox measures.

2. "The cost (of the foreign debt) was reduced considerably. The services profile is more in accordance with the country's ability to pay; being even better than before the crisis of 1982, with which it will no longer be an obstacle to the future development of Mexico and will permit sane and sustained growth and fulfillment of our foreign obligations." "In this way [with restructuring], we will resolve the problem of Mexico's foreign debt during this *sexenio* and the beginning of the next. The maturities between 1985 and the year 2000, including the need to refinance them, as well as the requirements for new money until the year 1990, have been calculated so that they may be financed through the market on the assumption that Mexico will continue its recuperation and enter a period of sustained growth." Secretary of Finance and Public Credit, *Notas sobre la Restructuración de la Deuda Externa de México*, Mexico City, 1985.

5

Mexican Foreign Debt: Old Lessons, New Possibilities

Thomas J. Trebat

Carlos Salinas de Gortari, head of the new administration in Mexico, will inherit from Miguel de la Madrid a greatly improved foreign exchange position. De la Madrid in December 1982 was faced with the exhaustion of Mexico's foreign exchange. Barring disaster, Salinas will enter office in December 1988 with foreign exchange reserves at near-record levels. Capital formation, not foreign debt management as such, will be the critical problem facing his administration.

Deciding how to deal with the debt will require an assessment of how key external constraints will shape Mexico's policy options.

The World Economy. Positive as well as negative shocks are possible. Oil prices could slump disastrously, but global oil supplies could tighten again in the 1990s resulting in windfall gains for Mexico. Manufactured export growth could collapse in a global recession, but continue to boom if a recession is averted.

Need for Foreign Savings. Can domestic savings in Mexico be mobilized to reduce the present dependence on external savings? How much foreign capital will the Mexican economy require to meet its growth objectives in the 1990s?

The Situation in the Less Developed Countries (LDCs). Global debt management in the late 1980s stumbles from crisis to crisis. Debt relief schemes may figure importantly in the workout of the global debt problem in some Latin countries. How should Mexico react? By seeking the same concessions from creditors as those obtained by other LDCs or by seeking rewards through more cooperative policies toward creditors?

Future Sources of Capital. The nature and sources of foreign capital for Mexico in the 1990s must also be carefully considered by policymakers. What can be done to attract more foreign investment? Will the International Monetary Fund and World Bank be willing and able to play important roles as providers of financing? Is it realistic to anticipate voluntary inflows of private capital during the next *sexenio?*

Changes in the International Economy. Evolving patterns of world trade and payments demand careful consideration by the Mexican authorities. The United States in the 1990s will seek to redress the international trade imbalances of the 1980s through investment in manufactured exports. How will Mexico fit into this process? Economic policies and diplomatic efforts stressing trade integration with the United States and Canada could wind up being much more important to Mexico in the 1990s than equivalent efforts to reduce the burden of the existing debt.

Historical Background

Mexico between 1950 and 1980 registered important economic and social progress, even though growth became increasingly bumpy in the Echeverría and López Portillo years.[1] Most of this progress was achieved on the basis of fairly modest (even at the time) inflows of foreign resources. External public debt was only on the order of US$4 billion at the outset of the Echeverría years in the 1970s.[2] Debt quintupled during the *sexenio* to more than US$20 billion; but since much of this can be attributed to the large capital expenditures involved in developing new oilfields in the early 1970s, the growth in debt was not disproportionate to expected future growth in output.

The dramatic growth of Mexico's foreign debt occurred in the López Portillo *sexenio.* The total debt (this time including debt of the private sector) quintupled again to more than US$100 billion. Yet this accumulation occurred during one of the greatest foreign exchange bonanzas in Mexican history. On the strength of oil prices, merchandise exports increased from US$5 billion in 1977 to US$21 billion in 1982.

Mexico spent all of its oil windfall almost immediately and worse, leveraged its expected future income from oil in order to borrow massively from the international banks. A particularly virulent strain of the "Dutch disease" broke out in Mexico as the oil abundance held up the value of the Mexican *peso* and encouraged imports, a process of import desubstitution.[3] Spiralling current account deficits in the early 1980s were financed through chaotic, increasingly desperate international borrowing which banks were, at first, willing to accommodate. When banks finally became wary in 1982, Mexico's foreign exchange reserves quickly dissipated leading to the August moratorium.

Mexico's Debt Management Policies

Mexico's influence on debt policies in other Latin countries stems from the coherence (by comparison to the more erratic records of Brazil and Argentina) of Mexican debt management. By accurately reading the shifting "mood" of the creditors, Mexico usually has led the way in extracting concessions and, as a result, continuously has redefined for other indebted countries the boundaries of the "conventional" approach to debt management.

The conventional approach took shape during the first phase of Mexico's debt refinancing in 1982–83. The first phase was marked by an unprecedented degree of cooperation between creditors and a large-scale provision of "new money."

Mexico signed a three-year Extended Fund Facility with the IMF in December 1982. The Fund agreement paved the way for a massive restructuring of both principal and interest on Mexico's commercial bank debt. Commercial banks eventually were persuaded to provide new financing of US$8.8 billion in the period 1983–84. This financing amounted only to about 45% of interest due to commercial banks in this period.[4]

Commercial bank debt totalling US$23.1 billion (including both short- and medium-term obligations of the public sector) was restructured. Both the interest rates charged on the new loans (1 3/4% over prime or 1 7/8% over London Interbank Offer Rate [LIBOR], plus a 1% commission) and the relatively short amortization periods (eight years with four years of grace) attached to the rescheduled maturities belied the confidence at the time of both Mexican authorities and the commercial bank creditors in the ability of the Mexican economy to recover creditworthiness quickly.[5]

The second phase of the Mexican debt negotiations, in 1984–85, produced a long-term rescheduling of the principal amounts of most of Mexico's external debt. The "Multiyear Rescheduling Agreement" (MYRA) affected amortizations of medium-term debt of the public sector falling due in 1985–90 in the amount of US$48.7 billion. This total included almost US$24 billion in amortizations that had been rescheduled previously in the first phase of the restructuring. Interest charges on the debt were reduced across the board on the consolidated debt to an average of 1 1/8% over LIBOR.

Hailed at the time as a breakthrough in the debt management process, the MYRA was in fact only a very modest next step which reflected the reality of Mexico's payments ability in 1984–85. Mexico's foreign exchange cashflow had improved since the nadir of 1982, but the country was barely able to meet its interest obligations. Complying with the mountain of amortization payments in 1985 and beyond was out of the question without a large inflow of fresh commercial bank lending.[6]

After the second phase of the restructuring of Mexico's debt, the main concern of both Mexican authorities and commercial bank creditors was to maintain the flow of interest on the long-term loans. While the MYRA made no explicit reference to new money, the third phase of the debt restructuring, in 1986–87, brought to the surface the implicit understanding that large amounts of new money from creditors could be made available in the event of a contingency. Few at the time of the MYRA signing in 1985 could have anticipated that the contingency would arise so quickly, however. A major earthquake in Mexico City in late-1985 coincided with a period of weakness in oil prices. By mid-1986, Mexican oil prices had already dipped below US$8 per barrel. (The official Mexican projections underlying the MYRA agreement had assumed an average price per barrel of US$27 in 1986). The cashflow crisis of 1986 led to the largest "rescue operation" yet in the debt management process, a US$12 billion "package" of new financing.[7] The rescue operation included a quickly negotiated 18-month standby program with the IMF involving about US$1.7 billion in Fund assistance. "Quick disbursing" policy-based loans from the World Bank were added in support of the various Mexican government programs. By September an agreement was reached with official government creditors to reschedule US$1.8 billion in maturing obligations and to refinance 60% of interest coming due to official creditors in 1986–87. The package also marked the first significant loan from the Japanese government, a US$1 billion loan from the Japan EXIMBANK.

This show of official support had been orchestrated by the United States (Federal Reserve Chairman Paul Volcker had taken an active role) to prod commercial banks to cooperate. The detailed financing arrangements—particularly the decision to divide Mexico's US$12 billion financing request equally between official and private bank creditors—had been worked out in secrecy by the Federal Reserve, the Treasury, the IMF, and the new Mexican finance authorities. The deal was presented as a *fait accompli* to senior executives from the leading creditor banks at a meeting hastily convened in Washington in late July 1986. Implicit but unstated in the Mexican presentation was that commercial bank participation more or less along the lines suggested was the only means to avoid unilateral Mexican default.

The detailed negotiations between Mexico and the banks that followed were contentious, but by the end of September 1986 had resulted in agreement to provide US$6 billion in new money to be disbursed in 1986–87. (The amount included US$1 billion in cofinancing with the World Bank.) The bank negotiations were also significant for two other concessions to Mexico. First, the lending spreads on the bulk of Mexico's public sector debt (US$43.7 billion) were reduced below the psychological barrier of 1% over LIBOR (the actual margin negotiated was 13/16 of 1%). Second, these bank negotiations marked the first appearance in any Latin rescheduling of contingency lending. Banks agreed to provide additional new money beyond the $6 billion if oil prices again collapsed or if Mexican economic growth failed to recover to a minimum level by early 1987.

An Assessment

Mexico's foreign debt policy since 1982—one of "muddling through" or "wearing down the debt"—has exacted a heavy cost on the economy. (See Table 5.1). The incipient recovery of GDP in 1984–85 was cut short by the earthquake and the collapse of oil prices. After seven years of muddling through, per capita GDP in Mexico is still 15% below the level of the early 1980s. Gross fixed capital investment in Mexico has slumped to a point that what capital formation does take place only replaces capital that is wearing out. Unemployment, even among the professional classes, rose sharply even as the total labor force has continued to surge.

The muddling through strategy has failed so far to return Mexico to voluntary capital markets, the stated purpose of the Baker Plan— a scheme under which Mexico is supposedly the showcase example. A review of the major ratios of external creditworthiness reveals little progress in wearing down the debt and, consequently, in attracting new voluntary credits. (See Table 5.2). The ratios of debt to exports and debt to GNP have remained the same or deteriorated since 1983. The same is true of the proportion of export earnings preempted by interest payments, although this indicator did begin to improve in 1987.

But the "muddling through" approach did bring some important benefits to Mexico. The strategy restored foreign exchange liquidity, converted many billions of dollars of short-term loans into quasi-equity investments by banks in Mexico, and provided de facto for a partial refinancing of interest payments to creditors.

Whatever its shortcomings, Mexico's debt management prevented foreign trade from collapsing by keeping trade credits in place. In

TABLE 5.1
Growth and Investment in Mexico, 1962-1988

	1982	1983	1984	1985	1986	1987
Real GDP (% Change)	-0.5	-5.3	3.7	2.8	-3.8	1.1
Per capita GDP (% Change)	-3.1	-7.6	1.2	0.5	-6.0	-1.1
Fixed Investment (% Change)	-15.9	-27.9	5.5	6.4	-11.6	0.0
Private (%)	-17.3	-24.2	9.0	13.4	-8.8	-0.2
Public (%)	-14.2	-32.5	0.6	-4.4	-16.8	0.4
Gross Domestic Investment (% of GDP)	21.6	17.0	17.7	19.6	18.4	
Gross National Savings (% of GDP)	22.5	20.6	20.0	19.6	17.4	
Net Foreign Balance (% of GDP)	0.9	3.6	2.3	0.0	-1.0	

<u>Source</u>: IMF, International Financial Statistics, various issues.

TABLE 5.2
Indicators of Mexico's Debt Service Burden, 1982-1987

	Total debt (US$ billion)	Net debt (% exports)[a]	Debt (% of GNP)	Interest (% of exports)
1982	91.1	329	55	44
1983	94.0	317	66	36
1984	95.3	273	56	36
1985	97.4	314	55	35
1986	101.5	409	80	36
1987	104.6	317	78	27

[a]Net debt is total external debt net of official international reserves. Exports of goods and services.

<u>Source</u>: Author's computations on the basis of data provided by the Banco de México.

fact, Mexico's non-oil export growth record has far exceeded expectations. Non-oil exports are now almost 60% of the total and still growing rapidly. Investment in the nontraditional export sector is an important exception to the overall picture of low investment in Mexico. (See Table 5.3).

The debt strategy could also be looked upon as a way for Mexico to buy time until an eventual rise in oil prices comes to the rescue. Oil prices in the late 1980s have rebounded from the dismal lows of 1986, but it is unlikely that they will rise much beyond the US$15–$US20 range before 1990. Yet at some point in the 1990s, another worldwide energy squeeze is possible, even probable, and it is likely to hit hardest in the United States. The potential leverage effect of oil on Mexico's debt servicing capacity cannot be ignored. For the sake of illustration, if at some point in the 1990s Mexican oil prices again reach US$32 a barrel (a price that would still be well below the peaks of the late 1970s), the resulting increase in oil revenues would exceed the entire interest bill due to banks in 1988. While it seems unrealistic to focus on only the potential for help from oil and non-oil exports—after all, oil prices could decline in the 1990s—the muddling through strategy does at least provide some basic protection for Mexico in the event of unanticipated pressures on the country's cashflow. This was most clearly demonstrated in the 1986 rescue operation, but it is true of the decade as a whole. (See Table 5.4). In the 1983–88 period, bank creditors provided new money on average sufficient to cover almost one-third of interest obligations to banks. During the same period, the net lending of official creditors to Mexico doubled, from US$13.5 billion in 1983 to US$27 billion in 1988.

Policy Options for Mexico

Faced with such mixed results from past debt strategy, Salinas now faces three broad sets of options regarding debt policy. First, Mexico could strike out on its own, determine what it could "afford" to pay, and impose a unilateral settlement on creditors. Peru under Alan Garcia has followed this path. Second, Mexico could seek a so-called "political solution" to the debt whereby the burden of the debt would be somehow shifted to industrial governments, which would in turn impose a settlement on creditor banks. Third, the Salinas government could build upon the "conventional" approach of the past five years with aggressive policies to attract voluntary capital to Mexico.

Authorities will probably waste little time in rejecting the first option of unilateral action. It is difficult to believe that such action—a partial repudiation, for example, or a below-market interest rate—

TABLE 5.3
Structure of the Balance of Trade, 1984-1988
(US$ billion)

	1984	1985	1986	1987[a]	1988[b]
Trade Balance	14.1	9.7	5.9	9.8	8.4
Exports	25.4	23.0	17.3	22.0	22.4
Oil	16.6	14.8	6.3	8.6	7.8
Non-Oil	7.6	6.9	9.7	11.9	13.1
In-bond	1.2	1.3	1.3	1.5	1.5
Imports	11.3	13.2	11.4	12.2	14.1
Memo Item:					
Non-Oil Export Growth (% Change)	7.0	-9.2	40.1	22.7	10.1
Non-Oil Exports (% of Total)	30.0	30.0	56.0	54.0	58.0
Oil Exports (million barrels per day)	1.53	1.43	1.29	1.34	1.30
Oil Export Price (US$ per barrel)	26.8	25.3	11.8	16.2	15.0
Foreign Exchange Reserves (US$ billion)	7.2	4.9	5.7	12.7	

[a]Estimated.
[b]Forecast.

Source: Institute of International Finance, Internal Documents.

TABLE 5.4
Interest Payments and New Money, 1983-1987

	Interest to banks (US$ billion)	New money from banks (US$ billion)	New money (% of interest)
1983	8.7	5.0	57.5
1984	9.8	3.8	38.8
1985	8.3	0.0	0.0
1986	6.6	0.0	0.0
1987[a]	5.9	4.4	74.5
1988[b]	6.1	1.1	18.0
Totals	45.4	14.3	31.5

Note: New money allocations by year are approximate as are interest payments to banks. New money for 1988 includes disbursement of US$500 million Growth Contingency.

Source: Author's computations on the basis of data provided by the Banco de México.

would be accepted by creditors without some type of retaliation. The option ignores the problem of obtaining new credits in the future and squanders Mexico's unique bargaining power to extract concessions and new credits from creditors. Besides, an arbitrarily imposed settlement, e.g., a ceiling or cap on debt service as a percentage of exports, could result in fewer resources for Mexico in the future than by simply muddling through with occasional new money support.

The second option—a "once and for all settlement"—is no doubt receiving serious attention in Mexico City as officials seek ways to capture for Mexico the secondary market discount on Mexican debt.[8] Mexican interest in a nonconventional approach has grown against the backdrop of large U.S. bank reserves against LDC debt and a spate of international proposals—some from academic observers, some from the floor of the U.S. Congress, some from commercial banks— for the creation of an International Debt Discount Facility which would dispense debt relief at the cost of banks and taxpayers in industrial countries.

A negotiated once and for all solution would be in Mexico's long-term interest, but the United States and other industrial country governments have neither the financial nor political means necessary to mount an international debt rescue effort. An internationally sponsored debt rescue could hardly be limited just to Mexico and would require several hundreds of billions of U.S. dollars in industrial country support for the LDCs. This does not appear to be in the cards, no matter who wins the November 1988 elections in the United States, so Mexican authorities are likely to reject the second option as unrealistic.

This leaves the third option—a conventional approach to the debt coupled with policies to attract new resources to Mexico. Mexican authorities can hardly be expected to be enthusiastic about a set of policies that appears to be more of the same. But, as I argue below, the Salinas government will probably arrive at the conclusion that policies which emphasize cooperation with creditors offer the best hope for the future.

Secondary Markets and External Debt

Theoretical and practical considerations limit the possibilities for a comprehensive working out of the Mexican debt on the basis of large secondary market discounts. The overriding characteristic of the Latin debt crisis of the 1980s has been the absence of an international bankruptcy court, the equivalent of a Chapter XI in the U.S. bankruptcy code. As Dooley has pointed out, this means that it is impossible in the case of sovereign debt to define the "property rights" of the existing creditors so that the loss, if any, can be allocated equitably among them.[9]

The existence of a secondary market for discounted Mexican debt introduces a further complication. The discount on the debt is the market's signal that existing creditors have sustained a significant loss on their loans to Mexico. Yet, since no forum exists to fix the loss on the existing bank creditors, the market price takes on much broader significance as a proxy for the discount to be applied to all liabilities of Mexico. Since it is difficult or impossible to subordinate old claims on Mexico to new claims, potential new creditors of Mexico have every reason to believe that eventually they, too, can be made to share in the loss sustained by the existing creditors. Following this argument, potential new creditors (e.g., a foreign investor or a domestic resident contemplating purchase of a domestic obligation of the Mexican government) must immediately write down the value of the initial investment to reflect the possibility of sharing in the loss signalled by the secondary market discount. In particular, foreign and domestic corporations will demand a much higher than "normal" return on investments in physical capital before committing funds to investment projects in Mexico. In consequence, investment will fall below, probably well below, levels that could be reached in the absence of a secondary market discount.

The intrinsic link between existing and new creditor groups is that all are acquiring claims on the same source of repayment, in this case the future output of Mexico. As long as the possibility of loss exists for some group of creditors (e.g., the commercial banks) the same possibility exists for other creditors as well. Investors in physical capital can be taxed heavily or denied access to foreign exchange. Holders of domestic currency debt can see the values of their investment eroded by repudiation or currency reform.

Since the debt crisis in 1982, the flow of new foreign direct investment to Mexico has understandably slowed to a trickle, despite the loosening of investment regulations. Capital flight has also been a serious problem during the period. If, as is likely, these investors are reacting to the risk signalled by the large market discount on Mexican debt, then the best debt strategy for the Mexican government would consist of policies that cause the secondary market price to rise (the discount to fall).

Practical difficulties also stand in the way of a broad-based debt strategy based on the secondary market valuation of Mexican debt. The foremost involves getting all bank creditors to agree to accept a large loss on their existing claims. Many will refuse to do so at a price that is advantageous to Mexico. Those who do agree to the exchange will insist on some type of "credit enhancement" (e.g., a U.S. government or World Bank guarantee for their remaining principal and interest exposure). Such a large-scale public bailout does not seem likely, and it would be unwise for foreign debt policy to count on its occurrence.[10] Another practical objection to the debt-buyback schemes (i.e., Mexico using secondary market valuations to repurchase its own debt) is the illusory nature of the secondary market discount. As any one bank elected to exchange its debt for bonds, thereby reducing Mexico's debt, the price of the debt in the secondary market would tend to rise as the collectibility of the loans not exchanged for bonds would rise. As the secondary market price rose, the Mexican government would not be able to buy back the bank debt as cheaply as originally envisioned. Unless forced to do so many banks would elect not to participate, as they would reap capital gains simply by staying on the sidelines and holding on to their loan claims. The dilemma of a deeply discounted debt-buyback scheme as the basis for Mexican foreign debt policy can be stated as follows. A large amount of Mexican debt could be retired at secondary market prices only if the debt remained cheap. But if the debt remains cheap, new creditors will avoid acquiring new claims on Mexico. The net gains for Mexico in this game would be marginal at best, possibly even negative. The present cycle of low investment and low growth would persist.

Attracting New Money to Mexico

The new Mexican administration will need more deliberate policies to speed up the return of voluntary capital to Mexico. Ways must be found to deal with the major shortcomings of the Baker Plan approach: inadequate levels of external financing to support Mexican economic reform and an unrealistic timeframe for the economic reforms to take root. Examples of specific policy actions can be grouped under three headings: a) transforming the nature of bank claims; b) attracting new money from banks and other private sources; and c) tapping official sources of capital.[11]

Transforming bank claims. The Mexbond scheme in February 1988 was an important first step toward the voluntary transformation of claims into bonds or local currency claims. The scheme was far from successful, primarily because it offered too little to creditors in exchange for what Mexican authorities hoped would be a large amount of debt forgiveness. (The principal on the Mexbond is secured by a long-term U.S. Treasury obligation, but the interest on the bond remains a Mexican risk for participating banks).

In the future, voluntary bond conversions with modest credit enhancements (e.g., partial World Bank guarantees) could result in a larger volume of debt forgiveness by banks wishing to get out of the business of international lending. Debt-equity arrangements—conversions of bank debt into equity in Mexican corporations or mutual funds—will need to be reexamined in the next Administration. Authorities to date have been very cool to debt-equity programs, fearing inflation, capital flight, and nationalist reactions.[12]

Concerns about side effects are warranted; however, experience in other countries (Chile is the leading example) has shown that debt-equity programs can transform bank debt into claims more easily serviced, and that the conversions can be important both in absolute size and as catalysts for complementary private sector investments. Mexico's limited experience to date with debt-equity conversions suggests a strong interest by banks and foreign investors in acquiring real assets in Mexico, even at the cost of an upfront discount on the debt being converted. Authorities have chosen in 1988 to concentrate on antiinflation efforts; but if these prove successful, the debt-equity program in Mexico should promptly be restored.

Attracting New Money. The advantage of strategies that emphasize new money rather than relief on the old debt is that they open up the possibility of much larger inflows of resources in the future. Mexican strategies to attract new money could be variations on the Mexbond theme. It would make more sense to use Mexico's large foreign exchange position to collateralize new resources from lenders, for example, rather than old debt. Escrow arrangements or sinking funds might also serve a useful purpose in reducing risk for new investors or lenders. The rules governing the debt-equity program could be loosened if creditors are able to supplement the converted funds used in the investment with fresh resources from abroad.

Tapping Official Sources. The time could be right for Mexico to push for a major expansion of import financing lines from official export credit agencies in support of new private sector investments. Japan, the major surplus country, has announced its willingness to recycle at least US$30 billion to the indebted countries. No Latin country has yet pressed the issue and no new Japanese financing has yet materialized in the hemisphere. Mexico is well placed to press the point with Japan, especially in view of the strategic interests of Japanese corporations in Mexico. The new Mexican government could also do more to tap new, more innovative types of assistance from the multilateral agencies. Greater use could be made of World Bank guarantees to increase the flow of new private lending and to enhance debt-bond exchanges. The time seems right for the IMF to develop new lending facilities to protect indebted countries against swings in international interest rates, and Mexico could be the leading candidate.

Conclusions for the Bilateral Relationship

Although not a stated objective of policy on either side of the border, a framework of bilateral consultation and cooperation on international financial issues has resulted from the debt crisis. The U.S. has used policies ranging from direct financial assistance, its influence in multilateral agencies, and moral suasion with private U.S. banks to provide critical assistance to Mexico during the last decade. Mexico has responded by eschewing unilateral actions on debt and exercising a moderating influence on debt policies elsewhere in Latin America. With the passage of time, it will be seen that these Mexican actions prevented serious shocks to the U.S. and world financial systems.

But the economic and social costs have been disturbingly high and now Mexico stands at a crossroads. The new administration must decide either to reaffirm these moderate policies on debt management or to strike out in new directions to reduce the burden of the external debt. Options are being considered in Mexico City, but the assessment in this chapter concludes that Mexico's foreign debt policy will continue to emphasize moderation, cooperation, and compromise.

From a sheer practical viewpoint, the country's cash position is now much improved in comparison with the situation six years ago. More importantly, the competitive position of Mexico in the world economy has been strengthened; the economy is now much more outward-oriented than before. Over the next *sexenio* Mexico will be subject to the pushes and pulls of many external forces; positive as well as negative shocks are possible. The world economy itself is changing. If economic policies are the right ones, Mexico will have an important opportunity to take part in a major expansion of U.S. trade in the 1990s. Policymakers who mull over these considerations will probably conclude that muddling through on the foreign debt may be the only way to proceed after all.

But if new inflows of foreign capital sufficient to change the bleak picture of investment and growth in Mexico are not forthcoming, it will be politically impossible to sustain in the early 1990s the economic reforms of the 1980s. By that point, unilateral action on the foreign debt and inward-oriented economic policies may be the only policy choice remaining, instead of one among several options.

The United States has a strategic interest in political moderation and successful economic policy in Mexico. Mexico is the geoeconomic hinterland of the United States and, unless Mexico deals itself out of the game, it can reinforce the expansion of U.S. trade and investment in the 1990s. But a Mexican recovery must be a specific policy objective of the United States. Bringing lagging Mexico along in an industrial revival on the North American continent means speeding up Mexico's return to more normal financial market conditions and more normal investment levels. Even in an era of budget restrictions, the United States will have to find ways to encourage increased flows of private and official capital to Mexico. The "wear down the debt" approach of the Baker Plan era must be complemented by policies to boost trade with, and investment in, Mexico.

The best hope for the next decade is that Mexico and the United States will go from the framework of financial cooperation that has emerged from the debt crisis to one of much closer integration on trade issues. Mexico must look to the trade sector of its economy for dynamism in the 1990s. Both countries share a need to improve trade and investment performance; the dollar's decline gives them the opportunity. This can and should be done in partnership, taking advantage of the complementarity of the two economies.

Notes

1. For background on this period, the reader is referred to Luis Rubio and Francisco Gil-Díaz, *A Mexican Response*, Priority Press Publications, New York, 1987; Albert O. Hirschman, "The Political Economy of Latin American Development: Seven Exercises in Retrospection," *Latin American Research Review*, XXII:3, 1987, pp. 7–36; Thomas J. Trebat, "Mexico's Foreign Financing," in Musgrave, editor, *Mexico: A Perspective for the Next Decade*, pp. 33–70; Edward F. Buffie and Allen Sangines Krause, "Economic Policy and Foreign Debt in Mexico," in J.D. Sachs, editor, *Foreign Debt and Economic Performance*, Summary Volume, University of Chicago, Chicago, forthcoming 1988.

2. For a viewpoint on the early growth of Mexico's external debt, see Adrian Lajous, "A Note to Mexico's Creditors: No More Loans, Please," *Wall Street Journal*, October 2, 1987.

3. Hirschman, *op. cit.*, pp. 17–18.

4. Commercial banks provided US$5 billion in new money for disbursement in 1982–83 and, upon further negotiations in late 1983, an additional US$3.8 billion which was disbursed during 1984.

5. The external obligations of the Mexican private sector were also swept up in the 1982 moratorium and subsequent restructuring. The rapid pace of devaluations in 1982 had put a heavy strain on the cashflow of most Mexican private corporations. The private sector was also vulnerable to pressures from nervous foreign creditors anxious to call back in their loans to all Mexican borrowers by any means available. Some of the private debt was assumed by

the sovereign with the nationalization of the Mexican banks in 1982. The bulk of the private sector foreign debt (a total of US$12 billion) was rescheduled with creditors via the FICORCA system which provided forward foreign exchange cover for Mexican private corporations.

6. In fact, Mexican authorities had originally intended to propose a "Multiyear New Money Agreement" to go along with the MYRA, but were persuaded at an early stage in the negotiations by their commercial bank advisors to drop the idea.

7. This third phase of the debt restructuring was also important in marking the economic policy ascendancy of Salinas and the demise of Jesus Silva Herzog. How their respective positions on Mexican foreign debt policy in general, and the wisdom of the rescue package in particular, influence this critical reshuffling is not yet clear. In the weeks prior to the launching of the rescue in July 1986, Silva Herzog had adopted an increasingly hardline public posture on the need for more equitable burden-sharing between Mexico and its bank creditors. Mexican finance authorities, under Silva Herzog's direction, had gone so far as to prepare a scheme that would effectively have suspended interest payments in foreign exchange to bank creditors as of July 1, 1986. Silva Herzog's departure from office coincided with dismissal of the plan to suspend interest.

The contingency facilities were a US$1.2 billion "investment support" facility which was tied to oil prices and a US$500 million economic growth facility. The investment support facility was not disbursed as Mexican oil prices in 1986–87 stayed well above the trigger price of US$9 per barrel. However, Mexican finance authorities announced in early 1988 their intention to draw on the economic growth facility funds as Mexican GDP in 1987 (measured by the growth of industrial sector GDP) did not surpass the target rate of 3.5%.

8. Rubio and Gil Díaz, *op. cit.*, pp. 49–50. Also "Urgente, Ajustar la Deuda Externa a su Valor de Mercado: Pedro Aspe (SPP)," *El Financiero*, October 23, 1987.

9. Michael P. Dooley, "Market Valuation of External Debt," *Finance and Development*, March 1987, pp. 6–9.

10. This type of debt exchange is probably only feasible in the context of a Kenen-like International Debt Management Authority (IDMA), under which some international agency stands willing to exchange its obligations for external debt, thereby providing the credit enhancement. While an IDMA of some type may be an ideal solution for Mexico, budget constraints in the United States and the capital constraints of the World Bank make it unlikely to occur. See "Statement of Peter Kenen," Hearings Before the Subcommittee on International Finance and Monetary Policy of the Committee on Banking, Housing, and Urban Affairs, United States Senate, March 26, 1987, Washington, D.C., Government Printing Office, 1987. Felix Rohatyn suggested a version of an IDMA to be operated on a bilateral basis between the United States and Mexico. See Felix Rohatyn and Roger Altman, "Confront the Mexican Problem," *Wall Street Journal*, November 26, 1986.

11. These and other options are discussed in detail in William R. Cline, *Mobilizing Bank Lending to Debtor Countries,* Institute for International Economics, Washington, D.C, 1987; Stanley R. Fischer, "Resolving the International Debt Crisis," unpublished, August 1987; "Restoring Market Access: New Directions in Bank Lending," Institute of International Finance, Inc., Washington, D.C., June 1987.

12. A total of US$2.1 billion in debt-equity applications had been approved by December 1987 with another US$600 million in pending applications. However, the program has been suspended several times to discourage greater volume.

6

Recent U.S.-Mexico Trade Relations: Positive Results and Increased Cooperation

Brian Timothy Bennett

Mexico is now engaged in transforming the structure of its international trade. This change is a fundamental part of Mexico's effort to move its economy away from a policy of import substitution and dependence on oil exports for foreign exchange earnings to a policy of export-led growth. Once the de la Madrid administration became convinced that export-led growth should be an important part of Mexico's economic future, it was clear that concrete measures, and not just rhetoric, were needed to make the change.

First, trade liberalization, combined with the reduction or elimination of domestic subsidies for Mexican producers, was needed to stimulate competition and force producers to respond to the market on the basis of price, quality, timely delivery and follow-up service: characteristics that were all too often missing among Mexican producers and products. Second, in order to respond most effectively to competitive pressure, Mexican producers needed access to lower cost imported raw materials, intermediate goods, and up-to-date machinery. Since late 1987, trade liberalization in Mexico has also increasingly taken on an antiinflation role.

An important by-product of the substantial trade liberalization implemented by the de la Madrid administration since July 1985 has been the reduction or elimination of numerous, longstanding bilateral trade irritants. Thus, as a direct result of a process undertaken by the Mexican government largely for reasons of its own internal economic development, trade relations between the United States and Mexico since early 1985 have entered their most active phase ever and become increasingly cooperative and productive. To the extent that the trade liberalization implemented to date can be sustained and even expanded, together with the continued resistance to protectionism in the United States, good trade relations should continue, with positive spin-offs for the overall bilateral relationship. Although the final outcome of the ongoing structural adjustment process in Mexico obviously is not yet known, it is already clear that the focus on fostering export-led growth has magnified and strengthened the interdependence of the U.S. and Mexican economies, and will continue to do so.

The Recent Evolution of Mexican Trade Policy

Recognition of the need for a change in Mexico's development model was not unique to the de la Madrid administration. In response to the serious financial and economic crisis of 1976, the first years of the López Portillo administration included a conscious effort to move away from the import substitution model followed since the mid-1940s by rationalizing the system of trade protection in order to stimulate competition in the industrial sector. This first attempt at a partial internationalization of the Mexican economy culminated in Mexico's first application to the General Agreement on Tariffs and Trade (GATT) in late 1978 and the actual negotiation of a draft protocol of accession in 1979.

The year 1979 also saw the second oil boom, however. The increase in oil revenues, and the increase in international stature that accompanied it, undermined this first effort at restructuring the Mexican economy and overwhelmed the interest in structural adjustment, which was at that time rather narrowly based. Although López Portillo's 1979–1982 Global Development Plan and his 1979–1990 National Industrial Development Plan called for increased emphasis on export-led growth and some further reduction in the level of protectionism, increasing oil revenues seemed to many the best way to finance growth. As a result, forcing inefficient domestic manufacturers to become internationally competitive was perceived as less urgent. This, in turn, opened the door for the industrial groups opposed to more open trade to lobby (successfully in some cases, such as beer and consumer electronics) for a rollback of some of the trade liberalization measures already implemented.

The turning point in López Portillo's policy of leading Mexico increasingly into the international economy through export-led growth came with the decision of the Mexican economic cabinet in March 1980 to reject the protocol of accession (despite its extremely generous terms of entry) offered by the GATT Council. A few weeks before the vote, López Portillo reportedly stated in a speech that there were only two types of countries in the world: those with oil and those without. Although there were certainly a number of reasons (including opposition from labor unions, universities, domestic industry, and some dissatisfaction in the cabinet with the bureaucratic handling of the negotiation) why the majority of the economic cabinet decided against GATT accession, López Portillo's comment undoubtedly reflected the mental attitude of many of his cabinet members as well.[1] The confidence that flowed from increasing oil revenues diminished the sense of urgency with respect to structural adjustment and fueled Mexico's historical reluctance to enter into international agreements.

This oil-based growth and the confidence that went with it were shaken by the fall of oil prices in the second half of 1981. The consequent collapse of the Mexican economy in 1982, with its debt servicing moratorium and in the midst of a deepening international recession, led to the negotiation of an International Monetary Fund (IMF) loan in November 1982. The austerity program undertaken in conjunction with that loan included import restrictions. Thus, by the end of the López Portillo administration in 1982, the Mexican market had almost totally closed, trade relations between the United States and Mexico were tense, and the Mexican economy was once again in crisis.

Like his predecessor, de la Madrid spoke early on in his administration of the need for structural adjustment, including the need for a gradual opening of the Mexican economy. However, the first years were focused primarily on economic stabilization, with structural adjustment relegated more to talk than to action. In fact, the publishing of the National Program for Industrial Promotion and Foreign Trade (PRONAFICE) in 1984 raised serious questions within the U.S. government as to just what kind of structural adjustment Mexico had in mind. The planned policy of sectoral development programs, combined with a selective opening for imports, raised serious concerns among U.S. trade officials already frustrated in dealing with a large trading partner that remained outside GATT and the protective walls of protection.

It took slower than expected growth and rising inflation in 1985 to force the de la Madrid administration to conclude that substantial, fundamental structural reforms were indeed needed to restore sustainable future growth in Mexico. This led to the first significant trade liberalization measure under de la Madrid: removal in July 1985 of the import licensing requirements on over two thousand categories in Mexico's tariff schedule, representing about 37% of the total value of Mexican imports by value.[2] This was followed by the announcement in late November 1985 that Mexico would reapply for entry into GATT.

The decision to once again seek admission to GATT was of enormous importance. Since Mexican development and growth were targeted to become increasingly dependent on non-oil exports, GATT membership would enable Mexico to participate in and enjoy the benefits of the only multilateral instrument that lays down agreed rules for international trade. GATT membership would provide most favored nation status to Mexico in all the other GATT markets, while also providing a mechanism for redress should access to those markets be nullified or impaired. Also, with the initiation of the Uruguay Round of multilateral trade negotiations approaching, it made sense for the world's thirteenth largest economy—and one openly intending to become more of a world trader of manufactured goods—to participate in the formulation or reformulation of the rules of the game relating to trade in goods and services, trade-related investment measures, and intellectual property protection.

The practical benefits of GATT membership should not be overplayed, however. Mexico was already receiving most favored nation treatment for most of its exports, and GATT disciplines do not cover Mexico's four largest sources of foreign exchange earnings: oil, *maquiladoras*, tourism, and migrant workers. In addition, the U.S.-European Community trade disputes during the first half of the 1980s had exposed serious weaknesses in GATT's dispute settlement mechanism. It thus can be argued that the greatest immediate benefits to Mexico from the decision to reapply for GATT membership were symbolic and psychological. The decision symbolized to both the international banks (and the IMF and World Bank) and the Mexican people (especially industrial producers) that the de la Madrid administration was firmly committed to structural adjustment, including the concomitant trade liberalization. GATT membership itself served as a public guarantee that the announced policies of economic reform and trade liberalization would continue.

It is important to note that during the period of the GATT accession negotiations (February–July 1986), an evolution in general Mexican attitudes toward structural adjustment and trade liberalization became increasingly evident. This reflected growing acceptance of the need for Mexico to change course, including the necessity to become actively involved in the competitive world of international trade. The evolution probably can be attributed, at least in part, to the conscious effort of the Mexican government to consult closely with all appropriate industrial chambers and labor unions as it moved forward. These efforts at convincing the hearts and minds of key interest groups of the wisdom of the course that had been charted was helped substantially by the sudden and unexpected fall in oil prices in early 1986. The realization spread fairly quickly that there were actually few alternatives other than to expand Mexico's base of non-oil exports, which required economic reform and structural changes, including trade liberalization. Acceptance of this by all sectors of opinion was obviously not uniform in degree or timing. But it was widespread enough so that by the time the Mexican Senate ratified the Protocol of Accession, very little opposition was voiced and no raging debates took place, as they had in 1979–1980. Private sector interests contented themselves with cautioning the government to proceed with trade liberalization gradually.

Even prior to the conclusion of the GATT accession negotiation, the Mexican government unilaterally decided on a tariff reduction program to proceed in four stages—May 1986, February 1987, December 1987, and October 1988—over a 30-month period. This measure first reduced the highest Mexican tariff from 100% to 50%, and then immediately phased it down to 45%. The aim was to lower all 50% tariffs to 30%, all 40% tariffs to 25%, all 30% tariffs to 20% and all 25% tariffs to 20%. The 5% rate was to be abolished, with some items dropping to zero and others increasing to 10%. This was a surprising decision for a government to take while a trade negotiation (i.e., GATT accession) was still in progress, but it impressed U.S. officials as a good faith yet concrete sign of the direction the de la Madrid administration was headed.

The Mexican government did in fact implement the May 1986 and February 1987 tariff cuts as planned. Then, on December 15, 1987, as part of President de la Madrid's Pact of Economic Solidarity and Economic Strategy, the maximum applied tariff rate for Mexico was lowered to 20% from 40%, and new accompanying tariff categories of 5%, 10% and 15% were established. In addition, the 5% general import tax (another long-standing irritant to U.S. trade officials) was abolished. These stunning trade liberalization measures were taken for solid antiinflation reasons. Nonetheless, in one stroke they removed any criticism of Mexico as a country with excessively high tariffs. They lowered the weighted average tariff to 5.6%, about equal to that of Canada and close to that of the U.S. (3.1%), and left Mexico with a lower maximum tariff than many in the U.S. tariff schedule.

Two trade-related actions taken by the Mexican government in the last quarter of 1986 should also be mentioned. First, Mexico entered into discussions with Brazil and Argentina to explore the possibility of establishing a preferential trade agreement with those countries. These negotiations were unsuccessful basically because each of the three countries was looking to export to, but not necessarily import from, the others—an outcome that underlined the fact that the success of Mexico's economic restructuring was dependent upon the continuing ability of the U.S. market to absorb Mexican exports. Depressed markets in Latin America combined with slow growth in most developed countries meant that any major diversification of export markets was unlikely in the near future. Second, discussions with the United States in 1986 helped lead to passage of an amended patent and trademark law by the Mexican Congress in December 1986. This reflected recognition by the Mexican government that intellectual property protection is an issue with legitimate trade policy aspects, aside from its importance to the investment climate.

Successful negotiation in 1987 of the bilateral framework agreement for trade and investment represented a further important step in the rapid evolution of Mexican trade policy. As originally envisioned at the time the two governments signed a "Statement of Intent to Negotiate" on April 23, 1985, the framework agreement was to be a comprehensive trade agreement involving principles, tariffs, nontariff barriers, investment, services, and intellectual property protection. Mexico's entry into GATT in 1986 substantially altered the scope and content of the intended agreement. Instead, the two sides concentrated primarily on establishing a consultative mechanism which can be used to clarify respective trade policies, resolve specific disputes, or negotiate the removal or reduction of barriers.

For Mexico, this agreement reaffirmed its recognition of its continuing high degree of dependence on the U.S. market for its exports. For the United States, it provided a mechanism for addressing trade and investment issues with a country that is its third largest export market, yet a country with which bilateral discussions on such topics have often been difficult to arrange in the past. (In fact, U.S. requests for consultations on trade and investment issues had sometimes been viewed in Mexico as attempts to intervene in what were then considered internal affairs, and therefore denied). For both governments, the agreement provided a policy tool for use in managing commercial relations. It was a pragmatic acknowledgment of the fact that problems are normal in such a large bilateral economic relationship and should be addressed to the extent possible in a nonconfrontational, technical fashion. In sum, the agreement acknowledged the dependence and integration of the two economies and enabled the two governments to come to the table as equals to address trade and investment issues. It represented a maturing of the bilateral trade relationship.

The elimination of additional licensing requirements was announced in April, July, and October 1987. These measures continued the de la Madrid administration's trade liberalization program, brought Mexico into greater compliance with its GATT accession commitment to eliminate import licensing requirements to the fullest extent possible (a process the United States was closely monitoring), and satisfied part of the conditions attached to US$500 million trade policy loans granted Mexico by the World Bank in 1986 and 1987. By October 30, 1987, only 329 out of over 8,300 tariff categories were still subject to licensing requirements.

Combined with the December 15 tariff reductions referred to above and the elimination of official reference prices at the end of 1987, Mexico entered 1988 with its trade position liberalized to an extent that no one in or out of Mexico thought possible when the process was begun in earnest in July 1985. The extent and rapidity of the change has, in fact, blurred the vision of the casual observer and prevented full appreciation of just how far Mexico has come. It is also noteworthy that the change was conceived and implemented at the initiative of the de la Madrid administration, although the United States had consistently been urging such action in numerous high level meetings. The large World Bank loans supported, rather than initiated, this policy of trade liberalization by conditioning certain loans on compliance with the already announced intention of the Mexican government to eliminate many import licensing requirements (de facto quantitative restrictions in most cases) and rely upon tariff protection instead. What has in fact happened is that Mexico has exceeded the trade conditions attached to the World Bank trade policy loans.

There is understandably a widely shared feeling on the part of the Mexican government and the public that Mexico should receive some trade benefits from other countries in return for its actions. And Mexico will undoubtedly try to seek some form of credit in GATT for the trade liberalization it has unilaterally implemented. It will be difficult to obtain substantial trade concessions in bilateral negotiations during the Uruguay Round, since Mexico's trading partners all know that much of the trade liberalization was undertaken for Mexico's own economic good. Even so, some countries (primarily the United States) will be very interested in granting trade concessions in order to lock in as much as possible of the liberalization implemented to date. Aside from the unique opportunity presented by potentially numerous bilateral negotiations during the Uruguay Round, Mexico also should consider pursuing bilateral deals with the United States as opportunities arise during the ongoing liberalization process.

Bilateral Trade Issues

Several bilateral efforts were undertaken in the first half of the 1980s to improve U.S.-Mexico trade relations. The first two were aimed at providing some structure to the trade relationship in light of Mexico's rejection of GATT membership. Since the termination by an exchange of notes in 1950 of the Reciprocal Trade Agreement (1943–1950) which had been negotiated during World War II, there had been no formal mechanism or principles to govern commercial relations between the two countries.[3]

The first recent effort to improve trade relations was a U.S. proposal in the fall of 1980 to negotiate a notification and consultation agreement. This agreement would have obligated each side to notify the other prior to taking any trade action which might have an effect on the other, and required an opportunity for bilateral consultations prior to the implementation of the measure. The United States, in fact, already had a formal commitment to notify and consult with the Mexican government on any measure which might adversely affect its exports to the United States. This stemmed from the U.S. commitment under the Special Committee for Consultation and Negotiation (CE-CON) of the Organization of American States (OAS) to consult with OAS members prior to adoption of any measures that might adversely affect their exports to the United States or third countries. The proposed bilateral agreement with Mexico was an attempt by the United States to introduce greater reciprocity into the bilateral trading relationship. It was discussed bilaterally but not formalized due to lack of Mexican interest.

The second effort to improve bilateral trade relations was the establishment of a Joint Commission on Commerce and Trade (JCCT) in 1981. It followed a meeting at Camp David of Presidents Reagan and López Portillo and several of their cabinet officers in June 1981. That working meeting resulted in the formation of the JCCT and the Binational Commission.[4] More than anything, the Camp David meeting and the joint committees it established reflected President Reagan's desire (which had been expressed during his presidential campaign) to strengthen relations with Canada and Mexico. The JCCT, specifically, was formed as a high-level body to discuss trade issues, resolve commercial disputes, and implement measures to facilitate or expand trade.

A JCCT Technical Secretariat was formed and it established an extensive work program. Study groups on the computer, auto, petrochemical, and textile sectors were set up, as well as talks at the technical staff level on intellectual property rights, subsidies, trucking access, business visa reciprocity, customs regulations, access for U.S. agricultural products, U.S. participation in major construction projects in Mexico, cooperation on nuclear construction, and the sale of silver from the U.S. strategic stockpile. The study groups were to examine the possibilities of harmonizing trade and development objectives in certain sectors. The technical-level and cabinet-level bilateral talks were to focus on more specific problems.

Progress on all issues proved slow, and meetings quickly became more difficult to schedule as both sides became disenchanted with the prospects of advancing beyond previously stated positions. The JCCT suffered from the inability or unwillingness of either side to respond on tough problems. There was certainly grumbling among U.S. trade officials that the Mexican government was interested only in using the JCCT to resolve its problems (e.g., lack of injury test under U.S. countervailing duty law), while simply engaging in sterile discussion on issues of interest to the U.S. Undoubtedly, Mexican officials were making similar complaints. Commission success was further hindered by the lack of enthusiasm displayed by the incoming de la Madrid administration to this political creation of the previous administration. In addition, the economic crisis of 1982–83 forced Mexican policy members to address more immediately pressing problems than the list of U.S.-Mexico trade concerns.[5]

The end result was a short-lived JCCT. The last full Commission meeting (Cabinet level) was in July 1982; and all activities had ceased by the fall of 1983. The only concrete result was the Mexican government granting U.S. businessmen the right to travel to Mexico on a tourist visa. The failure of the JCCT, which has never been formally pronounced extinct, did, however, give impetus to the concept of a comprehensive bilateral framework agreement for trade and investment.

The third major effort to improve trade relations in the 1980s was the successful negotiation of an understanding on bilateral subsidies— a process that took three years prior to the formal signing on April 23, 1985. Mexico took the initiative on this issue since, not being a GATT member, its exports did not receive the benefit of an injury test under U.S. countervailing duty (CVD) law. In order for a U.S. manufacturer to have penalty duties imposed on Mexican exports of a particular product, it was simply necessary to prove that the Mexican producer received export subsidies or domestic subsidies with a trade effect. This was not difficult to do in light of Mexican subsidy practices at that time, and led to numerous affirmative CVD findings against Mexican exports. While the penalty duties were often small (less than 5%), the uncertain outcome hanging over the lengthy procedures was often enough in itself to disrupt trade. If Mexico was going to place increased emphasis on export-led growth, it needed to improve the protection its exports received in the primary destination for Mexican exports. (In 1984 almost 73% of Mexican exports went to the United States). The United States, in its turn, was interested in having the use of export subsidies eliminated by one of its largest trading partners and in introducing some GATT-like discipline into the bilateral relationship. In addition, the United States wanted to link certain improvements in the Mexican pharmaceutical decree, which was then in its final stages of preparation, to its agreement to provide Mexico the injury test under U.S. CVD law.

With respect to Mexico's accession to GATT, the manner and speed with which the Mexican government conducted its accession negotiations were key to making Washington policymakers take serious note of the fundamental changes taking place in Mexican economic policy. The U.S. government was pleased with President de la Madrid's announcement in late 1985, since it had been urging Mexico for over a decade to join GATT. The U.S. position reflected both a general belief that GATT participation should be as wide as possible and a specific belief that bilateral trade relations would be facilitated if both countries were subject to a common set of principles and obligations. The U.S. government was also wary, however, of how seriously the Mexican government would actually approach the accession exercise. The memory of the March 1980 rejection and previous Mexican attitudes were still fresh in the minds of key U.S. officials.

The wariness of U.S. officials about the new Mexican accession negotiation was heightened by growing U.S. concern over the functioning of GATT generally. The spread of "gray area" measures, the weakness of the dispute settlement mechanism, the lack of obligations undertaken by the "NICs," and free riding by developing countries in general were all major concerns. The United States was also aware that the Mexican protocol could set a precedent for certain other accession negotiations by developing countries that were on the horizon (e.g., China),[6] making them strongly disposed against any protocol of accession for Mexico that contained any derogations from GATT obligations. The United States was thus adamant that the 1979 protocol of accession negotiated by Mexico not serve as a basis for the current accession negotiation.[7] Too much had changed between 1979 and 1986. The 1979 Mexican protocol was negotiated in the concluding rush of the Tokyo Round of Multilateral Trade Negotiations; this time there were few distractions. Concerns about GATT, future accession negotiations, and the continued deterioration of the U.S. trade balance combined to make the United States take a firm attitude toward negotiation.

These points are all important because Mexico's GATT accession negotiation was principally a bilateral negotiation with the United States. GATT custom is to give great weight during an accession negotiation to the guidance of the applicant country's major trading partner(s). The Mexican negotiators quickly realized and accepted that their efforts to revive the 1979 protocol of accession and use it as the basis for a new protocol were unacceptable both to the United States and other developed country contracting parties. The serious, professional, and reasonable negotiating posture of the Mexican negotiating team favorably impressed U.S. trade officials.

The accession protocol provided for no exceptions from GATT rights or obligations, other than those already provided within GATT for developing countries. There were no phase-in periods (contrary to the belief of many people in Mexico) before any obligations were binding on Mexico; full membership was effective with the date of Mexico's entry into GATT. The protocol also called for all aspects of Mexico's national development plan to be conducted in accordance with its GATT obligations and contained a substantial set of bound tariff concessions.

Along with the contents of the protocol themselves, there were several other important benefits for the United States from Mexico's accession to GATT on August 24, 1986, as its 92nd contracting party. First, GATT membership represented an important psychological leap forward for Mexico as it officially accepted the fact that the Mexican economy could no longer be isolated from the international trading system. Second, it promoted the beginning of a gradual but favorable reassessment of attitudes among U.S. trade officials toward Mexico. Other key results from the U.S. perspective were the commitments by Mexico in the GATT Working Party Report on Mexican Accession to eliminate the use of official reference prices for customs valuation purposes (a longstanding bilateral trade problem), and to add an injury test to the provisions of the new (January 1986) Mexican trade law dealing with safeguards, countervailing duties, and antidumping.

Despite these negotiated improvements in the trade environment with the third largest U.S. trading partner,[8] however, there was a widespread attitude among U.S. trade officials to wait and see if there would be any backsliding on Mexico's part vis-à-vis its newly accepted GATT obligations. Memories of short-lived past trade liberalizing actions by the Mexican government were still vivid. On August 13, 1986, the United States did move to recognize the progress made by Mexico to date by lifting the six-year-old embargo on all imports of tuna and tuna products from Mexico.[9] Beyond this most U.S. officials seemed unwilling to go, until the process of trade liberalization had cut deeper and made more of a commercial impact.

It was in this "show-me" atmosphere that the final stages of the General Review of the U.S. Generalized System of Preferences (GSP) vis-à-vis Mexico was conducted. Mandated by the Trade and Tariff Act of 1984, the General Review required the U.S. administration to examine the future levels of duty-free benefits to be accorded the program's beneficiary countries—taking into account the level of market access and intellectual property protection, investment policy, and workers' rights. With Mexico, the exercise quickly focused on U.S.-perceived problems with Mexico's 1976 Patent and Trademark Law. U.S. complaints included lack of any patent protection whatsoever in certain subject matter (e.g., pharmaceuticals and alloys), the short patent term (10 years), patent lapse provisions, trade secret protection, and trademark linkage. Bilateral discussions were aided by the fact that the Mexican government was, in any case, considering amending the law to improve both the investment climate and the protection for Mexican inventors.

The persistent, and even aggressive, manner in which the United States pursued the subject reflected the mandate outlined in President Reagan's September 1985 trade policy speech. In that policy statement, President Reagan made it quite clear that the United States would aggressively pursue protection of its intellectual property both bilaterally and internationally. Although the de la Madrid administration did submit comprehensive amending legislation in September 1986, the amended law approved by the Mexican Congress in December 1986 fell short on certain provisions of particular importance to U.S. economic interests. The greatest shortcoming in U.S. eyes was the postponement for ten years (until January 1997) of patent protection for certain products (including pharmaceuticals and chemicals). This additional ten-year window for the continued counterfeiting in Mexico of certain U.S.-developed products infuriated the United States and led President Reagan, on January 2, 1987, to announce his intention to remove from Mexico on July 1, 1987, US$200 million of duty free benefits under the GSP. In retrospect, it can be argued that this partly failed negotiation can be attributed to the failure of senior officials within both governments to appreciate the political requirements of each side in this traditionally delicate area.

After this tough beginning, however, 1987 developed into a year that has put U.S.-Mexico trade relations on a solid footing. There is an adage that problems between nations are more often managed than solved. However, 1987 saw a lot of bilateral trade problems solved and actions in trade relations that spoke just as loud as words. Continued dismantling of the system of protectionism in Mexico and the successful negotiation of the bilateral framework agreement were the keys.

Elimination by Mexico of an important number of remaining licensing requirements in February, April, July, and October of that year served as confidence building measures (although not necessarily intended as such) and solidified the belief among U.S. policymakers that de la Madrid intended to stand firm on his course of trade liberalization. The significant import duty reductions announced in mid-December 1987 were further affirmation of this, regardless of the primary motive (anti-inflation) behind the action. The selection of Carlos Salinas de Gortari as the PRI presidential candidate was also viewed by U.S. officials as a firm signal that structural adjustment accompanied by trade liberalization would remain a fundamental tenet of Mexican economic policy. Although the main reason for accelerating trade liberalization in Mexico in 1987—the gravity of the domestic economic crisis—was viewed with concern by the United States, the measures taken as a result of this crisis were welcomed.

The bilateral framework agreement, described earlier in this chapter, was viewed by the United States as an important complement to the principles and mechanisms provided both countries by their membership in GATT. It addresses the fact that GATT does not cover all trade issues and covers investment issues inadequately, and that the bilateral trade relationship is of increasing economic and strategic importance. Although by no means a free trade arrangement (FTA), it does provide both sides a forum to clarify misunderstandings, negotiate the reduction of trade barriers, and attempt to resolve any commercial disputes. Its pragmatic simplicity is intended to help the mechanism survive the political life of the current U.S. and Mexican administrations.

The agreement quickly provided benefits. Its signature on November 6, 1987, in Mexico City by Mexican Secretary of Commerce and Industrial Development, Hector Hernández, and the United States Trade Representative, Clayton Yeutter, was followed by the formalization in December of negotiated agreements involving steel, beer, wine, distilled spirits, agricultural seeds, chocolate confectionery, and textiles, among other products. The 12.4% increase in the 1988 U.S. quotas for Mexican steel represented the first time the United States had negotiated any meaningful increases in any quota arrangement in its current steel import program. Elimination of the Mexican quotas on beer, wine, and distilled spirits along with the negotiated elimination of the import licensing requirement on numerous other items represented important market access improvements of interest to the United States.

The new, four-year (1988–1991) textile agreement with Mexico was the most generous textile agreement negotiated by the United States in 1987. It was preceded by a unilateral opening of the Mexican apparel and finished product market to a potential US$240 million of U.S. apparel exports. This partial opening of the Mexican apparel market was the first real relaxation of that market in decades. Previously apparel imports had only been permitted in the border zones and in tourist areas. All these measures combined to represent concrete evidence of the growing recognition within both governments of the mutually beneficial results that could flow from cooperative trade relations.

Conclusions

Current Mexican economic policy is showing results. Mexican manufacturing exports increased almost 38% in 1986 over 1985 levels, and registered an additional 39% increase in 1987. Obviously, this improvement is due not just to structural adjustment but also to a depressed domestic economy and an undervalued Mexican *peso*. Questions do remain as to how extensively the adjustment process has been actively embraced within the Mexican manufacturing sector, and how many companies that are now exporting will maintain an export orientation once the Mexican economy recovers or should the Mexican government stop supporting the undervaluation of the Mexican *peso*.

Despite the beneficial effects of debt-equity swaps and the Morgan Guaranty Trust–Mexican Government–U.S. Treasury collateralized debt exchange scheme, Mexico must still earn substantial trade surpluses to finance its debt. Weak and protected markets in the European Community and the rest of Latin America, along with a Japanese market difficult to penetrate, mean that Mexico is and will remain dependent primarily on the U.S. market for the success of its economic development program. Mexico should still prod the European Community and Japan to improve market access for Mexican exports and assist in their promotion. However, the major preoccupation of Mexican trade policy is and will be bilateral relations with the United States. Issues of critical importance to Mexico are and will be the health of the U.S. economy and the fate of protectionist trade legislation in the United States.

The U.S. market is, with a few important exceptions, open to imports from Mexico. Over 80% of Mexican exports to the United States enter at a duty rate between 0 and 5%. There are no section 301 measures against Mexico, and the only section 201 measures affecting Mexico relate to quotas on stainless steel imports.[10] (These quotas have, in practice, not proven particularly restrictive for Mexico). Mexico is now the fourth largest beneficiary of the U.S. GSP program, sending over US$1.5 billion worth of products into the United States duty free under the program's provisions. The steel and textile quotas have been significantly increased as of 1988. The meat embargo is under technical review, and prospects are good that the meat inspection system problem will be resolved and the U.S. market reopened to Mexican exports before the end of 1988. The embargo on fresh avocados appears to be technically justified because of seed weevil infestation in Mexico, although the two sides are likely to discuss in the future the possibility of permitting exports from designated pest-free zones. Antidumping and countervailing duties are not considered protectionist by the United States, as they involve the imposition of penalty duties to offset the value of an unfair trade practice but do not involve denial of market access. Finally, the U.S. system of sugar quotas has had little impact on Mexico since it consumes almost all of its own domestic production.

Although the U.S. market is in fact pretty well open, there is still a widespread perception in Mexico that the United States is a highly protected market. This perception, caused largely by the continuous consideration of protectionist legislation by the U.S. Congress throughout the 1980s, and by a misunderstanding of the role of antidumping and countervailing duties in international trade law, can be just as much a disincentive to exporting as formal trade barriers. It places an additional educational burden on the Mexican government as it tries to encourage small and medium size producers to get on the export bandwagon.

This burden should not be underestimated, since the threat of protectionist action is likely to remain a constant in Washington into the foreseeable future in light of the likelihood of continuing large U.S. trade and current account deficits. The Omnibus Trade Bill is now the major preoccupation of Mexico (and all the rest of the trading partners of the United States); but the continuing interest in "fair trade" and strong action among much of the congress will lead to serious consideration annually of potentially trade-restrictive legislation.

This continuing threat at a time of increasing interdependence confirms the need from this point forward in the bilateral trade relationship for what Riordan Roett calls in Chapter 1 "a steady and permanent process of consultation and negotiation." The bilateral framework agreement provides the means for both sides to do just that in a low key manner.

The United States for its part should examine whether improvements in market access for Mexican exports are possible. This could include an examination of possibilities for extending additional GSP benefits to Mexico, or for entering into FTA negotiations. Mexico's benefits under the U.S. GSP should certainly increase in 1989 as a result of the U.S. decision in late January 1988 to graduate (i.e., remove) South Korea, Taiwan, Hong Kong, and Singapore from the U.S. program as of January 1, 1989. Even so, the two governments should consider negotiating certain trade-related concessions by Mexico in return for additional GSP benefits of interest to Mexico.

The United States should also terminate the countervailing duty orders on nine products which enter the United States duty free but for which no injury test was provided, as required by GATT.[11] Further, the United States should amend its Superfund legislation to eliminate the three and a half U.S. cents differential in tax rates between domestic and imported crude oil and petroleum products. Mexico successfully challenged this in GATT, with the GATT Council recommending in June 1987 that the United States eliminate the GATT-illegal discrimination. The United States should also maintain U.S. tariff items 806.30 and 807.00, which complement the *maquiladora* operations.[12]

The FTA option has certainly received a lot of attention since conclusion of the U.S.-Canada FTA negotiations, including reference to such a possibility in President Reagan's final State of the Union address on January 25, 1988. Although the U.S.-Canada FTA presents a competitive challenge to Mexico, the disparity in development levels and the need for Mexico to adapt to and digest much of the structural adjustment and trade liberalization already undertaken make any serious FTA discussions premature. It is worth noting, though, that the economic restructuring and trade liberalization now being implemented in Mexico are the very types of measures that lay the necessary groundwork for any possible future FTA.

A strong and continuing U.S. interest in blending multilateralism and bilateralism in its trade policy—as indicated in written comments by Treasury Secretary James Baker in January 1988 mentioning a U.S. interest in forming a free-trading club of nations along the lines of the U.S.-Canada FTA[13]—will force a quicker consideration of a U.S.-Mexico FTA than otherwise would happen. Actual negotiation of any additional FTAs by the United States will probably be put on hold until the outcome of the Uruguay Round is clear. Should that outcome be unsatisfactory or partially satisfactory, it is very possible that the United States in the 1990s will pursue additional FTAs (such as with Japan, Taiwan, or Singapore). In order to protect its share of the U.S. market, Mexico would be forced to give serious thought to negotiating a similar arrangement. In the meantime, the United States needs to give serious thought to Mexican government interest in negotiating sectoral arrangements (partial FTAs, in a sense). By combining several sectoral FTAs with the fact that 51% of Mexican imports now enter the United States duty free, the two governments could approximate an FTA (which is not a common market, contrary to common belief) without taking on the political resistance to a full-blown FTA negotiation.

For Mexico's part, maintenance of the trade liberalization already implemented, combined with some additional measures, is the key to maintaining bilateral trade relations on a solid and cordial basis. This will not be easy as Mexican producers work their way through the painful and not always successful structural adjustment process. Although there seems to be little serious questioning within Mexico of its appropriateness at this point in Mexico's development, there is some grumbling about the speed of the market opening. The "losers" in this process will be putting enormous pressure on both the current and the next Mexican administration to slow it down. Only time will tell whether this rapid change in levels of trade protection can continue to be managed. There are some restraints, though, on Mexican backsliding: conditioned IMF and World Bank loans, GATT obligations, continuing low oil prices, and the possibility of retaliatory U.S. action against Mexican exports.

Serious trade problems, of course, still need to be addressed. Issues such as the use of local content and export performance requirements, copyright infringement, inadequate patent protection, the pharmaceutical decree, majority ownership limitations on foreign investors, and trucking access remain problems of major concern to the United States. Also, should Mexico eventually align with certain other LDCs within GATT to obstruct progress within the Uruguay Round on important new issues such as investment, intellectual property and services, the atmosphere for bilateral trade relations would certainly be soured. For Mexico, steel and textile quotas, fresh avocado and meat embargoes, protectionist legislation, and the treatment of labor services (e.g., migrant workers) are important concerns.

The question of whether debt-equity swaps will be considered countervailable (i.e., a subsidy with a trade effect) possibly lurks in the future. Also looming is a possible adverse U.S. reaction to third country (especially Asian) investment in *maquiladoras* (in-bond export operations). While most parties in the United States now understand that these are a function of Mexican law and regulation, extensive Asian investment in them could lead to calls for import restraints and pressure on the current U.S. policy that supports such investment.

The trade liberalization implemented in Mexico since July 1985, the bilateral framework agreement, and the cooperative, even friendly, relationship developed in recent years between U.S. and Mexican trade officials auger well for continuing cooperative and productive trade relations. The challenge for the United States is to more consciously and consistently recognize the economic and strategic importance to the United States of the restructuring of the Mexican economy and the success of the process to our southern neighbor's future stability. Mexico's task is to stay the course by keeping its market open, promoting exports, and continuing to reduce subsidies to domestic industries. The responsibility of both countries is to utilize the new framework agreement as a management tool for bilateral trade and investment relations. The challenge for both is to maintain cooperative and pragmatic trade relations amid the swirl of other difficult and deeply contentious issues such as drug enforcement and Central American policy.

Notes

These are views of the author and not necessarily of the U.S. Trade Representative or the U.S. government.

1. In fact, shortly after the decision not to enter GATT, announced by López Portillo on March 18 (Mexico's National Oil Day), López Portillo and several of his cabinet members suggested that Mexico use its oil leverage to negotiate bilateral trade agreements with its major trading partners. In other words, they believed trade concessions could be obtained without the entanglements and obligations of a truly international agreement.

2. Throughout 1983 all of the more than 8,000 Mexican tariff categories were subject to import licensing requirements, or "prior import permits" (PIP). These PIPs were the primary policy tool used by Mexican governments to control imports. Starting in January 1984 the de la Madrid administration began a gradual elimination of licensing requirements, often increasing the applied tariff as the PIP was eliminated. The significance of the July 25, 1985, action was rapid acceleration of the liberalization process.

3. An interesting note on the Reciprocal Trade Agreement is that it was used as the model for the U.S. proposals that became GATT. See Robert E. Hudec, *A Brief History of GATT's Legal Policy Toward Developing Countries*, a working paper presented before an October 16–17, 1986 meeting of the study

group on the Integration of the Developing Countries into the World Trading System, Council of Foreign Relations, in New York.

4. The Binational Commission, which still meets every 12–18 months, has a broad mandate to deal with bilateral issues. It is cochaired by the U.S. Secretary of State and the Mexican Secretary of Foreign Relations, with other cabinet members participating.

5. The JCCT was further hindered by the fact that it was jointly chaired on the U.S. side by the Office of the United States Trade Representative and the U.S. Department of Commerce. During the early 1980s relations between these two cabinet agencies suffered as the Commerce Department actively lobbied within both the Administration and the Congress for the formation of a Department of Trade and Industry.

6. The U.S. concern proved well founded, for a delegation of Chinese trade officials traveled to Mexico City to meet with the senior Mexican GATT negotiators on the topic of the GATT accession process shortly after Mexico's accession to GATT.

7. Mexico's 1979 Draft Protocol of Accession basically excluded Mexico from any GATT obligations with respect to both the agricultural and industrial sectors. In addition, the tariff concessions called for in that protocol covered substantially less than half the trade that the 1986 protocol provided for. The tariff concessions also included tariff bindings as high as 60%, 80% and 100%, along with 10- and 12-year phase-out periods for certain licensing requirements. See GATT Documents L/4849 of October 26, 1979, and L/4849/ADD.1 of November 28, 1979.

8. In 1986 and 1987, Mexico was the fourth largest U.S. trading partner (based on total trade turnover, which represents the sum of imports from + exports to) after Canada, Japan, and West Germany.

9. The U.S. embargo on imports of all tuna products from Mexico was imposed in July 1980 in response to two U.S. laws (in a sense, a double embargo), one of which is related to porpoise protection (the Marine Mammal Protection Act of 1972) and is administered by the U.S. Department of Commerce; the other is related to fisheries conservation and fishing boat seizures (the Fishery Conservation and Management Act of 1976) and is administered by the U.S. Department of State.

10. Section 301 of the Trade Act of 1974 concerns (1) the enforcement of U.S. rights under trade agreements and (2) U.S. response to foreign violations of international trade rules or foreign trade practices which restrict or discriminate against U.S. commerce. Section 201 of the Trade Act of 1974 involves determinations as to whether imports into the United States of an article in increased quantities are a substantial cause of serious injury, or threat thereof, to the domestic industry providing a like or similar article.

11. The nine products are fabricated automotive glass, bricks, carbon black, cement, iron construction castings, lime, litharge, polypropylene film, and toy balloons.

12. U.S. tariff provisions 806.30 and 807.00 permit the export of U.S. items offshore for processing or assembly, with duty paid upon their re-entry into the U.S. only on the value added abroad.

13. James Baker: "The Geopolitical Implications of the U.S.-Canada Trade Pact," *The International Economy*, January/February 1988, pp. 34–41.

PART THREE

Key Bilateral Issues

7

Undocumented Immigration: Research Findings and Policy Options

Jorge A. Bustamante

An important obstacle in the way of a mutual understanding between Mexico and the United States about undocumented immigration is ideology. There is a Mexican ideology and a United States ideology about this migratory phenomenon which has had an important influence on the last hundred years of bilateral relations between the two countries. I begin the chapter with a discussion of these ideologies and how they contrast with reality. I then discuss the research and policy questions that need to be addressed before any informed policy choice on the issue of undocumented immigration can be made by Mexico. I follow this with a summary of research findings on the issue from the Zapata Canyon Project at El Colegio de la Frontera Norte. I end with some policy options.

Ideologies versus Reality

A growing body of research literature shows increasing consensus on the notion that undocumented immigration from Mexico is the result of the interaction between a demand for cheap labor from the United States and a supply of it from Mexico.[1] There is, however, a wide gap between this consensus within the scientific community of both countries and U.S. public opinion.

According to the research of Celestino Fernandez, U.S. public opinion views undocumented immigration from Mexico as a negative for the American people[2]—a silent invasion, a national threat, the cause of a variety of public calamities such as a loss of control of U.S. borders, a burden for U.S. taxpayers because of illegal aliens' abuse of welfare and other public benefits, a cause of unemployment, even a cause of drug traffic.[3] The contrast between U.S. public opinion and the economic realities of undocumented immigration is illustrated by the divergence between the statement of William Colby, former head of the CIA, that Mexican immigration could become a more serious threat to the United States than the Soviet Union,[4] and the conclusions of the *Economic Report to the President: February 1986*, that undocumented immigrants produce more benefits than costs to the U.S. economy.[5]

These contradictions between the ideology and the economics of undocumented immigration from Mexico to the United States are reflected also in the contradictions between the objectives and written text of the U.S. legislation on immigration—Public Law 99–603, known as the Simpson-Rodino Law—and the realities of the international labor market.

The most important reform introduced by the Simpson-Rodino Law is "sanctions to employers" who knowingly hire an undocumented immigrant. The predominant ideology of immigration would indicate that the United States is interested in closing the door to undocumented immigrants. Economic realities, however, dictate something different. On the one hand, there is the written text of sanctions to employers with loopholes big enough to render these sanctions inapplicable. On the other hand, there is the loud voice of west coast growers crying labor shortages. Perhaps the biggest loophole in Public Law 99–603 regarding sanctions to employers is in subsection (4) of Section 274A (b):

Copying of Documentation Permitted. Notwithstanding any other provision of law, the person or entity may copy a document presented by an individual pursuant to this subsection and may retain the copy, but only (except as otherwise permitted under law) for the purpose of complying with the requirements of this subsection.

Thus, an employer could be found in full compliance with the new law if he or she signs an INS form I-9 stating that an alien who is applying for a job and has produced a legal document demonstrating eligibility to work in the United States, regardless of the existence of such a document. It amounts to the word of the employer against the word of the alien employee that determines whether or not he or she has complied with the law attesting to have seen and verified a paper document shown by the job applicant who is not a citizen of the United States.

I am not suggesting that all U.S. employers will be taking advantage of this loophole. I am suggesting, however, that full use of this loophole might render sanctions to employers inapplicable. I am also arguing that the text of the law as it stands today reflects an inherent contradiction in the new legislation on immigration between the negative perception of the presence of undocumented immigrants in the United States and, simultaneously, an objective need for their labor.

Growers of Northern California and the State of Oregon blamed the Simpson-Rodino law for a labor shortage early in the summer of 1987.[6] According to Oregon's governor, the acuteness of such a labor shortage was becoming a threat to the state economy to the point that he was ready to declare a state of emergency. Senator Pete Wilson of California demanded in Washington a relaxation of border enforcement in order to facilitate the border-crossing of undocumented migrants in order to apply for a Special Agricultural Workers (SAW) visa.[7]

The new legislation was not yet fully enforceable when several reforms had been already made to the text of the law signed by President Reagan on November 6, 1986. The first reform moved the cutoff date to apply for a SAW visa from May 1986 to July 26, 1987.[8] INS officials had been saying since February of 1987 that a decline in the number of apprehensions indicated that the Simpson-Rodino Law was working. The joy went sour when the newly opened offices for the reception of applicants for "amnesty" (i.e., legalization), under a self-financing bureaucratic design, were receiving for the first two months less than 10% of the expected numbers of undocumented migrants. The INS amnesty program was saved from bankruptcy in early August 1987 with a partial budgetary increase of 33% over what they had requested, after conspicuous INS reports in June of the same year that apprehensions were again on the rise.

One aspect of the Mexican version of the ideology of emigration was conspicuously illustrated during the first quarter of 1987, when rumors swept the country that the United States was preparing a massive deportation operation to begin on May 5. The public alarm in Mexico about the Simpson-Rodino Law was as high as the ignorance of the politics underlying it and its written text. "Mexico-U.S. border in state of siege" read the headline of one of Mexico City's major newspapers in early May. All kinds of motives were given for the Simpson-Rodino Law. The most common one in the streets of Mexico City was that President Reagan had decided to teach Mexicans a lesson for their deviant behavior on Central America.

Obscured by the two ideologies, the true picture of the Mexican migrant going north in search for a job was only perceived by the main actors: the American employer whose hiring practices were seemingly indifferent to any legislative changes on undocumented immigration, and the migrant worker more ready to pay attention to the labor market laws of supply and demand than to the politics of immigration on either side.

Policy and Research Questions

There is no way to produce a rational policy about a phenomenon that results from the interaction of factors in two countries, unless the countries involved share the political will to define, approach, evaluate, negotiate, and become obligated on a bilateral basis. This is equivalent to saying that there is no way to reach a rational policy on a truly bilateral question from a unilateral perspective. That is why, no matter how strongly one country feels about a problem of shared causes and consequences with another country, a unilateral policy will be limited if not counterproductive. Unfortunately, this is the situation with respect to the undocumented immigration from Mexico.

From the Mexican perspective, any policy on this issue has to take into account not only the above-mentioned contrast of ideologies but also the fact that the United States has already a stated policy in the form of legislation: Public Law 99–603. Thus, any policy decision in Mexico should start by asking about the impact such new legislation has had on the conditions that shape the undocumented immigration phenomenon.

The United States Congress decided, with the approval of the President, to create the "Commission for the Study of International Migration and Cooperative Economic Development" as part of Public Law 99–603 (Section 601). This decision would have been preferred in Mexico as a precedent and not as a consequence of legislation; nevertheless, it does represent a step toward a bilateral approach to the issue. However, it is important to point out that Section 601 refers to a domestic Commission chartered to consult "the governments of Mexico and other sending countries in the Western Hemisphere." That is, the new law still takes a unilateral U.S. approach to an issue that it explicitly recognizes as bilateral and multilateral. To consult with another government is not equivalent to negotiating with another government.

It is desirable that Mexico welcome such consultation, but the United States should be prepared to understand that any Mexican response to the consultative purposes of such a Commission should not be construed as an action in compliance to the objectives of Public Law 99–603, but as a response to Mexico's own objectives in conducting bilateral negotiations. As a sovereign country Mexico should not respond to the authority of a foreign law, regardless of its merits. Thus, the consultation ordered by Section 601 of the new law does not escape the basic problem of the contrasting ideologies discussed above.

Given the new U.S. legislation on immigration, Mexico could address the policy issue in a variety of ways, depending on the changes in undocumented immigration brought about by the new Public Law 99–603. Therefore, an assessment of the changes that are expected should precede any policy decision.

Such an assessment was the objective of the Zapata Canyon Project at El Colegio de la Frontera Norte.

The Zapata Canyon Project

When, at the beginning of 1986, we were looking at the possibility that the Simpson-Rodino Bill would become legislation, and at the need to collect data to assess its effects, we were confronted with two constraints. First, any conventional survey at ports of entry of undocumented migrants as they were expelled from the United States would be very costly. Second, whatever measurement was attempted should start early enough before the approval of the immigration reforms to allow before-after comparisons. We had to design a data collection that was less costly than a conventional survey, and we had to design it soon.

The basic research design we chose views the undocumented immigration phenomenon in the context of an international labor market. In this context, U.S. demand for undocumented immigrants is determined jointly with Mexican supply, and legislation-induced changes in demand will be reflected in changes in supply. In other words, any impact of the Simpson-Rodino Law on undocumented immigration should be observable in the flow of migrants across the Mexico-U.S. border.

Research conducted at COLEF has shown that 48% of the total flow of undocumented migrants crossing the 2,000 miles of the Mexico-U.S. border goes through the City of Tijuana.[9] This is because more than 50% of all undocumented immigrants end up in the highly dynamic economy of the State of California. The same research has also shown that 70% of that flow goes through a single place—called Zapata Canyon on the Mexican side and the "soccer field" on the American side.

The Zapata Canyon is an esplanade at the bottom of the Ottay Mesa hills just facing north from the edges of Colonia Libertad where

Tijuana borders with San Isidro in San Diego County. Its topography makes photography an effective tool for registering observations about the high variability of the concentration of people in the esplanade of the Canyon. Here one does not have the common methodological problem of elucidating who is undocumented and who is not. Because the whole esplanade is in U.S. territory and there is no other way to get there from Mexico but by crossing the imaginary line of the international border illegally, anyone captured by camera is undocumented. And every picture represents a sample of the flow.

After analyzing several options, we decided on three pictures a day. The last of the three is taken 10 minutes before sunset; the second, one hour earlier than that, and the first, one hour earlier than the second. This timing is because undocumented immigrants do not move north by the clock, but by sunlight. When it begins to get dark the previous quietness is transformed by the elusive movements of the vans of the U.S. border patrol and the undocumented immigrants, to the sound of helicopters combing the canyons with powerful search lights and loud speakers blaring *"detenganse"* (stop).

This three-photograph sequence has been taken daily since August 11, 1986. The number of men, the number of women, and the number of children in each picture is systematically recorded and fed into a computer through software that allows probabilistic estimates to be made of the volume and the intensity of the crossing of the daily flows of undocumented immigrants.

Preliminary findings are available from the first stage of this project.

Findings

Graph 7.A1 provides background for the discussion. It is based on data from previous research and depicts the seasonal variations of the statistical data on apprehensions produced by the INS on a monthly basis for the 1972–1977 period. It is important to note that statistics on apprehensions by INS do not account for individuals but for different events of apprehension. Therefore, statistics of apprehension cannot be construed as indicators of the volume of undocumented immigrants. They reflect the combination of at least three factors: (1) INS apprehension capacity in terms of manpower and infrastructure, (2) INS apprehension policy at the U.S.-Mexico border in terms of the location of border patrol resources, and (3) the actual volume of undocumented immigrants. There is no way to determine the weight of each of these three factors from the available data. The fact that INS statistics of apprehension are the most quoted source in the U.S. mass media for estimates about the number of undocumented immigrants[10] suggests how ill-informed the American public are about this question.

Graph 7.A2 shows the highest number of undocumented immigrants entering the United States of the three pictures taken every day over a nine-month period. The abundance of peaks in the graph derives from the pattern of repetition of the same individuals making a second or third or nth attempt to enter the United States through the Zapata Canyon, after being expelled by the U.S. border patrol.

The Zapata Canyon project will continue until December 30, 1988. This will allow us to make comparisons between the same months of more than one year, including several months before the Simpson-Rodino legislation was approved.

Graph 7.A3 sheds some light on the ideology of migration in Mexico. There were widespread rumors about a "massive deportation" campaign, which supposedly was going to be launched by the U.S. government beginning on May 5, 1987. Graph 7.A3 depicts the highest number of undocumented immigrants recorded at Zapata Canyon for the month of May 1987. It shows a slight decline in the period before the fifth of May. It is possible that this short-lived downward trend was due to fears provoked by rumors that the United States would conduct massive deportations. Whatever the case may be, however, the trend stopped its decline after May 5, when the only new action taken by the U.S. Immigration Service was to start receiving applications for legalization under the new law.

Graph 7.A4 makes a methodological point, showing the variations in the numbers found in each of the three photographs taken daily at Zapata Canyon. Each photograph captures a moment of the concentration or gathering of undocumented immigrants already in U.S. Territory, while they wait for dusk to continue their northbound journey, seeking to elude the U.S. Border Patrol. The peak is always reached within the two-hour span covered by the three daily pictures. In periods of low levels of the flow, the earliest take is always the lowest and the latest is the highest. In periods of high levels of the flow, however, the second take shows the highest number; by the third take some undocumented immigrants in the second take have already left.

These findings give us an empirical basis for estimating what we call the "speed" of the flow, which is equal to the difference between the numbers recorded by each photograph at one-hour intervals. When the second take is the highest, it means that the flow is going faster. Combining the "speed" of the flow with what we call the "intensity" of the flow (the actual number of undocumented immigrants in each picture) allows us to estimate probabilistically the volume of the flow corresponding to each particular day. Since the flow at Zapata Canyon consists of approximately 70% of the total flow through the municipality of Tijuana—which, as noted, gets across close to 50% of the total flow crossing the U.S.-Mexico border—whatever impact some event makes on the flow of undocumented immigrants from Mexico to the United States can be expected to show up in the procedural recordings of the Zapata Canyon Project.

Graphs 7.A5 to 7.A9 record the highest number found daily from the series of photographs for the same month of two different years. This is the first time that a comparison of data about daily characteristics of the undocumented migratory flow of the same month of different years has been available. The only source of data produced on a daily basis about undocumented immigration has been the INS. It would be desirable to make comparisons between the data from the two sources. However, we have failed so far to obtain INS statistics on a daily basis for the San Diego district. The importance of being able to make comparisons of day-by-day data produced under homogeneous conditions for subsequent years stems from the question of the impacts of Simpson-Rodino on the undocumented immigrant flow.

Graph 7.A5 shows an increase of 10% in the monthly average of daily figures of November of 1987 over those of November 1986. Graph 7.A6, however, shows a reverse trend, which is maintained through the months of January (Graph 7.A7), February (Graph 7.A8), and March (Graph 7.A9). These graphs suggest that no significant changes have taken place in the flows of the same months of 1986, 1987, and 1988, respectively. This finding could be interpreted as showing no significant impact of Simpson-Rodino on the undocumented northbound flow at Zapata Canyon, at least up to March 1988, although it is premature to make such a judgment until the end of the warning period about sanctions to employers at the end of the summer of 1988.

The absence of any significant impact on the undocumented migratory flow as measured by the Zapata Canyon Project is reinforced when the weekend days of the two months compared in these graphs are made to coincide. The weekly trends within the same month are strikingly similar, with the peak of the flow tending to be the highest on weekend days.

Graph 7.A6, in comparison to the graphs for other months, shows a cyclical pattern that has occurred for decades, with the lowest levels in the month of December. Even though the international labor market has diversified quite significantly over the last decade, the traditional pattern of returning for Christmas has not changed.

This pattern of return used to be associated with agricultural seasons, when the U.S. demand for undocumented migrant labor was predominantly in agriculture and the supply from Mexico was predominantly peasants from rural communities. Times have changed. U.S. labor demands have shifted more toward services. And the socioeconomic profile of the Mexican undocumented immigrant has also shifted from a peasant to an urban dweller, with higher educational levels than the national average. Outmigration to the United States has long ago ceased to be like an escape valve for poverty and unemployment, to become a drain of increasingly skilled human capital.

The main factor in this very important change has been the spectacular increase in the costs of migration to the U.S.-Mexico border and to the United States from the traditional areas of outmigration of the central northwestern part of the country. The higher the cost of migration the lower the likelihood of a poor peasant getting to the United States, unless his travel expenses and the service of a "coyote" or smuggler are financed in dollars by a relative already in that country. Higher costs of entry to the U.S. labor market for undocumented immigrants have become an important factor of de facto selectivity, with the better off more likely to reach that labor market. This is not to suggest a change of peasant migrants into a "brain drain." But it is to suggest a trend toward a more skilled, better educated, more urban type of undocumented immigrant, in a drastic change from the past.

In every January of the last decades there has been an increase in the northbound flow of undocumented immigrants crossing the U.S.-Mexico border. As Graph 7.A7 shows, the months of January of 1987 and 1988 were not exceptions, in spite of the approval of the Simpson-Rodino legislation in November 1986. One could expect to see a decrease from January 1987 to January 1988 if the new immigration legislation was having any effect. Instead, the monthly averages increased by 16% over the period.

The fact that the month of January marks the beginning of a cyclical upward trend in each year, plus the fact that no significant change has occurred in this pattern over time, plus the fact that the volume increased from January of 1987 to the same month of 1988, all add further strength to the assertion that the new immigration legislation has not yet made any significant impact on the inflow of undocumented immigrants from Mexico to the United States.

Graph 7.A8 confirms the persistence of the cyclical upward trend at the beginning of the year. The increase between the average volumes of the flow shown in the month of January is about the same as in the month of February (17%).

The downward swing in the flow in late February 1987 shown in Graph 7.A8 was due to a very heavy rain. These torrential rains are not common in a desert area but when they happen, usually in the winter, they can drastically affect outdoor activities. Graphs 7.A9 and 7.A10 include the latest data available when this chapter was written. These graphs reinforce the arguments presented before in regard to the absence of any Simpson-Rodino impact on the flow of undocumented immigrants at Zapata Canyon. Both graphs show a decrease in the flow during the last part of 1987 in comparison with the same months of 1986. This decrease was also detected by INS authorities, who claim it indicated the success of the new immigration legislation.

We found a different reason for the apparent decline. Besides taking the three daily photographs, we have been interviewing systematically randomized samples of the people that appear in the daily pictures. These interviews indicate that many undocumented immigrants already in the United States are deciding not to go back home for their yearly winter visit, because of the increasing costs of their return to the United States. The decline shown in the months of September, October, and November of 1987, compared to the same months of 1986, was not of newcomers but of returnees. This explains why there was an upsurge in the volume of the flow in December of 1987 in comparison to the same month of 1986, and also why this upsurge continued through March 1988.

If this interpretation is correct, a prediction can be made that the decline in the volume of the flow from September to December will be repeated, whereas the pattern of increase in the volume shown in the first months of 1988, in comparison with the same months of 1987, will tend to diminish toward the summer months, when the yearly flow reaches its cyclical peak. This prediction assumes that the Simpson-Rodino legislation will continue to have no significant impact into the flow of undocumented immigrants, even after the period of receiving applications has ended and full enforceability of sanctions to employers has begun, later in 1988.

Toward Some Policy Options

In assessing the impact of Public Law 99–603, or Simpson-Rodino, on the flow of undocumented immigrants from Mexico, one should distinguish between (1) the enforceability of sanctions to employers and (2) the policies of border enforcement executed by the INS. Both policies preceded the new immigration law and tend to change depending on how sensitive INS enforcement policies are to regional or national economic and political changes or pressures. The appointment of the Commissioner of INS at the national level as well as most regional commissioners has always been political. Enforcement policies of INS differed, for example, between the regimes of Leonard Chapman under President Nixon and of Leonel Castillo under President Carter. INS official estimates for the total of undocumented immigrants in the United States dropped from 20 million under Chapman to 4 million under Castillo in less than a five-year period.

The distinction between the final outcome of Simpson-Rodino and the INS enforcement policies is important because of the possibility of a significant change in U.S. border enforcement policies, depending on the health of the U.S. economy (particularly in terms of unemployment and regional economic differences). INS border enforcement policies can be expected to be more stringent if the United States economy enters into a recession in late 1988.

The same reasoning suggests that Mexico should develop two different strategies—one on the assumption of a U.S. economy still in expansion toward the end of 1988; the other on the assumption of a U.S. economy entering into a recession, with high interest rates, higher unemployment, and more protectionism. In the latter scenario, expectations of bilateral negotiation on the question of migrant workers would be minimal and probabilities for massive departures would be higher. In the former scenario, Mexico should be prepared to offer the United States a bilateral negotiation as an alternative to the failure of Simpson-Rodino. Pressures in favor of such an alternative might come from a likely expansion of underground markets of fraudulent documents, which could become attractive for organized crime at the U.S. border cities.

Both format and content should be different from those of bilateral negotiations regarding the migratory workers. In terms of the format, a tripartite participation from both sides with the respective representatives of organized labor, organized employers, and government could be explored. This format should be preceded by the promotion of separate bilateral meetings between each of these pairs of representatives, which at the present time show no visible interest in discussing the question of undocumented immigrants in a bilateral context.

The main objective of these separate bilateral meetings would be to come up with common definitions about the same phenomenon so as to facilitate future bilateral negotiations.[11]

These separate meetings should be followed by a bilateral agreement between the two governments to organize a bilateral commission whose main objective would be to conceptualize and assess major costs and benefits for the two countries deriving from undocumented migration.

Findings from this bilateral commission should then be the basic material for the formal negotiation of a bilateral agreement. This formal negotiation should be conceived as the last stage of a difficult but necessary process of bilateral discussions within the logic of the format discussed above. Formal negotiations should be conducted by the tripartite format, with the respective representatives of organized labor, business, and government from each country.

The basic notion from which the Mexican negotiations should proceed was given in the political context of the Mexican Senate Hearings on Migratory Workers which took place throughout 1985: outmigration of Mexican workers to the United States is, in the long run, contrary to the national interest because no national development project could be based on the constant exportation of the Mexican labor force. The other basic notion derived from these Senate Hearings was that, in the short run, Mexico is not in any position to stop, or even significantly reduce, the outflow of migrant workers to the United States. Because of this limitation Mexico should pursue, with dedication and skill, a bilateral negotiation with the United States on this matter.

Finally, bilateral negotiation from the Mexican perspective should be targeted toward the maximum protection of the human and working rights of Mexican migrant workers while in the United States and their safe return to Mexico. Also to be discussed are working conditions, number and qualifications of migrants, length of stay in the United States, social security benefits, sectors of the U.S. economy that draw workers, and specific regions of destiny. Among other important elements of a bilateral agreement should be the expected content of a concerted rational solution obligating the two countries to fulfill their responsibilities under it. This can only be achieved with the shared consciousness that the migration of workers from Mexico to the United States could be transformed with intelligence and a sense of justice, from a problem that troubles bilateral relations to an opportunity of international cooperation between two countries in order to better face the challenges of the increasingly interdependent world economy of the twenty-first century.

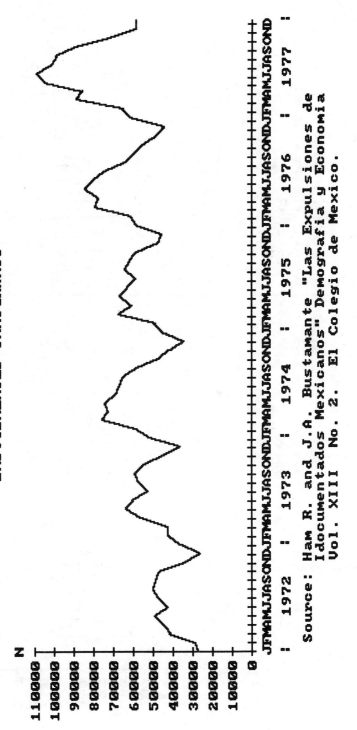

Graph 7A1

I.N.S. ANNUAL STATISTICS OF APPREHENSIONS OF MEXICAN
UNDOCUMENTED IMMIGRANTS

Source: Ham R. and J.A. Bustamante "Las Expulsiones de
        Idocumentados Mexicanos" Demografía y Economía
        Vol. XIII No. 2. El Colegio de México.

Graph 7.A2

FLOW OF UNDOCUMENTED IMMIGRANTS FROM MEXICO

Highest number recorded per day during the months of
September, 1986 through May, 1987

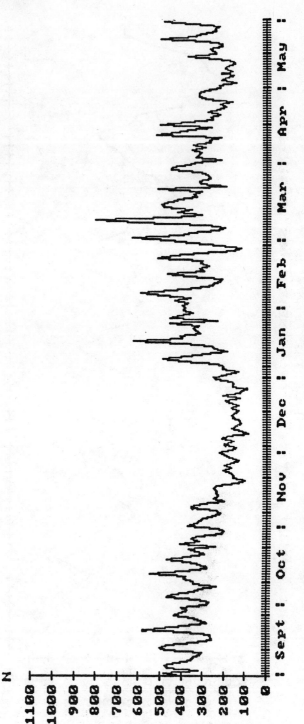

N

1100 · 1000 · 900 · 800 · 700 · 600 · 500 · 400 · 300 · 200 · 100 · 0

: Sept : Oct : Nov : Dec : Jan : Feb : Mar : Apr : May :

Source: Zapata Canyon Project. El Colegio de la Frontera Norte.

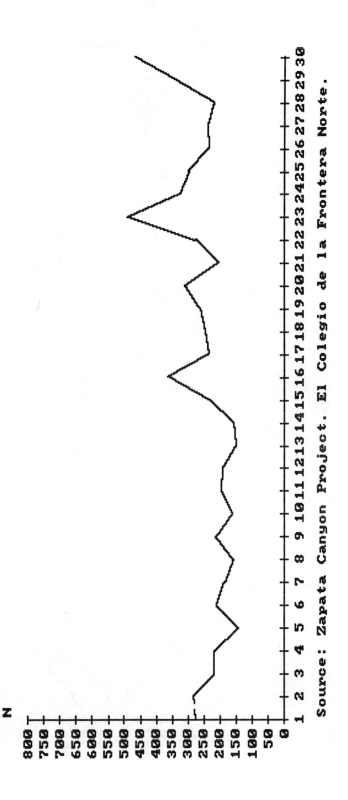

Graph 7A3

FLOW OF UNDOCUMENTED IMMIGRANTS FROM MEXICO

Highest number recorded per day in the month of May, 1987

Source: Zapata Canyon Project. El Colegio de la Frontera Norte.

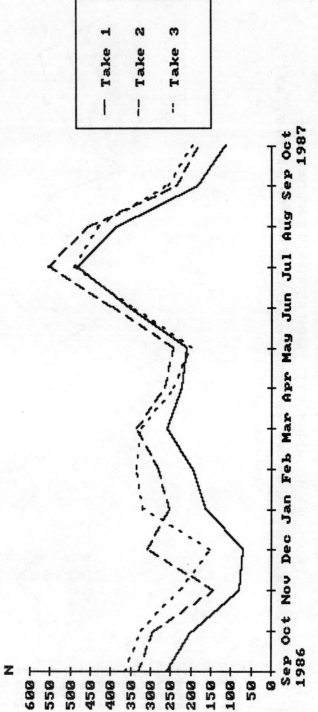

Graph 7.A4

FLOW OF UNDOCUMENTED IMMIGRANTS FROM MEXICO

Monthly average of daily recording from the photograph series.

Take 1
Take 2
Take 3

Source: Zapata Canyon Project. El Colegio de la Frontera Norte.

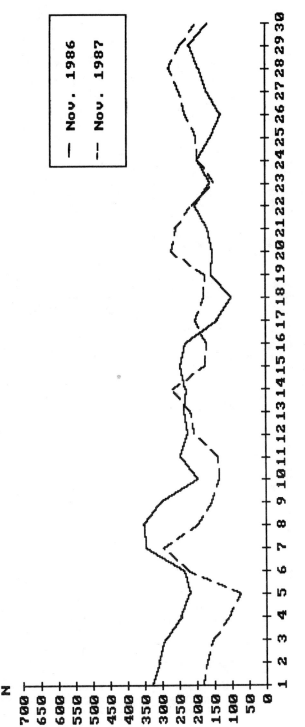

Graph 7.A5

FLOW OF UNDOCUMENTED IMMIGRANTS FROM MEXICO

Highest number recorded per day in the months of

November of 1986 and 1987

— Nov. 1986

-- Nov. 1987

Source: Zapata Canyon Project. El Colegio de la Frontera Norte.

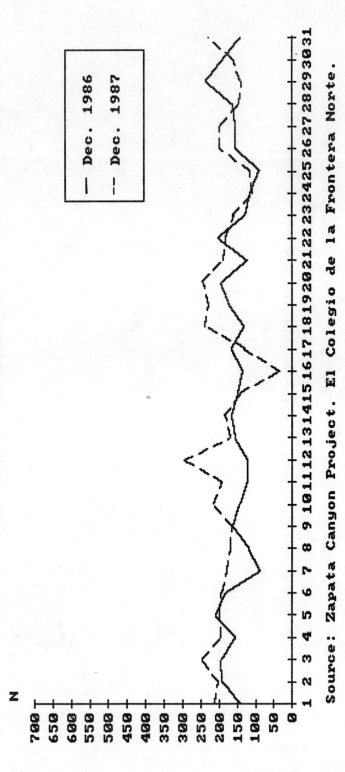

Graph 7.A8

FLOW OF UNDOCUMENTED IMMIGRANTS FROM MEXICO

Highest number recorded per day in the months of

December of 1986 and 1987

— Dec. 1986

-- Dec. 1987

Source: Zapata Canyon Project. El Colegio de la Frontera Norte.

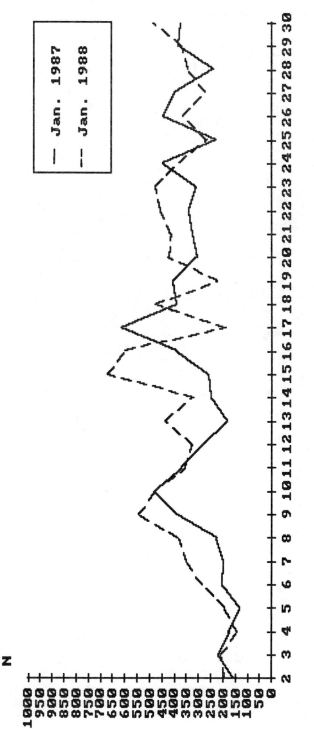

Graph 7.A7

FLOW OF UNDOCUMENTED IMMIGRANTS FROM MEXICO

Highest number recorded per day in the months of

January of 1987 and 1988

— Jan. 1987

-- Jan. 1988

Source: Zapata Canyon Project. El Colegio de la Frontera Norte.

Graph 7A8

FLOW OF UNDOCUMENTED IMMIGRANTS FROM MEXICO

Highest number recorded per day in the months of

February of 1987 and 1988

—— Feb. 1987

-- Feb. 1988

Source: Zapata Canyon Project. El Colegio de la Frontera Norte.

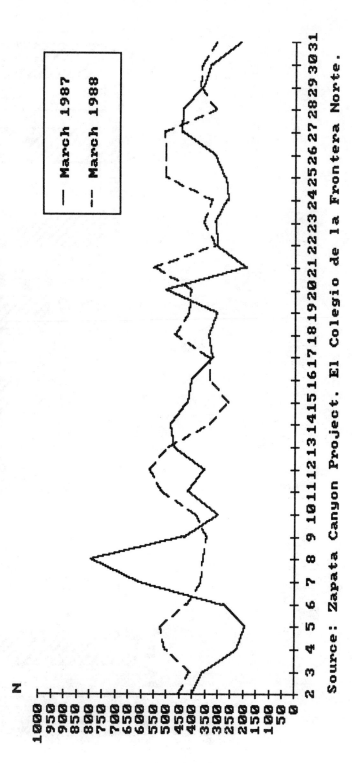

Graph 7.A9

FLOW OF UNDOCUMENTED IMMIGRANTS FROM MEXICO
Highest number recorded per day in the months of
March of 1987 and 1988

March 1987
March 1988

Source: Zapata Canyon Project. El Colegio de la Frontera Norte.

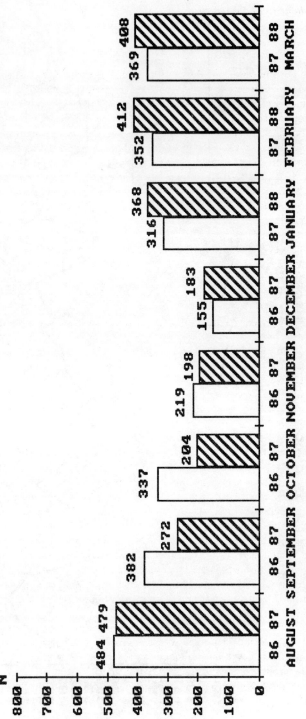

Graph 7.A10

FLOW OF UNDOCUMENTED IMMIGRANTS FROM MEXICO

Monthly averages of the highest number recorded per day

(Totals)

Source: Zapata Canyon Project. El Colegio de la Frontera Norte.

Notes

1. In my doctoral dissertation (Jorge Bustamante, *Mexican Immigration and the Social Relations of Capitalism,* Department of Sociology, University of Notre Dame, 1975) I produced the concept of "commodity migrant" within a theoretical context of undocumented immigration as a result of an international labor market. Along the same lines see Clark M. Reynolds, "Labor Market Projections for the United States and Mexico and Their Relevance to Current Migration Controversies," Food Research Institute Studies No. 17, Stanford, CA, 1979; Richard C. Jones, editor, *Patterns of Undocumented Migration,* Totowa, NJ, Rowan and Allanheld, 1984; Michael J. Greenwood and John M. McDowell, *Journal of Economic Literature,* Vol. 24, December 1986, pp. 1638–1772.

2. Among the various articles in which Celestino Fernandez of the University of Arizona-Tucson has published the results of extensive research on the process of public opinion formation about the presence of the undocumented immigrant from Mexico, see "The Border Patrol and the New Media Coverage of Undocumented Immigration During the 1970's: A Quantitative Content Analysis in the Sociology of Knowledge," *California Sociologist,* 5, 1982, pp. 1–26.

3. Jorge A. Bustamante, "Mexican Migration: The Political Dynamics of Perceptions," in C.W. Reynolds and C. Tello, editors, *U.S.-Mexico Relations: Economic and Social Aspects,* Standford, CA, Standford University Press, pp. 259–276.

4. C. Fernandez, *op. cit.*

5. See, in particular, chapter 7 of the U.S. Council of Economic Advisors' *Economic Report to the President, February 1986,* Washington DC, Government Printing Office, 1986, pp. 223, 227, and 233.

6. *Wall Street Journal,* June 5, 1987.

7. A radio program sponsored by the U.S. Immigration and Naturalization Service (INS), broadcast from Irvine, California on June 18, 1987, included the telephone participation of Senator Pete Wilson from Washington, D.C., in which he asked the INS and the U.S. Border Patrol to relax border enforcement.

8. The announcement of this change of dates was made by Mr. Alan Nelson at a press conference in Washington, D.C. on June 22, 1987.

9. Tijuana is located at the upmost northwest tip of the Mexican border with the United States. Tijuana's economy is very much integrated into the economy of San Diego. It shares some of its tourism. Legal border crossings at the U.S. gates between Tijuana and San Diego amounted to about 35 million during 1986.

10. This has been documented by Celestino Fernandez *op. cit.*

11. Other more specific proposals relating foreign debt and undocumented immigration for bilateral negotiations have been suggested elsewhere in an essay published in Susan Purcell Kaufman, editor, *Mexico in Transition: Implications for U.S. Policy,* New York, NY, Council of Foreign Affairs, 1988, pp. 69–80.

8

Mutual Ambivalence Mutually Misunderstood: Mexico-U.S. Immigration Issues

Michael S. Teitelbaum

For 15 years now, immigration issues have both animated and complicated Mexico-U.S. relations—*animated* because there are few exchanges as emotionally powerful as are the movements of large numbers of people from one nation to another; *complicated* because these emotional effects are both positive and negative, leading to deeper understanding and ties, while generating fears and animus.

The leitmotifs of both Mexican and U.S. views on immigration have been ambivalence and misunderstanding. These general tendencies have been exacerbated, in both countries, by contention and exaggeration that has poured from the pens (and more recently from the word processors) of committed advocates. Such contentions rose to their highest volume during debate about proposed changes in U.S. immigration law.

Although it is true that such overstated views have tended to dominate the press and public debate in both countries, the purpose here is to present—as neutrally as possible—the core of the more measured perceptions of immigration issues as they have been seen by informed observers in Mexico and in the United States. Since 1986–1988 has been a period of important change, such developments are discussed here with a view to how immigration issues may affect future relations between the two countries.

Quantitative Facts, Semi-Facts, and Uncertainties

No full coverage of quantitative immigration data is either possible or appropriate here, but the groundwork for understanding the policy debate can be laid with a few paragraphs of summary.

Legal immigration by Mexican nationals to the United States has averaged 65,000 per year since 1980.[1] This represents the largest number of legal immigrants from any country, and about 11.5% of the global total. Such numbers are put into comparative perspective by noting that during the 1980s legal immigration to the United States from the whole of Western and Eastern Europe averaged almost exactly the same as that from Mexico alone. As will be seen below, disproportions between Mexican and European migration are largely due to the unintended consequences of U.S. immigration reforms adopted during the 1960s to eliminate the blatantly racist elements of the earlier National Origins Quota system.

The above figures relate only to legal immigration. In addition, an unknown number of Mexican nationals have migrated unlawfully to the United States, many for temporary stays, many permanently. The reason for the uncertainty about the size of this undocumented (or illegal, or unauthorized)[2] flow is its largely clandestine nature.[3] The magnitude and permanence of such unlawful migration has been a point of contention between the two governments and among nongovernmental advocates. However, there would be broad agreement that the numbers involved are nontrivial, with back-and-forth movement numbering in the hundreds of thousands a year at a minimum. The number of Mexican illegal migrants taking up permanent residence in the United States is agreed to be much smaller, but cumulating to at least one million by 1980.[4] Some responsible observers believe this resident population is substantially larger; few think it smaller.

Thus, even such minimalist estimates of illegal permanent immigrants, when combined with Mexico's status as the leading country of origin for legal immigration, illustrate why Mexico-U.S. immigration has risen to policy salience in a way that the far smaller movements from other countries have not. There are a few exceptions to this point, such as the highly politicized migrations from Cuba, Haiti, and Central America and the ethnically energized advocacy about recent illegal migrations from Ireland.

U.S. Perceptions

It has been remarked that U.S. attitudes toward immigration often have been characterized by ambivalence.[5] On the one hand, Americans have romanticized immigration and described the United States as a unique "nation of immigrants," apparently in ignorance of the fact that its percent foreign-born is considerably lower than that of many other countries such as France, Canada, Australia, Israel, and Kuwait. On the other hand, immigration frequently has been perceived as a threat to unity and coherence of an already turbulent society, especially when immigration is large, lacks diversity as to nationality, language, religion, etc.; and/or is heavily concentrated in enclaves.

Mainstream U.S. opinion perceives recent migration from Mexico, and especially its illegal form, as a significant problem warranting public policy attention. Indeed, Mexican illegal migration may have received, if anything, disproportionate attention in the American debate given that approximately half of all illegal immigrants are thought to come from countries other than Mexico.

At least four streams of thought underlie this American concern about Mexican illegal immigration. First are general worries that American sovereign control of her borders has been breached, to the extent that prominent opinion leaders of diverse political views speak of having "lost control of our borders." Precisely this characterization has been embraced by William French Smith, a conservative stalwart and former Attorney General in the Reagan Administration, and by Father Theodore Hesburgh, one of the country's most respected liberal humanitarians who for many years served with distinction as Chairman of the Commission on Civil Rights.

Second, the American labor movement is offended by an uncontrolled influx of workers from a country where prevailing wages are 80–90% lower than those in the United States. Such migrants are perceived as a pool of willing labor available to undercut hard-won gains by the domestic labor movement, especially during a lengthy period of economic and political stress.

Third, there are general concerns about the rapidly growing linguistic minority of Spanish-speaking residents, and a belief that most illegal immigrants are Spanish-speaking. Such concerns are particularly prominent in the context of low levels of domestic childbearing and the heavy geographic concentration of immigrants in only a few states and metropolitan regions, both of which contribute to a fear of being "swamped." It is fair to say that bilingual policies adopted by politicians and jurists at the urging of such linguistic groups have generated, rightly or wrongly, powerful political opposition at the grassroots.[6]

Finally, there are humanitarian concerns about the development of an exploitable underclass who, given their unlawful presence, are unwilling to file complaints about violations of employment regulations such as minimum wage and occupational safety, not to mention abuses of their basic human rights. For this reason, there are many political liberals who support policies aimed at limiting illegal immigration.

It should be obvious that the debate about illegal immigration has cut across traditional political lines, generating extraordinarily odd political alliances and a great deal of rhetoric. Notwithstanding such evidence of dissonance and extended stalemate among the political elite, all available evidence from public opinion polls suggests that adoption of measures to control illegal immigration has long had the support of a very large majority of the public, typically in the range of 70–90%.[7]

At the same time, there are other forces in the United States that did not see illegal migration from Mexico as a serious problem, or considered the proposed solutions to be worse than the problem. Economic interests were prominent among these, but the perspective was considerably broader, including at least the following:

- regionally concentrated employer interests, especially fruit and vegetable growers in California
- two or three Hispanic political groups claiming to represent Mexican-Americans or even all Hispanic-Americans
- groups such as the American Civil Liberties Union that described themselves as defending the civil liberties of immigrants and/or minorities
- regional and academic groups who shared Mexican viewpoints on the subject (see below), and some foreign policy specialists for whom domestic U.S. concerns were subordinate to possible foreign policy complications.

There was also awareness in Washington about Mexican official concerns, and as the domestic debate unfolded about proposed reforms, there were several official attempts by executive and legislative branch officials to seek Mexican comments. For reasons discussed below, these proved to be unproductive.

With the passage of the Immigration Reform and Control Act of 1986, the broadly held domestic views described above may be said ultimately to have prevailed. However, it has been often remarked that U.S. politics since the 1970s has become increasingly a contest of small but well-financed interest groups, and immigration policy was no exception to this pattern. Indeed, for nearly ten years the debate on U.S. immigration issues was successfully controlled by unlikely coalitions of such groups, many of which had long been bitter antagonists in other policy spheres. While these groups were unable to achieve affirmative defeat of the proposed legislative actions, they were able to delay action for many years via parliamentary blocking tactics, and the California growers were able to triumph even within the 1986 reforms.

Mexican Perceptions

As viewed from north of the border, the mainstream of Mexican opinion over the past decade, both official and nonofficial, has seemed to favor the continuation of the status quo—but with important ambivalences and concerns. Continuation of relatively easy access for Mexicans to the U.S. labor market provided a source of highly paid employment to Mexicans seeking opportunities unavailable at home. This was the so-called "safety valve," often remarked upon by Mexican commentators and their U.S. supporters. Some nontrivial fraction of U.S. earnings returned to Mexico as remittances, contributing both to foreign currency reserves and to improved conditions of living. In addition, such migrations allowed for the maintenance of family ties across borders and might also increase Mexican leverage in the U.S. political system.

Undocumented Mexican migration to the United States was acknowledged to have both costs and benefits, but most Mexican observers saw the phenomenon as on balance a positive factor for both countries. The U.S. economy was seen as needing and benefiting from Mexican workers, especially those with low skills and wages, and hence the flow was caused heavily by demand factors north of the border, and only secondarily by labor force and economic trends within Mexico. Moreover, Mexican undocumented workers were seen as occupying discrete segments of the U.S. labor market that were not attractive to U.S. workers, and hence to generate no unfair job competition or displacement. From this perspective, those in the United States who saw undocumented migration as contributing to depressed wages and underemployment among low-skilled U.S. citizens were "scapegoating" undocumented Mexicans for problems generated by U.S. society.

Whatever the impacts of Mexican migration, it was typically seen in Mexico as essentially beyond the control of governmental actions—an unstoppable tidal movement driven by structural attributes of the global economy, subject only to attempts at the margin to manage and optimize. Should such marginal efforts be made, they must be the product of bilateral negotiation rather than "unilateral" U.S. legislation. Moreover, Mexican officials noted that the Mexican Constitution guarantees the right of citizens to emigrate, and pointed to U.S. criticism of Soviet restrictions upon such outmovements by its citizens. In a similar vein of concern about human rights, Mexican officials from the president down emphasized what they described as the basic human right to migrate internationally for employment.[8] Finally, some Mexicans argued that special historical rights attached to such migrations by Mexicans, since their main U.S. destinations lay in territories (California, Texas, etc.) that had been Mexican until 1848.

Mexican ambivalence and concern arose from the reality that many undocumented Mexican workers experienced various forms of mistreatment, ranging from discrimination to exploitation. At the same time, a powerful sense of Mexican nationalist pride was offended by the spectacle of hundreds of thousands of citizens departing voluntarily to work and live in the colossus to the north. The ambivalence was especially acute on the political left, which saw such migration as yet another form of economic and political dependency upon the United States. Meanwhile, conservative religious elements in the Mexican Catholic Church worried about the weakening of religion, morality, and traditional family commitments among those participating in the northward migration to the secular culture of the United States.

More recently, there has been some concern in Mexico about the growing "brain drain" of professionals to the United States; the changing profile of Mexican migrants, from the less to the more skilled, means that the costs to Mexico in terms of lost human capital are rising. Finally, there has also been a sometimes muted Mexican concern about undocumented migration into Mexico from Central American countries such as Guatemala and El Salvador, with quite divergent characterizations of such migration (ranging from bona fide refugees to undocumented migrants displacing Mexican workers) arising from different sectors of the Mexican elite.

Effects of Ambivalences and Misunderstandings

The mutually held ambivalence, and the mutual misunderstandings that resulted, have not been constructive forces in U.S.–Mexico relations. Mexican commentators and officials interpreted the U.S. stalemate on immigration reform achieved by interest group blocking tactics as reflecting broad political support for continuation of the status quo. The general view seemed to be that passage of employer sanctions was politically impossible, opposed as it was by the odd alliance of California growers and Mexican-American politicians. In part for this reason, Mexican officialdom generally declined to enter into discussions solicited by U.S. representatives concerning the shape of U.S. immigration policy. Several such initiatives were undertaken by the Department of State, the U.S. Congress, and the Immigration and Naturalization Service; all were politely rebuffed. In part this response reflected Mexican reluctance to be seen to interfere in a U.S. domestic political matter, in part it also reflected fear of being drawn in and thereby coopted into a participant's role in the process.

The contours of Mexican responses generally included acknowledgment of U.S. sovereign rights to control immigration, and a description of the phenomenon as one driven by the U.S. economy rather than by aspects of Mexican development. At the same time, Mexican officials and (especially) journalists exercised with some enthusiasm their right to criticize abuses reportedly experienced by undocumented Mexicans in the United States.

The general Mexican belief that employer sanctions would be blocked by employers and Mexican-American politicians, coupled with Mexican unwillingness to engage in serious discussions of proposed reforms, led to the Mexican leadership's being caught substantially off guard on at least two occasions when employer sanctions suddenly moved forward legislatively—in 1982 and again in 1986. In the first of these cases, when the Immigration Reform and Control Act of 1982 (known as the Simpson-Mazzoli bill) suddenly passed the U.S. Senate by a large majority and was brought forward to the floor of the House of Representatives very late in the legislative session, the Mexican Senate was galvanized into expeditious adoption of a strongly worded resolution on "this grave matter that negatively affects our good neighbor relations," expressing its "alarm and concern for the repercussions which will impact both countries if the Simpson-Mazzoli legislation is passed." Mexican undocumented migration to the United States was a transcendent matter that "should not be considered from a unilateral perspective, but rather should be treated from a bilateral and even multilateral perspective."[9]

Given that the bill was at that moment pending before the House of Representatives and that previous U.S. requests for Mexican governmental comment had been politely rebuffed, this Mexican statement was seen in Washington as a rather crude attempt to intervene in the American legislative process. However, one informed Mexican observer argues that the Mexican Senate resolution derived from a resolution of a parliamentary conference held earlier that same month in Brazil, in which he was the principal expert on international migration, which embraced a recommendation to "encourage both origin and destination countries to negotiate bilateral or multilateral agreements in respect of international migration."[10]

In the end, the Mexican Senate's resolution probably had little effect in either direction; the fact that only a few days remained in the U.S. legislative session meant that delaying tactics could be successfully deployed by the already mobilized interest groups mentioned above. Their success in killing the 1982 legislation reinforced Mexican observers' belief that such measures could not be adopted by the U.S. political system. One result was that when similar legislation emerged again in 1986 as the Simpson-Rodino bill, its ultimate adoption took the Mexican government substantially by surprise.

Reading the Tea Leaves: Early Assessments of the Effects of the *Simpson-Rodino Act*

Like all its predecessors, the Simpson-Rodino bill's main approach to restraining illegal immigration is to reduce the "magnet" of high-wage employment in the United States, principally by making employers liable for the knowing employment of illegal aliens (measures known by the shorthand phrase "employer sanctions"). Enacted in November 1986, the Simpson-Rodino Act incorporated a set of phased implementation dates, including:

- for employer sanctions for nonagricultural employers, a 12-month phase-in of penalties such that no penalties would result for violations until December 1, 1987
- for employer sanctions for agriculture, an additional 12-month delay in sanctions, such that no penalties would result for violations before December 1, 1988
- for all employers, sanctions that apply only to hirings after November 6, 1986; continued employment of illegal aliens hired before this date is mandated as lawful.

Obviously it is impossible to reach firm assessments concerning the long-term effects of legislative measures that phased in recently for nonagricultural employers, and will not become effective for agriculture until near the end of 1988. Several interim assessments have been offered, however, and two of these illustrate both the difficulties and the differing perceptions involved.

Jorge A. Bustamante, a leading Mexican analyst of Mexican migration trends to the United States, reports in Chapter 7 of this volume on the results of a novel method for studying the rate of flow of illegal migration through the Zapata Canyon or "Soccer Field" sector of the U.S.-Mexico border between Tijuana and San Isidro. The approach selected involves counts of migrants taken from a set of three daily photographs of this area; such counts have been made from August 1986 onward. On the basis of such data up to late 1987, Bustamante perceives no downward trend, which he finds consistent with an unchanged continuation of the longstanding seasonality of such Mexican migration to the United States. He also describes as shedding "some light on the ideology of migration in Mexico" the data for the month of May 1987. He perceives only a short-lived decline, which he attributes to "rumors [within Mexico] about 'a massive deportation' campaign," which was going to be launched by the U.S. government beginning on May 5. He finds a slight decline in the period before the fifth of May. But says "the trend stopped its decline after May 5, when the only new action taken by the U.S. Immigration Service was to start receiving applications for legalization under the new law." From this, and similar evidence he suggests that "the new immigration legislation has not yet made any significant impact on the inflow of undocumented immigrants from Mexico to the United States."

A leading U.S. analyst of immigration trends, David S. North,[11] examines more conventional data drawn from apprehensions of illegal aliens at the southern border through August 1987. North emphasizes the limitations of apprehension data, but argues that they can provide useful evidence if treated carefully. Because the number of apprehensions is affected not only by the flow but also by the intensity of enforcement effort, North standardizes the raw apprehension data by the number of shifts of Border Patrol personnel policing the border (the "linewatch" function in Government parlance).

In the ten months following the November 1986 passage of the Simpson-Rodino Act, apprehensions-per-agent-per-shift fell 27%. However, this reversal of trend diminished over the period, with levels in July 1987 having increased back to those a year earlier, particularly in the western region. North attributes this summer increase to reports widely broadcast by West Coast U.S. growers that there would be severe labor shortages during the summer. This interpretation is consistent with more recent data, showing sharply lower figures for August-October 1987 than for the comparable period in 1986.

North also notes a 31% decline in the number of smuggler vehicles seized over comparable periods pre- and post- Simpson-Rodino,[12] and scattered evidence ("straws in the wind, not solid statistical evidence") suggesting an unusually heavy flow of undocumented migrants out of the country. North considers the possibility that the decline in apprehensions resulted from the record height of the normally shallow Rio Grande River in the winter and spring of 1986–87. He notes that geographically any such effects could occur only in Texas and especially around El Paso and Del Rio, and that 65% of the linewatch activity from which his data are drawn takes place over dry land to the west of the Rio Grande border area.[13]

On the basis of this preliminary analysis, North concludes tentatively that:

Illegal migration across the southern border has declined. . . . As a result of the new law, nearly one-half million illegal entries apparently were not made during the first ten months after enactment. There were also scattered indications of a rise in the flow of illegal aliens from the country. IRCA has created some pressures to reduce the resident illegal migrant population—as well as discouraging the arrival of new illegal migrants—thus producing some movement towards a primary objective of IRCA: the discouragement of illegal migration.[14]

It has always been extraordinarily difficult to develop credible data on undocumented migration; the same is true for other clandestine phenomena such as child abuse, tax evasion, or the cultivation and use of illicit drugs.[15] Moreover, given the sharp legal shift, even the creative approaches of Bustamante and North cannot offer us enlightenment concerning possible transitional effects, such as undocumented Mexicans choosing not to return home for Christmas 1986, or staying on to claim the legalization benefit. Finally, it is important to emphasize the fact, sometimes misunderstood in both countries, that the employer sanctions provision did not take effect until December 1987 for nonagricultural employers, and will not be activated for agricultural employers until December 1988. For all these reasons, it is too much to ask that firm conclusions be drawn now as to the effectiveness of the Simpson-Rodino Act in reducing undocumented migration, though periodic interim assessments are highly desirable.

Reading the Crystal Ball: Mexico-U.S. Migrations in the Future

There is agreement on both sides of the border that adoption of the Simpson-Rodino Act has changed substantially the context of Mexico-U.S. migration trends, as well as the tenor of public discussion concerning them. No one can foresee the future other than hazily, but at least three important matters in prospect are worthy of mention:

- reforms in U.S. law on legal immigration
- the Mexican economic crisis
- protectionist pressures in the United States.

Reforms in U.S. Law on Legal Immigration

As noted above, Mexico is not only the largest source country of undocumented or illegal migrants to the United States, but also the largest single source country for legal immigrants, accounting for 66,533 in 1986.[16] This may be compared with the 62,512 legal immigrants from the whole of Europe, comprising some 27 countries with a combined population nearly six times as large as Mexico's (ca.

500 million vs. 84 million). Note that the above immigration numbers from Mexico do not include any illegal immigrants legalized under the Simpson-Rodino bill, a large percentage of whom appear to be from Mexico.[17] The only other country coming close to Mexico was the Philippines, with some 52,558 legal immigrants in 1986. Overall, some 84% of legal immigrants now come from Latin America and Asia; only 16% are admitted from the rest of the world combined, including Africa (3%), North and West Europe (5%), South and East Europe (5%), and Canada and Oceania combined (about 3%).

Meanwhile, U.S. law appears to be quite evenhanded, for each country of origin is allocated an equal number (20,000) of numerically limited visas, with minor anomalies for certain colonies and territories. How can the apparent discrepancy of apparent evenhandedness and actual inequality be explained?

In part the discrepancy is due to differences in demand for immigrant visas. For self-evident reasons, greater demand comes from those countries with much lower wage levels than those prevailing in the United States, and especially the ones that have longstanding cultural, political, or economic ties. Much of this demand component is beyond the control of U.S. policy.

However, there is also an important difference in the supply of immigrant visas, deriving from what may be described as a perverse "law of the unintended consequence" that afflicts U.S. immigration law.[18] Put briefly, the major reforms in U.S. law adopted in 1965 incorporated a provision that had the effect, unintentionally, of making it easier for would-be immigrants from Latin America and Asia to obtain immigrant visas than for comparable persons in Europe or Africa. The intention of these reforms was to repeal the blatantly racist National Origins Quota system of 1952 and earlier—hence the adoption of an equal number of numerically limited visas for each country of origin.

In addition, visa preferences were shifted toward family reunification. The intent of many of the proponents of this shift was to increase the visas available to immigrants from traditional countries of origin such as Italy, Ireland, Greece, and Poland. Thus, although the reforms allocated 20,000 visas to each country in its numerically limited categories, certain then-small categories were exempted from all numerical restrictions. In particular, unlimited admission was continued for immediate family members of U.S. citizens—indeed this category was expanded to include parents as well as spouses and minor children of U.S. citizens. Both supporters and opponents of this provision stated that its main effect would be to continue the European dominance of immigration to the United States, although visa barriers would be eased for migrants from Southern and Eastern Europe.[19]

Unintentionally, this exemption of immediate family of U.S. citizens—intended by its sponsors to be of small size and focused upon European immigrants—became an unlimited entitlement provision used primarily by immigrants from Latin America and Asia. This numerically exempt category now accounts for some 37% of all legal admissions, and the numbers have been rising briskly, averaging a 7% annual increase over an extended period. In 1976 there were about 100,000; in 1985 nearly 205,000—a doubling in less than 10 years. The latest data for 1986, show an increase of over 9% per annum in this unlimited category. A large percentage of these unlimited admissions come from countries such as Mexico, the Philippines, South Korea, India, all of which routinely exceed the apparent per country ceiling of 20,000.

Overall, family reunification (both the immediate and extended family forms) have come to swamp the other categories of legal immigration: in 1986, nearly three quarters (72.1%) of legal immigrants were admitted under the immediate and extended family categories. Only 17% were categorized as refugees, and many of these too were admitted for reasons of family ties. Remarkably, less than 9% were admitted on the basis of education or skills needed by the American economy; even in this small category, nearly half were accompanying family members.

The net result is that current policy is now widely described as discriminatory, even if unintentionally so; in particular, it discriminates against would-be immigrants from Europe and Africa, and in favor of immigrants from Asia and Latin America. It is now far more difficult for a would-be immigrant from Ireland, England, or Italy to obtain an immigrant visa than for one from Mexico, the Philippines, or Jamaica. National comparisons offer striking examples: in 1986, there were ten times as many legal immigrants born in Jamaica (19,595) as in Ireland (1,839); eight times as many born in the Dominican Republic (26,175) as in Italy (3,089); four times as many in Colombia (11,408) as in Greece (2,512); and so on.

Notwithstanding the above, some regional and/or ethnic interest groups are advocating that more than 20,000 numerically limited visas (the typical number advocated is 50,000) be allocated to Mexico only, on grounds such as physical contiguity and historical ties,[20] a move that would do away with even the appearance of nondiscrimination by national origins. Meanwhile, stimulated in part by the immigration activism pursued by Mexican-American political groups over the past ten years, other ethnic groups have now mobilized to reverse the unintended effects of the 1965 reforms. In 1986, Irish-American activists were able to incorporate an amendment allocating 10,000 special visas on a first-come first-served basis to nationals of countries "disadvantaged" by the 1965 reforms. This provision resulted, in early 1987, in an embarrassing flood of well over 1,000,000 visa applications for these 10,000 visas.

These interest groups and others are now pressing for more substantial revisions of legal immigration laws, aimed at countering the current law's unintended discrimination in favor of nations from which the most recent immigration streams have come. At the urging of such groups, Senators Kennedy and Simpson have introduced legislation, and other bills are sure to emerge. Given the uncertainty that attaches to U.S. Congressional action, it is anybody's guess as to how such initiatives will develop over the coming year. As this debate proceeds, however, it is important to note that all available data on U.S. public opinion consistently show only a tiny percentage (between 4% and 7% in the 1980s) favoring increased levels of legal immigration, while large majorities (49% to 66% in the 1980s) favor lower immigration numbers.[21]

The Mexican Economic Crisis

An extended discussion of the Mexican economic crisis is found in earlier chapters of this volume. For purposes of considering future immigration prospects, however, it must be understood that since the Mexican economy entered its crisis in 1981, there has been essentially no real economic growth but 18% growth in the labor force. Mexican projections indicate a continuing labor force growth of 3.2% per year to the year 2000, with the total labor force increasing from about 28 million in 1987 to about 40–42 million in 2000. Based upon historical experience, such labor force growth requires annual economic growth of 5.3% to keep constant current levels of unemployment and underemployment.[22]

Such growth clearly is possible for Mexico, which from World War II until the 1980s averaged about 6% growth, establishing it as one of the jewels of economic success in the Third World. Unfortunately, Mexican leaders of the 1970s were induced by rapid labor force growth—and seduced by high and rising oil prices—into expenditure and investment policies that now appear to all concerned to have been unwise. Both government and private sectors enthusiastically took on very high levels of international debt on the basis of Mexican oil reserves (from equally enthusiastic lenders, it should be said), policies that are described by current Mexican leaders, from President de la

Madrid on down, as "mistaken judgments."[23] Such policies were accompanied by events and trends clearly well beyond Mexican control: a steep worldwide recession, falling oil prices, historically high real interest rates, and a destructive earthquake.

Taken together, these factors combined to create a profound economic malaise: Mexico's total foreign debt now exceeds US$100 billion. Debt service now accounts for some 6% of Gross Domestic Product and 65% of the federal budget. Annual inflation exceeds 150%. Real wages have fallen by half, and unemployment and underemployment appear to be up sharply.

Mexican Fears Concerning U.S. Protectionism

Mexico's strategy to cope with such staggering problems, stemming from mistaken judgments and bad luck, reflect major departures from longstanding policy and depend critically upon the absence of protectionist measures in the United States. Mexico is now engaged upon a dramatic restructuring of her economy. The longstanding Mexican policy of protectionist tariffs and quotas in support of import-substitution policies has been replaced by rapid opening of the Mexican economy to international competition, symbolized by Mexican accession to the General Agreement on Tariffs and Trade (GATT) in 1986. Two important trade agreements have been concluded with the United States, Mexico's leading trading partner. Policies that long deterred foreign investment have been relaxed, though limitations of various kinds continue. The exchange rate of the Mexican *peso*, so overvalued during the oil boom, has been dramatically (some might say traumatically) depreciated; in 1981 there were 24 Mexican *pesos* to the U.S. dollar; in early 1988 there were approximately 2,400.

As a result of these trends and policies, Mexico is rapidly becoming one of the lowest-cost producers in the world, and is depending heavily upon increasing export-led growth. For this reason, Mexican officials express special concern about rising sentiments of protectionism in the United States. They recognize that these are directed primarily toward what are perceived as unfair trade practices among Asian nations such as Japan, but fear that the U.S. Congressional process will fail to link trade policy issues to other matters such as migration and that Mexico's planned export-led recovery might be unintentionally wounded by such measures aimed elsewhere.

Conclusion

There is no disagreement that the capacity of the Mexican economy to generate sufficient employment for its burgeoning labor force depends critically upon its ability to escape from the economic stagnation and crisis of the 1980s and to reestablish a trajectory of sustained high economic growth. The United States has an important role to play, given its status as Mexico's largest trading partner; and, generally speaking, Mexican observers describe U.S. policies over the past several years as constructive and supportive. There remain, however, the uncertain effects on Mexico of rising protectionist sentiment in the United States, even though these are driven by domestic political concerns and directed principally at trade imbalances with countries other than Mexico.

Mexican migration pressures, both internal and international, will be heavily influenced by the pace and nature of economic recovery and advance within Mexico, which in turn may be substantially affected by trade policies adopted by the United States. Meanwhile, the extent to which Mexican migration pressures are directed toward the United States will depend upon the effects, intended and unintended, of the 1986 immigration reforms. Notwithstanding continued opposition by some interest groups, U.S. immigration policies seem likely to continue their shift toward rectifying the failures and unintended inequities of past legislation.

To this observer, the Mexican government has appeared to have been less than fully informed as to the contesting, and often chaotic, domestic forces influencing U.S. policy on both immigration and trade. It is fair to say that the U.S. policy process in both the trade and immigration spheres has been marked by its general unpredictability, by the high level of interest group influence, and by the weakness of connection between policy elements. The unpredictability and internal contradictions in U.S. immigration policy that so perplex Mexican observers are outcomes of these characteristics.

Moreover, the border represents a conceptual as well as a geographical dividing line. North of the border immigration is overwhelmingly seen as an issue of United States domestic policy, and one involving immigration from many countries. To its south, the focus of the Mexican government is upon Mexican migration to the United States, often seen as an historical and essentially uncontrollable flow that is subject only to bilateral or multilateral negotiation for its management. For these and perhaps other reasons, past Mexican responses to official U.S. inquiries have proved to be less than forthcoming, and in the longer run unproductive.

Recently, however, there have been signs of change. In December 1987, the U.S. Commission for the Study of International Migration and Cooperative Economic Development was cordially welcomed in Mexico City by President de la Madrid. Moreover, the president responded positively to the U.S. Commission's proposal for the establishment of a Mexican counterpart commission. Joint research projects are currently under active discussion between the two counterpart commissions, and the overall tone of communication has been both warm and constructive.[24]

Such developments are very promising, but it must always be remembered that each of the two governments holds strongly to the view that *its* immigration policy is a fundamental aspect of national sovereignty (indeed, the same may be said of all governments). Given the deep sensitivities involved, neither can be expected to enter into bilateral or multilateral negotiations about its immigration policy with the several immigrant-sending countries to its south. Nonetheless, one may hope that future U.S.-Mexico dialogue on migration issues will be marked by mutual understanding concerning the other's perceptions and concerns, and by a willingness for constructive exchanges of views directed toward harmony rather than contention.

Notes

1. Data on legal immigration are derived from U.S. Department of Justice, Immigration and Naturalization Service, *Statistical Yearbook of the Immigration and Naturalization Service, 1986*, Washington, D.C., U.S. Government Printing Office, 1987, Table 3.

2. Even the choice of adjective has been a prominent point of contention among advocates. In this chapter, the various terms are used interchangeably, with no attachment implied to one or another advocacy position.

3. For a discussion of such uncertainties, see M.S. Teitelbaum, "Intersections: Immigration and Demographic Change and Their Impact on the United States," in Jane Menken, editor, *World Population and U.S. Policy: The Choices Ahead*, New York and London, W.W. Norton, 1986, pp. 150–153.

4. See, for example, Robert Warren and Jeffrey S. Passell, "A Count of the Uncountable: Estimates of Undocumented Aliens Counted in the 1980 United States Census," *Demography*, 24(3), August 1987, pp. 375–393; Frank D. Bean, Allan G. King and Jeffrey S. Passell, "The Number of Illegal Migrants of Mexican Origin in the United States: Sex Ratio-based Estimates for 1980," *Demography*, 20(1), February 1983, pp. 99–109; Manuel García y Griego and Leo F. Estrada, "Research on the Magnitude of Mexican Undocumented Immigration to the U.S.: A Summary," in A. Rios-Bustamante, editor, *Mexican Immigrant Workers in the U.S.*, Los Angeles, Chicano Studies Center, University of California, Los Angeles, 1981, pp. 51–70.

5. See, for example, Charles B. Keely, *U.S. Immigration: A Policy Analysis*, New York, The Population Council, 1979, Chapter I.

6. Numerous local actions have been initiated in opposition to bilingual policies. For example, in 1984 in California, ballot Proposition 38 entitled "Voting Materials in English Only" was initiated with a petition of over

600,000 signatures, and passed by a 72% majority despite nearly universal opposition by Democratic and Republican politicians.

7. See, for example, Rita L. Simon, "Immigration and American Attitudes," *Public Opinion*, July/August 1987, p. 49.

8. See, for example, Peter H. Smith, *Mexico: the Quest for a U.S. Policy*, New York, The Foreign Policy Association, 1980, p. 26.

9. Reprinted in U.S. Congress, *Congressional Record* December 17, 1982, p. H10256.

10. Jorge A. Bustamante, "International Migration and Foreign Policy: Comments from a Mexican Perspective," in Lydio F. Tomasi, editor, *In Defense of the Alien, Volume VI*, New York, Center for Migration Studies, 1984, pp. 238–239. The quoted recommendation is from *Brasilia Declaration on Population and Development*, Section 14, issued by the Western Hemisphere Conference of Parliamentarians on Population and Development, 2–5 December 1982, Brasilia, Brazil.

11. David S. North, "Immigration Reform in Its First Year," Washington, D.C., Center for Immigration Studies, November, 1987.

12. *Ibid.*, p. 17.

13. *Ibid.*, pp. 17–19.

14. *Ibid.*, pp. 3, 19.

15. On the drug issue too, there are longstanding disagreements between the governments of Mexico and the United States, as may be seen in other chapters of this volume.

16. *Immigration Reform, op. cit.*, pp. 25–27.

17. All data on legal immigration by country of birth are taken from *Statistical Yearbook, op. cit.*, Table 3.

18. Other countries have also experienced unintended consequences from their immigration policies. The West German government certainly did not intend to have a large-scale permanent immigration when it opted for its "guest worker" program. The governments of France, Belgium, and other West European countries did not intend to stimulate powerful right-wing political movements when they adopted their immigration and refugee policies. The Canadian government did not intend that its generous refugee policies encourage Tamils and Sikhs resident in Western Europe to pay unscrupulous freighter captains thousands of dollars per head to drop them in lifeboats off the Canadian coast. The governments of Kuwait and other Arab labor-importing states of the Persian Gulf never intended that their migrant labor policies would make them minorities in their own countries, a fact of major political significance in this strategic and turbulent region.

19. David M. Reimers, "An Unintended Reform: The 1965 Immigration Act and Third World Immigration to the United States," *Journal of American Ethnic History*, 2, Fall, 1983, pp. 15–18.

20. For example, see American Assembly for the Southwestern Region, *Population and Immigration Policy: Mexico, Central America and the U.S. Southwest*, Woodlands, TX, Center For Growth Studies, 1987, p. 9.

21. *Immigration and American Attitudes, op. cit.*, p. 48.

22. Saul Trejo, Colegio de México, personal communication, December 1987.

23. Meeting with President de la Madrid, Mexico City, December 3, 1987.

24. The U.S. Commission, established in 1987 under the terms of the Simpson-Rodino Act (and of which the present author is a Commissioner), has the following charge: "The Commission, in consultation with the governments of Mexico and other sending countries in the Western Hemisphere, shall examine the conditions in Mexico and such other sending countries which contribute to unauthorized migration to the United States and [shall explore] mutually beneficial, reciprocal trade and investment programs to alleviate such conditions."

9

Mexico in Transition and the United States: Old Perceptions, New Problems

Sergio Aguayo

The combined effect of economic crisis, foreign debt, illegal immigration, political changes, differences over Central America, and drug trafficking has focused U.S. attention on Mexican affairs. Although the views expressed are as diverse as U.S. society, there is a consensus that Mexican events may culminate in a threat to the national security of the United States. Therefore, it is in the best national interest of each country to take a critical look at its perceptions of the other.

In the past, periods of U.S. attention (in 1946–47 and 1951–54, for example) have been followed by periods of neglect. That is changing. The number of U.S. correspondents accredited in Mexico has increased significantly: 26 in 1975, 33 in 1981, 58 in 1983, and 92 in 1987.[1] Predictably, press coverage of Mexico has increased; the *New York Times* published 51 articles about Mexico in 1980, 137 in 1982, and 192 in 1986.[2] A similar trend is evident in the *Washington Post,* in the three main T.V. networks, and in congressional debates.[3]

In recent years some private U.S. foundations have allocated considerable amounts of financial resources to strengthen research programs on Mexico.[4] In addition to academic researchers, many government officials in several agencies monitor Mexico. Some are in Washington, D.C.; others are scattered throughout Mexico, a country where the United States maintains its "largest diplomatic mission in the world."[5] Mexican events are also followed closely by the hundreds of U.S. companies that together have US$10 billion in direct investment in Mexico.

Clearly, a substantial number of individuals and groups in the United States are watching Mexico. They share some basic assumptions but also have their own interpretations of Mexican events. On the one hand this means that, contrary to what some Mexicans maintain, there is not a "master plan" to portray Mexico either one way or another. On the other, such diversity not only reflects the kaleidoscopic nature of U.S. society, but is also a manifestation of a new phenomenon: governments have lost their monopoly of bilateral relations. What was "a pragmatic, elitist and airtight" relationship has evolved into a multiplicity of relations among entrepreneurs, academics, members of religious orders, labor unions, and so forth.[6]

In the United States there is a widespread belief that "few people in the U.S. seem to understand Mexico very well, despite our long and close relationship."[7] This self-deprecating attitude is unsound. In the United States there is a very good understanding of Mexico. The problem is that Mexico is usually perceived within the limits imposed by the dominant U.S. world view, at the heart of which is the overwhelming belief that the U.S. experience is the best possible for any society.

The most fundamental objective of the United States for Mexico is an "independent, strong and prosperous," and politically stable nation, with which to "maintain friendly relations" and to ensure "maximum cooperation" at all possible levels.[8] Today, there are growing doubts as to whether these objectives will continue to be feasible. It is feared that the Mexican economic crisis might increase political instability, which could result in a deterioration of relations, with a negative impact on U.S. interests.

Trying to discuss the perceptions of all the Mexican topics followed in the United States in this small space would inevitably entail some superficiality. Therefore, I have selected the central aspects of three issues that have been constantly mentioned as part of the national interest and security of the United States and Mexico: the economic crisis, the stability of the political system, and the impact of drug trafficking on bilateral relations.

The Mexican Economic Crisis: Analysis and Prescriptions

The general U.S. understanding of the Mexican economic crisis is accurate. But two misconceptions persist in the academic, press, government, and business communities: that the Mexican government is largely responsible for an economic crisis that can affect U.S. interests; and that Mexico's best option lies in the privatization and opening of its economy.[9]

Some analysts reduce this estimate of government responsibility by citing external factors including the collapse of oil prices, the instability of interest rates, the deterioration in the terms of trade, the 1985 earthquake, and population growth.[10] None of these factors, however, has changed the belief that state intervention in the Mexican economy generates inefficiency and corruption. This perception is a consequence of Mexican reality, but it is also a natural corollary of the U.S. faith in capitalism.

Analysts also agree that Mexico's economy must grow, and that growth can only be achieved with "genuine economic reforms" much along the lines of those agreed upon by a representative group of U.S. experts on Mexico assembled by the Stanley Foundation. They concluded that the government must bring corruption under control, raise the level of efficiency, and cut back on public expenditures. Further, "inefficient parastatal enterprises should be sold; import licenses should be cut back; concrete changes in foreign investment laws should be enacted; and investor confidence should be restored so that capital flight can be reduced. Without these reforms, the Mexican economy will remain underdeveloped."[11] In short, the privatization and opening of the economy to trade and development are the magic solutions.

A unique aspect of the current period is that, for the first time in recent history, the administration of Miguel de la Madrid shares these ideas and has been implementing some of these recommendations.[12] It is not surprising that we hear praise for Mexico's new economic policy; former U.S. Ambassador to Mexico, John A. Gavin, has commented: the Mexican "President deserves admiration for having the strength to embark" on a program of reforms.[13]

Whereas U.S. analysts agree with the diagnosis and the prescribed cure, however, there are disagreements on the frequency of the dosage. Some urge the United States to put pressure on Mexico to bring the process to full completion.[14] Others deplore the fact that instead of receiving recognition for its efforts, the Mexican government faces a growing wave of criticism and a demand for more extensive and profound reforms.[15]

In any case, the policies applied by the so-called Mexican "technocrats" (and supported by the United States) have already had some political repercussions. For example, rifts have arisen within the ruling party, with some sectors highly critical of economic policies that, in their opinion, are leading inexorably to a greater integration of the two economies. In this context, the regime is vulnerable because it cannot denounce the existence of U.S. pressures. Ultimately, what is at stake is the role traditionally played by Mexico's nationalism.

The way in which a problem is defined influences the recommended solutions. In this case, if the central problem of the Mexican economy is believed to be state intervention and protectionism, the solution lies, first and foremost, in its privatization and opening. It follows that only positive things can come from domestic and foreign private investment. Without attempting to minimize the responsibility of the government, or to deny that part of the solution is to be found in private enterprise, I must emphasize that it is a very serious misreading of reality to ignore the fact that the private sector was partly responsible for the crisis.[16]

Most U.S. analysts (and the Mexicans who are in agreement with them) make the mistake of extrapolating the experience of the United States to other societies. It is unquestionable that the U.S. entrepreneur has played an important role in the success of capitalism in the United States; therefore, some seem to believe that any entrepreneur, anywhere, will be able to solve the problems of any nation.

Even when U.S. scholars recognize the growing importance of the Mexican private sector (correctly identified as the "most powerful political rival of the PRI")[17] they do not understand its nature or its complex relationship with the state. If they were to look deeper into the issue they would find that important segments of the Mexican private sector are also tainted by corruption and inefficiency, which have contributed to the economic crisis in Mexico. For example, the 1982 bank nationalization is often condemned, but there is not a single reference to the prior, harmful speculation of the private banks.

It can be argued that the Mexican private sector has been spoiled by easy profits, government subsidies, and protected markets. It must also be accepted that entrepreneurs have had some responsibility for the shameful state of Mexico's economy. Fernando Canales Clariond, a Monterrey entrepreneur who was candidate for governor of Nuevo Leon under the banner of the conservative National Action Party (PAN), thinks that one "predominant feature" of the Mexican private sector is the "lack of an entrepreneurial spirit; it is not willing to take the risks that come with a free market." He explains how the private organizations "demand a free market in public and then negotiate in private for the maintenance of their privileges . . . some denounce subsidies, but demand theirs" be maintained.[18]

U.S. observers do occasionally mention the weaknesses in Mexico's private sector. For example, Wayne Cornelius has written that during the oil boom, "investment by both the state and private sector was haphazard, inefficient and nonselective."[19] Another expert on Mexico, John Bailey, has observed that "also hampering the economy is an insufficiency of entrepreneurs, the nagging lack of groups—whether state or private—that are able risk-takers, innovators, and integrators. If the state enterprise system has shown little efficiency or innovativeness, the majority of Mexican industrialists have done little better."[20] But these are isolated references that do not give the problem the importance it deserves. The overwhelming belief persists that privatization is the only solution.

One cannot dismiss the possibility that the privatization and opening of the economy may solve Mexico's problems, and that the private sector will modify its distortions. However, that has not yet been proven, and it certainly cannot be assumed. So far, there has been a mystification of the private sector, a neglect of the possibilities presented by the social sector (most of the time ignored in U.S. analysis), and an outright condemnation of the state sector for its errors (some of which are real but others are overstated). If U.S. analysis of Mexico were to recognize the true nature of the private sector, the basic argument in favor of privatization would have to be adapted to a more complex reality.

The Political Transition in Mexico and the U.S. Dilemma

Contrary to the often heard statement that the United States is incapable of understanding Mexico, U.S. observers have been quite accurate in interpreting the Mexican political system. Surprisingly, the accuracy of this interpretation is not apparent in the formulation of policy recommendations. This is because the United States has been unable to address an old dilemma: how to reconcile democratic impulses with the defense of U.S. interests.

In the 1950s it was believed that Mexico would eventually become a Western type of democracy. In the 1960s and early 1970s Frank Brandenburg, Roger Hansen, and Susan Kaufman Purcell, among others, laid down the intellectual grounds for a different understanding: Mexico is politically different from the United States; it has authoritarian traits; it is presidentialist; and it is based on a corporative pact.[21]

Since then, it has been understood that the Mexican political class pragmatically and shrewdly uses all kinds of instruments to integrate, manipulate, coopt, control, or repress workers, peasants, bureaucrats, private enterprise, the press, and other political parties. The Mexican political system has been alien and antagonistic to the liberal paradigm. This really did not matter to U.S. observers as long as it remained strong, stable and, perhaps more important, capable of guaranteeing U.S. interests.[22]

The student movement of 1968 brought attention to the profound transformations of Mexican society, and also to some inadequacies in its political system. The gradual erosion of the foundations of the corporative pact continued into the 1970s and 1980s. These changes found a sophisticated and capable pool of analysts in the United States. For example, Wayne Cornelius, John Bailey, Susan Kaufman Purcell, and Richard Nuccio have given accurate general diagnoses of the political changes in Mexico. They have recognized the waning of the effectiveness and strength of the ruling party (PRI); the lessening importance of official organized labor; the alienation of the intellectuals, middle classes, and some private groups; the rift in the ruling circles; the emergence of independent labor and peasant organizations; and the growing strength of opposition parties.[23]

Other contributions include those of Roderic Camp and Peter Smith, demonstrating how the "technocrats have come to dominate Mexican politics over the past fifteen years or so;" Daniel Levy exploring the political effect of changes in socialization patterns; David Brooks calling attention to the appearance of new urban and rural social forces; David Ronfeldt offering insightful remarks on the differences in political time and the attitude towards contradictions in the two political cultures; and Edward J. Williams exploring the changing role of the army.[24] This impressive accumulation of knowledge disproves the belief that Mexico is inscrutable to foreigners.

In this list of authors, which is only a partial list of U.S. analysts with great insight into Mexico, there are differences in perspectives or emphasis. There are, however, some common denominators which are also shared by many Mexican analysts. The first one is a statement of fact: "Mexico stands on the brink of far-reaching transition." The second is the crucial question "Where is Mexico going?"[25] There are both pessimistic and optimistic answers.

In May 1986, Joel Brinkley wrote in the *New York Times* that "CIA reports have been warning for most of the last year that political instability and widespread violence could be the likely results if present trends in [Mexico] are not reversed." A few analysts concur with the forecast.[26] This perspective, however, is not shared by most of the U.S. government, academia, or the press. A high State Department official summarizes the view of the majority: "No one expects instability in the short run; we are concerned about the next decade."[27] This current stability perhaps explains the following paradox: Whereas in the economic dimension the crisis accelerated a consensus favoring profound reforms—even with U.S. encouragement—in the political one the consensus is to recommend caution and not to intervene, partly because the possible impact in the United States is not clear.[28]

There is another way of looking at the statement by the official quoted above. Few Mexicans following the United States are concerned about U.S. intervention in Mexico's affairs in the short run; many are concerned about the U.S. reaction to the changes that are going to take place over the next decade. There is the danger that a consensus in favor of intervention will gradually develop. In that sense, the perception of threat will become an actual threat to Mexico's national security.

Any deep political transformation has an ingredient of uncertainty. In the United States there is a feeling of danger in any process of change. For many U.S. observers, instability in Mexico is necessarily going to affect the United States negatively.[29] In the case of Mexico, the stakes are high because part of the U.S. global policy has been based on the assumption of a secure border with a country culturally alien but stable and friendly during times of crisis. A radical change in the established order is considered especially threatening, because rough estimates indicate that a secure southern border would cost at least one-tenth (around US$30 billion) of the military budget.[30]

Clearly, the main task for the United States is to reconcile change with national interest.[31] The problem here is not with Mexico; it is part of a U.S. tragedy: the political system of the United States is open and democratic in the liberal sense, but it is in a state of permanent tension with the defense of concrete U.S. interests in the world. Is it possible for a liberal democratic society to exercise its domination in an authoritarian way?[32]

This basic dilemma has apparently not been noticed by those studying Mexico. For example, a U.S. expert on Mexico has argued that "we should support democratic principles and fair elections in Mexico."[33] Yet, in a different piece the same author puts such a high premium on stability that she limits her support for democracy to telling the ruling party how it should reform itself.[34] Change, therefore, is seen not as true reform, but as a way to maintain the system; the benefits of democracy accrue only to the ruling elite.

The CIA analyst, Brian Latell, has written that "profound and fundamental change is inevitable over the next five to ten years." In some places he suggests his belief in democracy, only to conclude that if change "is orchestrated skillfully and benignly from the top, Mexico could pass through these years of crisis without suffering widespread violence or instability."[35] This is a deeply undemocratic conception, because it gives more importance to manipulation from the top than to society's need for self-determination.

There are other inconsistencies such as in the treatment of corruption, which was once overlooked and is now denounced, especially where the drug issue is concerned, but is still considered to be a contribution to stability;[36] or the treatment of Miguel de la Madrid, who is praised for his economic policies and then criticized for his weakness and powerlessness in the political arena, even though he has relaxed the authoritarian controls.[37]

Thus, the United States accepts the need for political change, and has a natural tendency to support it, but only if it is controlled and if it guarantees U.S. interests. This is evident in the response to the "Democratic Current," a splinter group from the ruling party that is creating a political phenomenon of unpredictable consequences. The Current has received a great deal of attention, partly because of its novelty. There is, however, another, more pragmatic reason. In a *Wall Street Journal* story, a U.S. expert on Mexico, Roderic Camp, considers the possibility that the PRI could split into two parties. For him "it's a great idea when you think about it. What you get are two parties at the center, both representing the establishment. So, the system doesn't go to a left extreme or a right extreme."[38]

Perhaps change will be controlled, perhaps not. Since U.S. reactions will have an impact on the nature of change, a fundamental challenge for the United States is to better understand that for many Mexicans democratization is unavoidable and desirable. However painful and difficult it could be in the short run, the establishment of a more plural and legitimate political system, perhaps along lines somehow different from those of the United States, can also be seen as the best guarantee of long-term stability, which is the central goal of the United States.

Drugs: The Clash of Two Corruptions

Of the multiplicity of issues in Mexico-U.S. relations, drug-trafficking is, by all accounts, the most divisive. The review of the problem shows that the old U.S. tradition of blaming others endures. Even though some U.S. sectors argue that Mexico's role in the drug issue is a national security problem for the United States, the Mexican perspective seems more credible. On the one hand, the consumption of drugs in the United States has created a national security problem for Mexico. On the other hand, the drug problem has affected the perception of other issues, and drug traffickers and users have had a profound effect on the bilateral relations.

The enormous complexity of the drug phenomenon reflects both the U.S. and the Mexican role. The U.S. role is to provide the wholesale and retail distribution of illicit drugs to a huge market of American consumers. In 1988 the General Accounting Office estimated that

"70.4 million people (37 percent of the population over 12 years of age) had used an illegal drug in their life-time and that 23 million people (12 percent) were current users."[39] This market is worth over US$100 billion a year.

Mexico's role is that of producer and transit route. There was an evident upsurge of these activities in the 1960s, and after some U.S. pressures (the most notable being Operation Intercept in 1969), Mexico increased its cooperation in stemming the drug trade. In the late 1970s and early 1980s its campaign against drug production and trafficking was often quoted as a success story to be emulated. However, the Mexican economic crisis, and changes in the worldwide production and distribution channels, have again increased Mexico's role. And, especially after 1985, Mexico has been constantly criticized in the United States.

Currently, Mexico's role is crucial because, according to a 1988 Report by the State Department, "Mexico is a major producer of cannabis [marijuana] and opium poppy and continues to be the largest single-country source of the heroin and marijuana available in the United States." Further, the "levels of U.S. bound cocaine transiting Mexico have significantly increased, and Mexico represents a major transit point for cocaine from South America."[40]

In the U.S. government, academia, and the media there are two alternative perceptions about Mexico's role in the drug problem. First, there are those who believe that the corruption of the Mexican government is so extensive that it endangers the program of drug control in Mexico and thus becomes solely a U.S. problem. Using recent precedents, they advocate pressures and sanctions because they believe these to be the only language understood by Mexican authorities. This group is also inclined to give weight to solutions on the supply side. The Mayor of New York, Edward Koch, is a representative of this school. He explicitly argued in a paid announcement in the *New York Times* that: "the cure [for the U.S. drug problems] will be found several thousand miles from Queens—in places like Mexico, Panama and the cadre of other nations that supply this country with" drugs.[41]

The second and more influential interpretation recognizes that official corruption in Mexico is a very serious reason for concern. However, sanctions or bashing are not recommended because they could aggravate Mexico's economic crisis, reduce the legitimacy of the Mexican regime, aggravate bilateral tensions, and limit Washington's influence.[42] Mexico's efforts are recognized publicly, but in private it is said that although Mexico is not cooperating, the consequences of applying pressure are even more damaging. Finally, it is believed that the root cause of the problem is demand. A recent General Accounting Office Report states that "an increasing number of experts believe that a higher priority and more resources must be assigned to reducing the demand for drugs."[43]

Recently there have been some remarkable changes in U.S. perceptions on the drug situation. In 1985–1986—after the assassination of the Drug Enforcement Administration (DEA) agent Enrique Camarena in Guadalajara—the bashing of Mexico became the rule. The U.S. Customs Director, William von Raab, set the tone: "the drug situation is a horror history, increasing logarithmically, and Mexico is doing nothing about it." He added that the Mexican government officials were "inept and corrupt" and that the "concern is now shared by the entire executive branch of government."[44]

As a matter of fact the Director of the DEA, the Assistant Secretary of State for Inter-American Affairs, Elliot Abrams, and the then-Ambassador to Mexico, John Gavin, were among those U.S. officials joining congress and the media in the chorus of public criticisms of Mexico. As a consequence, bilateral relations reached one of their lowest points in recent history.

Three years later, in 1988, there are some differences, as is apparent in the debate over certification. According to a 1986 law, the executive must certify every year if a country has or has not given "full cooperation" to the United States. If a country is "decertified" a number of sanctions follow. The executive also has a third option: certify on the grounds of national security considerations. After receiving the Report, Congress has 45 days to accept it or revoke it.

In 1988 the executive is divided about Mexico. This became clear when the president certified in March that Mexico "fully cooperates" with the United States. However, it was not a very convincing decision because it included a not-asked-for justification in which it was said that a "national interest certification has been weighed." The document also explicitly cited the reservations and opposition of some agencies (mainly U.S. Customs). Certification did not satisfy powerful sectors in the Senate who, taking advantage of the contradictions in the executive, were able to "decertify" Mexico in the 45 days they had to evaluate the president's determination.

The decision of the Senate marks the beginning of another round of bilateral tensions. However, it is worth noting that public criticism coming from the executive is remarkably milder than in 1985–86. The U.S. Customs Director, von Raab, is the only important official who has openly criticized Mexico. There also has been more moderation in other U.S. sectors.

It is not possible to establish with precision the circulation of ideas, but there are indications that Mexico (among other countries) is beginning to convince the United States that demand is the root cause. From a very defensive position in 1985–86, the Mexican government passed to a more aggressively vocal policy based on the denunciation of U.S. attempts to evade responsibility for a problem that has emerged as a result of demand in the world's largest drug market. In the last two years, the editorial opinion expressed in the *New York Times* that "the Mexicans have a point when they insist that the problem really begins with the demand for drugs in the U.S.,"[45] has become more widely accepted.

However, acceptance of this concept is still limited. Some of the most vociferous critics of Mexico seem to have a genuine concern about the devastating effects of drug consumption on U.S. society. Also, drugs have been used as another tool in the traditional conflict of power between Congress and the executive and is a 1988 campaign issue. The public's fear of drugs is being exploited, and fear sometimes generates irrational responses.[46]

Another, more serious, limitation is the U.S. self-image. One aspect of the U.S. dominant world view is the faith in the "American way of life." If it is accepted that drugs are a social illness and not a harmless amusement, then something is fundamentally wrong in the "American way of life" when some 70 million people have used drugs at some point in their lives. Perhaps for that reason, in the debate for the 1988 elections it is remarkable that most presidential candidates have not seriously addressed the demand side of the problem. In private, some campaign experts admit that this caution is due to the fact that drug users are also voters, and that it is easier to criticize a foreign government than U.S. society. So, while Mexican officials can be easily corrupted by drug money, the source of the money is a sector of the U.S. society equally prone to corruption.

It follows that Mexico is not creating problems for the United States; on the contrary, the demand for drugs in the United States is the most serious national security problem for the Mexican government. It is fueling corruption, creating private armies, and taking a heavy human toll.[47]

The extensive coverage and attention given by the U.S. mass media to the drug-related corruption of the Mexican government has highlighted the corruption and inefficiency of the Mexican government in the economic and political spheres.[48] The linkage between the perceptions of the different issues becomes evident.

For the time being the drug problem will continue to be the main problem in the relations between Mexico and the United States. The

most practical and obvious solution—legalization—is politically impossible in the short term.[49] It is hoped that the accuracy of U.S.
perceptions will continue to improve. If that does not happen, the
Mexican position will naturally get tougher. And, of course, the two
governments will continue to be limited by the autonomous actions
of private groups on both sides of the border.

Conclusions and Recommendations

Although this is necessarily a very limited review, one conclusion
is inescapable: the perception of Mexico in the United States is uneven.

- Concerning the economic crisis, the excellence of the analysis is
  flawed by distortions of the characteristics of, and the role played
  by, the private sector (both Mexican and foreign). There is a
  blind faith in the magic of market forces.
- When discussing the political system and its ongoing transition
  the analysis is good, but deteriorates rapidly when the need to
  suggest policy options arises. There are ambiguities and paralysis
  due to a dilemma inherent in the United States position: how to
  reconcile the faith in democracy and the defense of U.S. interests.
- In the treatment of the drug issue one finds two different interpretations: one puts the burden of responsibility on Mexico; the
  other recognizes this but gives weight to demand in the United
  States as the real cause. The drug problem also illustrates the
  reluctance of most U.S. analysts to recognize the role of the
  United States in Mexico and the importance of nongovernmental
  actors such as traffickers.

It is true that ideas articulated in world views do change over time.
The problem comes when there is an attempt to establish the factors
that create change. One concept that is particularly applicable to this
situation is that of potential consciousness, a working definition of
which was formulated by Lucien Goldmann:

> every group tends to have an adequate knowledge of reality; but its
> knowledge can extend only up to a maximum horizon which is compatible
> with its existence. Beyond this horizon, information can only be received
> if the group's structure is transformed; just as in the case of individual
> obstacles, where information can be received only if the individual's
> psychic structure is transformed.[50]

In other words, the structure of individuals and groups can be compatible or incompatible with the transmission or reception of information. One explanation for U.S. difficulties in understanding Mexico is that some information transcends the "group's maximum potential consciousness."[51] Although intelligence, training, and sensitivity do play a role, potential consciousness is also determined by other factors. E.H. Carr summarized them: "before you study the history, study the historian . . . before you study the historian, study his historical and social environment. The historian being an individual is also a product of history and society."[52]

The U.S. perception of Mexico has inevitably been distorted by the dominant U.S. world view. The basis of this world view is the overwhelming belief that the U.S. experience is the best possible experience for any society, which makes economic capitalism and political liberalism the yardsticks for the analysis of other countries.[53]

However, these ideas are not immovable. In the last decades there have been changes in the U.S. perception of some Mexican issues. In 1959, Robert Scott was reflecting a mainstream belief when he said that even if Mexico did not "yet have a 'perfect' political system," the country "had fulfilled the most basic requirements for a Western political system."[54] Barely 26 years later, in 1986, Susan Kaufman Purcell once again summarized another, but opposite, consensus: Mexico "never was a democracy."[55]

The role of the state in the economy is another example. During the 1960s, Arthur Schlesinger Jr., in a memorandum to President John F. Kennedy, suggested—against the established gospel—that even if "private enterprise" had a "most important role to play in Latin America," it was not "the sole engine to economic development."[56] C.L. Sulzberger complemented the idea in an editorial comment for the *New York Times*: the United States might very "well have to swallow many of" its "ideological preferences" and "recognize that a modified version of socialism might be the most effective form of government among Latin hands."[57] These were short-lived ideas. In the 1980s, state intervention in the economy is nearly unanimously rejected.

These changes are another manifestation of the transformations in the consensus behind U.S. national interests and security abroad, due to events as diverse as the civil rights movements, Watergate, the Cuban Revolution, the Vietnam war, and the impact of ideas generated in Latin America (mainly Dependency Theory and the Theology of Liberation). In the 1980s there is no consensus on a definition of U.S. national interest abroad or the policies that should be followed to defend it.

U.S. observers are becoming more sensitive and sophisticated and are making a systematic effort to grapple with Mexican (and Latin America) specificity.[58] So, as a general proposition, Mexico is far better understood now than in the past. At this point the United States does not need more information; it needs more introspection.

There is also a need for more serious scrutiny of the role played by the private sector in the genesis of the crisis and of the role of foreign investment in Mexico's development. Usually it is uncritically assumed that foreign investment has a positive influence on the host economy. This may be true, but it has yet to be proved that the privatization and opening of the economy are the solution to the crisis.

At the political level, the greatest challenge to the United States is to resolve the contradiction between democratic impulses and the defense of the established order. Such a task will gradually become imperative due to changes in Mexico. Also at the political level it would be useful to differentiate more clearly the role of elections. Voting is one important aspect of democracy, but change in Mexico is also taking place in the daily competition of organized social forces. The tendency to individualize history must also be resisted; in a number of analyses the threats to political and social stability are explained away as mismanagement by the president as an individual.

In relation to drugs the obvious recommendation would be to strengthen the trend that gives demand the attention it deserves. If Mexican corruption is so easily denounced, we Mexicans expect symmetry in the recognition of corruption in U.S. society.

It is also necessary to overcome the remarkable tendency of most U.S. analysts to ignore the impact of the United States on Mexico's life. As it is assumed that the U.S. role can only be positive, very little or nothing is said about negative implications. Granted, in Mexico some sectors exaggerate the impact of the United States. Nevertheless, it would be absurd to deny that the United States has played a role in the genesis of Mexico's problems. For instance, there is a noticeably short historical memory concerning the development of the foreign debt. Although Mexican frivolity played an important part, we must not overlook the aggressive irresponsibility of a large number of U.S. companies and banks wanting to do business with Mexico.

The global perspective should also be improved. The wealth of available information should be integrated in order to more clearly establish the linkages among issues. Looking to the U.S. perception of Mexico from this aggregate perspective, I would like to point out a number of inconsistencies that should be gradually corrected.

- In the United States it is considered healthy to reduce the economic presence of the state, and its power. However, at the same time it is desired that the Mexican government continue to pay the debt, impose austerity, reorder the economy, and preserve social stability. All these tasks require a strong state.
- It is also commonly believed that a democratic system and an economic recovery are compatible. It is usually overlooked that a recovery will revitalize the authoritarian and corrupt regime.
- Privatization and opening of the economy are seen as positive steps, but the impact that these policies might have on the political system is rarely discussed.
- Intervention is favored to accelerate economic change, but rejected at the political level. Having contributed to the readjustment of the economy, the United States seems to be losing its fear of Mexican nationalism. Mexican nationalism is increasingly perceived as a rhetorical recourse.[59]

These questions are difficult to explore because the Mexican transition is very rapid and the dynamics facing the United States and Mexico very complex. Thus, an increase in the dialogue between the two societies is also recommended because it will help to fill the gaps on both sides of the border. Also a glance at the field of "security studies" shows that in the case of neither Mexico nor the United States has there been any systematic thought about their respective national security roles.

In the United States, the basic assumption is that the United States and Mexico share common interests. Mexico tends to ignore the precise role of the United States in its own national security. In the literature about security one basic distinction is hardly ever made: there is an implicit differentiation between real and potential threats, but there has not been any explicit discussion of the theoretical or political implications of the concept of potential threats.[60] It follows, then, that it is fundamental for both Mexico and the United States to have an accurate and explicit differentiation between the *real*, or actual, and the *potential*, or hypothetical. In this realm, perceptions can play a crucial role.

Mexico is in transition; is that process either a threat to the national security or a challenge to the perceptions of the United States? Potentially, there are a number of threats to U.S. national security in the evolution of Mexican events, just as there are threats to Mexico in the evolution of events in the United States. However, it is not possible to determine which threats are real without first solving the most serious weaknesses in the U.S. understanding of Mexico. At this moment, erroneous perceptions are the most real and concrete threat to the security of the United States, and of Mexico.

Notes

1. Figures provided by the "Asociación de Corresponsales Extranjeros en México" in July 1987. I am including photographers because they also transmit images. It must be noted that some of the correspondents use Mexico as the basis to cover Central America.

2. These are total articles included under the heading "Mexico" in the indexes published periodically by the *New York Times*. Inclusion of the articles on Mexico listed under other headings increases the numbers to 277 in 1982 and 422 in 1986.

3. John Bailey, "Mexico en los medios de comunicación estadounidenses 1979–1986: inferencias para la relación bilateral," and Carlos Gonzalez Gutierrez, "México en el Congreso estadounidense: el debate sobre política interna," both articles in Gerardo M. Bueno, editor, *Mexico-Estados Unidos. 1986,* El Colegio de México, Mexico City, 1987.

4. In 1985 the main foundations channeled US$6.7 million into Mexican studies. Peter H. Smith, *Memorandum: the Study of Mexico in the United States,* Workshop on Cultural Relations, Bilateral Commission on the Future of United States-Mexican Relations, October 26, 1987. There are conflicting figures about the number of experts on Mexico. The *International Guide of Research on Mexico* listed 340 scholars for 1985; the Latin American Scholars Association, 518; and the National Directory of Latin Americanists, 1,400. El Colegio de la Frontera Norte/Center for U.S.-Mexican Studies, *Guía Internacional de Investigaciones sobre México,* COLEF-UCSD, Tijuana, 1986; and John H. Coatsworth, *Student, Academic and Cultural Exchanges Between Mexico and the United States: A Report with Recommendations,* Workshop on Cultural Relations, Bilateral Commission on the Future of United States-Mexican Relations, October 26, 1987.

5. *Embassy of the United States of America in Mexico,* United States Embassy, Mexico City, no date.

6. Guadalupe González, "Política interna y política exterior en el horizonte de las relaciones México-Estados Unidos," *América Latina Internacional,* vol. 2, no. 4, April-June, 1985.

7. Katherine Thorup, "Play it Smart with Mexico," *New York Times,* September 30, 1985. Similar statements can be found in pieces written by Richard Fagen (*New York Times,* January 6, 1985); James Reston (*New York Times,* September 29, 1985); and the editorial entitled "Stop Bullying Mexico," the *New York Times,* June 5, 1986. The opposite is also true because many Mexicans believe that ours is an inscrutable country. In my opinion, it is another manifestation of Mexican nationalism; being closed is a way to protect the nation against foreign intruders.

8. Department of State, "U.S.-Mexican Relations," *Gist,* Bureau of Public Affairs, Department of State, Washington, D.C., May 1984.

9. There are dozens of examples. Among others, see Brian Latell, *Mexico at the Crossroads. The Many Crises of the Political System,* Hoover Institution, Stanford, CA, 1986, p. 21. Susan Kaufman Purcell thinks that "the Mexican government was the main protagonist of the crisis in Mexico;" see *The Prospects for Political Change in Mexico,* Paper presented at the Conference on "U.S. Interests in Mexico: Agenda for the Next Decade," Washington, D.C., August 21–22, 1986, p. 27. According to Carlos Gonzalez "if there is a Mexican issue with consensus in Congress, that is the need of modernizing the economy" through a reduction of the state participation in the economy and an opening of the economy; *op. cit.,* p. 237. For official statements see *New York Times,* January 22, 1986.

10. See Wayne A. Cornelius, *The Political Economy of Mexico Under de la Madrid: The Crisis Deepens, 1985-1986* University of California at San Diego, Center for U.S.-Mexican Studies, San Diego, 1986, p. 2. Also see William P. Glade, "How Will Economic Recovery Be Managed?" and "Distributional and Sectoral Problems in the New Economic Policy," in Roderic A. Camp, editor, *Mexico's Political Stability: the Next Five Years,* Westview Press, Boulder, 1986.

11. The Stanley Foundation *U.S. Policy Toward Mexico. U.S. Foreign Policy Conference, 1986. Report Excerpt,* The Stanley Foundation, Muscatine, 1986, p. 4.

12. In 1986, the New York Times correspondent, William Stockton, wrote about the changes in the economy: "taken singly, all the government's economic moves do not seem particularly earth-shaking. As a whole, however, they reflect a significant policy shift as important as any since the Mexican revolution began in 1910." *New York Times,* February 16, 1986.

13. John. A. Gavin, "Mexico, Land of Opportunity. Will its Leaders Be Worthy of Its People?" *Policy Review,* winter 1987, no. 39, p. 34. For other examples of praise of the de la Madrid administration see Morton Kondrake, "Mexico's Next Revolution. The Machine and the Tiger," *New Republic,* February 23, 1987; and George Schultz's declarations to the New York Times, February 10, 1986.

14. In an editorial entitled "Another Movement of Truth for Mexico," the *New York Times,* stated that "now is the time to reduce both the state's role in the economy and the privileges of the PRI-favored few. Mexico's leaders may find it hard to ditch the main props of their power. But let them stare at the alternatives and *feel some friendly pressure from next door.*" June 11, 1986. Emphasis added.

15. Richard E. Feinberg, "United States Policy toward Mexico," *Statement Before the Senate Committee on Foreign Relations,* June 10, 1986, p. 3; and Katherine Thorup, "Play it Smart with Mexico," *New York Times,* September 30, 1985.

16. In this chapter I concentrate on the Mexican private sector. This does not mean that I accept the benefits of foreign investment. Its role has to be critically reviewed.

17. Sylvia Maxfield, editor, *Government and Private Sector in Contemporary Mexico,* University of California at San Diego, Center for U.S.-Mexican Studies, San Diego, 1987, p. 1.

18. As quoted in Sergio Aguayo, "Behind the Public Profile of Mexico's Private Sector," *Wall Street Journal*, December 18, 1987.

19. Cornelius, *op. cit.*, p. 31.

20. John Bailey, *Beyond De la Madrid: Alternative Futures of the Mexican Political Economy*, paper presented in Southwest Social Science Association-International Studies Association, San Antonio, Texas, March 20–23, 1986, p. 6. Some isolated characterizations of the Mexican private sector can be found in the U.S. press: *New York Times*, January 30, 1977, November 29, 1978 and October 23, 1986; *Businessweek*, December 10, 1984; *Wall Street Journal*, January 31, 1985; *Chicago Tribune*, November 25 and 26, 1986.

21. Roger Hansen, *The Politics of Mexican Development*, The John Hopkins University Press, Baltimore, 1971; Frank Brandenburg, *The Making of Modern Mexico*, Prentice Hall, New York, 1972; and Susan Kaufman Purcell, "Decision-Making in an Authoritarian Regime: Theoretical Implications from a Mexican Case Study," *World Politics*, October, 1973.

22. James Reston summarizes the mood when writing that with all its defects the ruling party, the PRI, "at least kept the peace and avoided a military dictatorship for over half a century." "The Mexican Time Bomb," *New York Times*, June 22, 1986.

23. Cornelius, *op. cit.;* Bailey, *op. cit.;* Kaufman, *The Prospects;* and Richard A. Nuccio, *Democratization and other Alternatives to PRI Rule. Some Considerations for U.S. Policy*, paper presented at Conference on "U.S. Interests in Mexico: Agenda for the Next Decade," Washington, D.C., August 21–22, 1986. Also see the works of Latell, Gavin, Smith, and Camp cited in previous notes.

24. Smith, *op. cit.*, pp. 107 and 110; Roderic A. Camp, "The Political Technocrat in Mexico and the Survival of the Political System," *Latin American Research Review*, Volume XX, Number 1, 1985, pp. 97–118; Edward J. Williams, "The Evolution of the Mexican Military and Its Implications for Civil-Military Relations," in Camp, *Mexico's Political Stability;* Daniel C. Levy, "The Political Consequences of Changing Socialization Patterns," in Camp, *op. cit.;* David Brooks, *Mexico. Whose Crisis, Whose Future?* NACLA. *Report on the Americas*, Volume XXI, no. 5–6; David Ronfeldt, "Preguntas y Reservas acerca del futuro de Mexico," in Gerardo Bueno, editor, *México-Estados Unidos. 1986*, El Colegio de México, Mexico City, 1987.

25. Peter H. Smith, "Leadership and Change, Intellectuals and Technocrats in Mexico," in Camp, *op. cit.*, p. 101. These quandaries are often found in the current literature on Mexico.

26. *New York Times*, May 25, 1986. An extremely alarmist perspective is the one of Sol W. Sanders, *Mexico: Chaos on Our Doorstep*, Madison Books, Lanham, MD, 1986.

27. Cited in Kondrake, *op. cit.*, p. 16. This idea is a constant. See, for example, Cornelius, *op. cit.*, p. 1; Kaufman, *The Prospects*, p. 19; *New York Times*, 22 October, 1986.

28. For an example of the consensus reached in different political currents see Esther Wilson Hannon, "Por qué la política exterior de México todavía irrita a Estados Unidos?" *The Backgrounder*, The Heritage Foundation, Wash-

ington, D.C.; and Kathryn L. Thorup, "United States Policy toward Mexico," *Statement before the Subcomitteee on Western Hemisphere Affairs,* Senate Committee on Foreign Relations, Washington, D.C. June 17, 1986.

29. Paul Ganster and Alan Swedler consider that "major disruptions and instabilities in Mexico . . . would surely be felt in the U.S., particularly in the four border states." "U.S.-Mexican Border Region: Implications for U.S. Security," paper presented at the Annual Meeting of the Western Political Association, Denver, CO, April 29, 1988, p. 1. Edward J. Williams argues that "outbreaks of political violence in Mexico" would "spill over the line to the U.S. side." See "The Implications of the Border for Mexican Policy and Mexican-United States Relations," in Camp, *op. cit.,* p. 22. An exception is the analysis of NACLA. In the left's perspective, "*la crisis* is the focus of energy. It impels the dynamic of society today, even though anything might happen tomorrow." Brooks, *Mexico* p. 13.

30. M. Delal Baer from the Center for Strategic and International Studies, made that estimation in the Roundtable "The Border and the National Security of the United States and Mexico." Annual Conference of the Western Political Science Association, Denver, Colorado, April 29, 1988.

31. Part of the problem is the unidimensionality of the dominant world view. For reasons that go beyond the scope of this chapter, most U.S. citizens are inclined to adapt to reality, having serious problems in integrating change at the epistemological or political levels.

32. Theoretically, domination can be exercised through the combinations of force or hegemony (i.e., the consent of those dominated). Both instruments are interrelated and have combined differently in the history of the region. Although the nature of U.S. political culture is more suited to domination through hegemony, in the nineteenth and some moments of the twentieth centuries, U.S. society has relied on force. The history of U.S.-Cuban relations after 1959 and the debate on Central America are excellent illustrations of the fluctuations in the use of different instruments of domination in the regional system. In the case of Mexico there is an additional complication in the intense interaction of two asymmetrically interdependent neighbors.

33. Susan Kaufman Purcell, "Support Fair Elections," *New York Times,* July 1, 1986.

34. For example, Susan Kaufman Purcell considers that "if political stability is to be maintained in the future, the PRI must devise new ways of relating to a more sophisticated labor movement" and that the "PRI must also find new ways of dealing with the peasantry." See "Mexico in Transition," in Susan Kaufman Purcell, editor, *Mexico in Transition. Implications for U.S. Policy. Essays from Both Sides of the Border,* Council on Foreign Relations, New York, 1988, p. 12.

35. Latell, *op. cit.,* pp. 12 and 31.

36. Peter Smith writes that a "a freewheeling system of patronage has its disadvantages, but one of its constructive consequences has been to give the ambitious a stake in the system," *op. cit.,* p. 111.

37. Latell thinks that "de la Madrid's style has certainly not strengthened the office of the Presidency," *op. cit.,* p. 27. In the Stanley Report it was

agreed that the President "has been criticized for not exercising strong leadership." For a criticism of these critiques see Sally Shelton-Colby, "Mexico-Bashing. The Latest Simple-Minded Sport," *Washington Post,* May 28, 1986. Obviously, there are some exceptions to this perception of the current Mexican president. Of those quoted in this chapter see Bailey, *Beyond de la Madrid,* and Kaufman, *The Prospects.*

38. *Wall Street Journal,* July 8, 1987.

39. Special Report from the Comptroller General of the United States, *Controlling Drug Abuse: A Status Report,* General Accounting Office/GGD-88–39, p. 5.

40. Bureau of International Narcotics Matters, *International Narcotics Control Strategy Report,* Department of State, Washington, D.C. March 1, 1988, p. 131.

41. *New York Times,* February 29, 1988.

42. A formulation of this position can be found in the *New York Times* editorial, "Where is Mexico's Pride?," March 22, 1985. More recent formulations of this position come from interviews with U.S. officials between January and April, 1988. An elaborate formulation can be found in a State Department Memorandum, *Why Mexico Should not be Decertified?,* May, 1988.

43. Special Report from the Comptroller General, *op. cit.,* p. 33.

44. *New York Times,* May 12, 1986.

45. *New York Times,* March 22, 1985.

46. Lawrence Smith, Democrat from Florida has been explicit: "It's a great issue, a great opening for the Democrats." Frank J.Fahrenkopf Jr., Republican national chairman also called drugs "a very legitimate issue for 1988." *New York Times,* March 14, 1988.

47. The candidate of the ruling party (PRI), Carlos Salinas, declared that "drug trafficking is the greatest challenge to Mexico's national security." *La Jornada,* November 13, 1987.

48. Basically, all the articles discussing drug problems highlight the corruption of Mexican officials. See, among others, Linda Gomez, "Harvest of Death," *Life,* March, 1988; Elaine Shannon, "The Drug Thugs," *Time,* March 7, 1988; and Terrence Poppa, "Crops of Corruption," *El Paso Herald-Post,* January 27–30, 1988.

49. An argument in favor of the legalization of drugs as a solution to the problem can be found in David Boaz, "Let's Quit the Drug War," *New York Times,* March 17, 1988.

50. "The Importance of the Concept of Potential Consciousness for Communication," in Lucien Goldmann, *Cultural Creation in Modern Society,* Telos Press, Saint Louis, 1976, p. 35.

51. *Ibid.* p. 34.

52. Edward Hallet Carr, *What is History?* Alfred A. Knopf, New York, 1963, p. 54.

53. Other elements of the dominant world view are confidence in the ability to shape history through techniques that proved successful in the United States; the ultimate value given to rationality, harmony, and utilitarianism; the definition of politics as interpersonal relations; the confidence in

action in and for itself; and a disdain for formal ideologies. For a fuller elaboration of the concept of world view and how it manifests in the United States see, Sergio Aguayo, "An Essay on the Evolution of World Views and Ideologies in the United States. Mexico as Reflected in the New York Times, 1946–1979," Unpublished Doctoral Dissertation, the Johns Hopkins University, Washington, D.C, 1984, Chapter I.

54. Robert E. Scott, *Mexican Government in Transition* University of Illinois Press, Urbana, IL, 1971, pp. 32 and 17.

55. Kaufman, *The Prospects*, p. 2.

56. Arthur Schlesinger Jr., "Report to the President on Latin American Mission, February 12–March 3, 1961," 10 March, 1961, p. 3, Typescript.

57. C.L. Sulzberger, "J.F.K. and Another Kind of Democracy," *New York Times*, June 30, 1962.

58. For an analysis of some of the factors that influenced the increase in the potential consciousness of different groups in the U.S. see Sergio Aguayo, "El conflicto centroamericano en la sociedad estadounidense," en *Mexico-Estados Unidos, 1983*, El Colegio de México, Mexico City, 1983.

59. The Stanley Report contains a revealing comment: "Unable to define the national interest in terms of concrete programs, President de la Madrid has cloaked his office in appeals to nationalist sentiments, just as other Mexican presidents have done before him." However, "Mexico cannot continue to hide behind jingoistic nationalism and wait for its domestic problems to be solved by the United States." Stanley Foundation, *op. cit.*, p. 8.

60. For example, the former Secretary of Defense, Harold Brown, builds his book on the following question: "What are the actual or potential threats to U.S. national security?" *Thinking about National Security. Defense and Foreign Policy in a Dangerous World*, Westview Press, Boulder, CO, 1983, p. 4.

10

Across the Rio Grande: Views from North of the U.S.-Mexican Border

William Watts

Our relations with Mexico are among the most important and complex ties that we maintain with any country. They are shaped by a mixture of shared problems, growing interdependence, and differing national interests and perceptions. Historical factors, cultural differences, and economic disparities add to the complexity of the relationship.[1]

Citizens of the United States view Mexico, their next-door neighbor to the south, with a mixture of good will, warmth, recognition of its appeal as a place to visit, a sense of respect, and awareness of Mexico's importance. Their views also show ignorance, naiveté, uncertain trust, condescension, and, in some quarters, fear and resentment. Popular attitudes are, on balance, more positive than negative. But they are complex and not easily pigeonholed.

It is probable that many Americans[2] take for granted their good fortune in having on both their northern and southern borders countries with whom relations are reasonably harmonious. Nowhere else on this globe do countries share lengthy borders that are as open and free of overt hostilities as those between the United States and Canada, and the United States and Mexico. To be sure, the Mexican-American territorial dividing line is increasingly the scene of friction brought about by problems related to illegal immigration and drugs. But compared to what is happening along the national boundaries between China and the Soviet Union, for example, the situation is far more manageable.

Over the years a number of opinion studies have sought to measure popular attitudes that Americans—both the public at large and specially selected "elite" or "leadership" groups—hold of Mexico and its peoples.

This chapter draws on several of those studies, assessing their content and considering possible policy implications.

A word of caution is in order at the outset. It is easy to read too much into the results of any given testing of public opinion. Surveys are, after all, a snapshot taken at one moment in time. They are subject to pressures brought on by current events, and even the wording of questions must be taken into account. Results contain a standard margin of error—plus or minus about four percentage points in virtually all the studies cited here.

What is found in any one survey does not provide an infallible road map for predicting the future, since events yet unknown will have their own inevitable influence. The interpretations of the data presented here are mine alone. The reader may well come to differing conclusions in looking at various tables and charts.

Another fact must be kept in mind. How well or poorly one country or another ranks in the eyes of Americans as a whole does not automatically translate into comparable standings in the attitudes and approaches of those who make and/or influence policy, whether in the halls of government or company boardrooms.

The more specific pressures that surround and influence public or private decision makers can push aside generalized perceptions that even those individuals may hold. It is also true, of course, that those generalized perceptions provide a backdrop against which policy is made. To the extent that such a backdrop is constructive and supportive, policy deliberations will proceed in a more positive setting.

Finally, the situation with Mexico is complicated by what might be called the "radar screen syndrome." Americans are bombarded daily, even hourly, by news and information from all corners of the globe. Not only is the flow incessant, but the problems being reported on frequently are not only large but also are events in which the United States is directly involved. This can mean that today's crisis is tomorrow's forgotten headline, already replaced by yet another situation of the moment. The fallout is that developments in Mexico and U.S.-Mexican bilateral ties command front-burner status and prime-time coverage only when the pot is boiling. Where sustained American attention is concerned, that is a reality which applies not only to Mexico but to virtually every country around the world, whether one is talking about the average citizen on the street corner or the president and his advisors in the Oval Office of the White House.

American Perceptions of Mexico: An Overview

Let us look first at how Americans compare Mexico to some other countries, in terms of such popularity ratings as like/dislike, warmth of feelings, and so forth. We look at other more substantive analyses in subsequent pages. What is most striking in these initial readings is the remarkably positive assessment held of Mexico. This may come as a surprise to many, since that evident popularity does not always come through in writing and reporting on Mexico, nor, for that matter, in policy making.

The Hemispheric Outlook

In virtually any random national survey of public opinion, Americans consistently rank Canada at, or next to, the top of the list of Western Hemispheric nations. Here, for example, are results from a 1984 testing of attitudes, as released in *The Gallup Report International*:[3]

I would like you to rate your opinion of several countries. Using a scale of one to seven where seven represents a country you like very much and one represents a country you dislike very much, how would you rate your opinion of the following countries. Remember, the higher the number the more you like the country and you may choose any number between one and seven. First, where on the scale of one to seven would you rate:

Like/Dislike: National Norm

Canada	6.1
MEXICO	4.6
Brazil	4.1
Venezuela	3.8
Colombia	3.7
Argentina	3.6
Chile	3.4
Nicaragua	2.5
El Salvador	2.5
Cuba	1.9

The range of opinion is remarkably wide. And while Canada did achieve the lead position, Mexico was not all that far behind, very solidly in second place. Geographic proximity surely played a role, but other factors to be considered later (including, for example, perceptions of importance to U.S. interests) also influenced American thinking.

With the exception of Canada, all countries were seen more positively either by black Americans and Americans of Hispanic origin, or both. Mexico was one of several where the racial differential was statistically meaningful (at least 0.4 points):

Race (Mean rating)

Nation	Total	White	Non-white	Hispanic
Canada	6.1	6.2	5.8	5.6
MEXICO	4.6	4.6	5.0	5.0
Colombia	3.7	3.6	4.2	3.7
Argentina	3.6	3.6	3.9	4.0
Chile	3.4	3.4	3.8	3.7
El Salvador	2.5	2.5	2.9	2.9
Nicaragua	2.5	2.5	2.9	3.0
Cuba	1.9	1.8	2.5	2.1

This could be a finding of growing importance for the future. The American political landscape is undergoing profound changes, not the least of which is the growing importance of minority and ethnic politics. The emergence of the women's movement and black power have been fundamental. More recently the voices of two groups have begun to be heard with increasing effectiveness: Americans of Asian and Hispanic origin. How will the latter community, many with direct ties to Mexico, see their role within the framework of U.S.-Mexican relations, and especially within the framework of bilateral tensions? The stresses on these individuals will be intense, caught as they can be between loyalties to their new homeland and warmer feelings toward Mexico than those of their U.S. neighbors.

Global Comparisons

On a global scale, Mexico also ranks well, as another 1984 *Gallup Report International* study made clear. This time, perceptions were recorded of 26 countries, using the same 1–7 point scale. Results are grouped below by tenths:[4]

Like/Dislike: National Norm

Group I (6.0–7.0):

United States	6.7
Canada	6.0

Group II (5.0–5.9)

Australia	5.7
Great Britain	5.3
Sweden	5.3
Japan	5.2
France	5.0

Group III (4.0–4.9)

Israel	4.6
MEXICO	4.3
Philippines	4.2
Taiwan	4.1
Poland	4.0
India	4.0

Group IV (3.0–3.9)

Brazil	3.9
South Korea	3.9
China	3.9
Kenya	3.9
South Africa	3.7
Nigeria	3.5
Saudi Arabia	3.4
Pakistan	3.4
Algeria	3.2

Group V (2.0–2.9)

Libya	2.7
Iraq	2.6

Group VI (1.0–1.9)

Cuba	1.8
Soviet Union	1.8

In this case, with the entire world as a backdrop, Mexico ranked at the upper end of the third echelon. In a repeat of what we saw in the hemispheric reading, Mexico placed well ahead of Brazil, and also outpaced a number of other key U.S. friends or allies.

In looking at countries ahead of Mexico, U.S. demography and history were apparently at play. The Anglo-Saxon connection was obvious, with Canada, Australia, and Great Britain in the forefront. The strong European heritage was also evident, as illustrated by the rankings of Sweden and France (although this does not always hold up, as we shall see shortly). Japan and Israel made special claims on the attention of Americans, as they continue to do in more recent surveys—the former because of its economic importance and growing influence on U.S. life styles and the latter because of the unique national linkage brought about by U.S. involvement in the creation of Israel, and the strong intellectual and other impact of the Jewish community in American life. Given these powerful sources of influence and their appeal to the attention of Americans, Mexico's relatively high ranking represented a strikingly positive assessment.

As might be expected, views of individual Americans about countries on the list were not uniform. Let us look at some of the more striking differentials concerning Mexico and a few others for comparative purposes. Only those variations that differed from the national norm by at least three-tenths of a point are considered here.

- Canada: Americans 18–24 years of age and those with less than a high school education were less positive.
- Cuba: Westerners and 18–24 year olds were above average in their positive views.
- Israel: Easterners were more favorable, probably reflecting geographic concentration.
- Mexico: The 18–24 year cohort was less positive than their seniors.
- Soviet Union: Southerners were more negative (in accord with their traditionally more nationalistic outlooks); 18–24 year olds were more positive.

The lower esteem in which Mexico was held by younger Americans, in contrast to their elders, deserves elaboration. One might conjecture that this portends a generational shift that will show up in more critical views about Mexico at the policy level in a few years, as this group moves into positions of influence and power in the United States. Perhaps, but a parallel example in another country recalls the caution against over-interpretation of the data recommended at the outset of this chapter. Opinion studies in Japan over the years have regularly shown greater skepticism about the United States and the U.S.-Japan connection among younger Japanese than their elders. As those younger men and women have matured, however, their views frequently have undergone a transformation. Indeed, many leaders and activists in the student demonstrations of 1960 against the U.S.-Japan Treaty of Mutual Security and Cooperation are today firmly entrenched in Japan's leadership elite, strongly committed to close bilateral relations. That is worth keeping in mind if one is tempted to project that today's younger Americans will be less friendly and supportive toward Mexico as they move up their career ladders.

Warmth

Another look at relative levels of like or dislike of certain countries, in this case translated into readings of "warmth," was taken in late 1986 by The Gallup Organization for The Chicago Council on Foreign Relations (CCFR). It was also highly favorable to Mexico:[5]

Next I'd like you to rate these countries on this feeling thermometer. If you feel neutral toward a country, give it a temperature of 50 degrees. If you have a warm feeling toward a country, give it a temperature higher than 50 degrees. If you have a cool feeling toward a country, give it a temperature lower than 50 degrees.

"Warmth" Readings
Mean Temperature (degrees)

	1978	1982	1986
Canada	72	74	77
Great Britain	67	68	73
West Germany	57	59	62
Japan	56	53	61
MEXICO	58	60	59
Israel	61	55	59
Philippines	n/a	n/a	59
France	62	60	58
Italy	56	55	58
Brazil	52	54	54
Poland	50	52	53
China	44	47	53
Taiwan	51	49	52
South Korea	48	44	50
Saudi Arabia	48	52	50
Egypt	53	52	49
India	49	48	48
South Africa	46	45	47
Nigeria	47	44	46
Nicaragua	n/a	n/a	46
Syria	n/a	42	34
Soviet Union	34	26	31
Iran	50	28	22

The high standing accorded Mexico in this reading—tied for fifth place with Israel and the Philippines (another special claimant for the attention of Americans), outdistanced only by America's principal allies and trading partners and leading a number of other traditional friends and allies—is impressive. The sense of "warmth" toward Mexico was matched in a July 1986 Harris Survey that registered American views of Mexicans as people: more than eight Americans in ten (83%) called "the people of Mexico" either "very friendly" (29%) or "somewhat friendly" (54%).

Trustworthiness

For a number of years one of Japan's leading newspapers, *The Yomiuri Shimbun*, has been measuring the degree to which Americans and Japanese consider various countries around the world to be trustworthy. Here are American responses, with the latest recorded in October 1987:[6]

Listed below are the names of 30 countries. Which five do you regard as especially trustworthy? (Multiple answers; only those countries mentioned by at least 5 percent of respondents are included):

"Trustworthiness"

	1979	1980	1981	1982	1983	1984	1985	1986	1987
				(percent mentions)					
Canada	69	77	72	73	74	75	76	70	73
UK	43	56	48	54	55	54	55	54	58
Australia	47	46	41	42	43	49	46	45	44
Switzerland	35	31	32	37	33	41	38	38	36
Sweden	30	24	29	31	31	33	28	31	30
France	29	27	21	22	29	32	27	23	25
FRG	24	28	24	21	23	26	28	24	24
Norway	22	16	15	20	19	20	22	23	23
Japan	17	22	26	18	23	23	24	23	20
Israel	14	18	15	12	17	17	17	17	17
MEXICO	18	17	25	16	16	17	20	14	15
Holland	16	12	13	19	14	17	13	14	15
Italy	13	9	8	12	13	17	15	12	13
New Zealand	13	11	9	14	14	12	14	12	13
Philippines	n/a	n/a	10	9	11	10	9	9	7
China	5	8	7	7	7	6	8	7	6
Brazil	6	6	5	5	5	7	5	5	5

On a positive note, Mexico stands either on a par with or ahead of several key U.S. partners. Those above it are distinguished by attributes noted earlier: the Anglo-Saxon/European connection and the special draw of Japan and Israel. Such a strong Mexican showing is in keeping with other indicators we have seen.

On a negative note, however, we should not overlook the fact that in the past two years the number of respondents that has picked Mexico as one of five "especially trustworthy" countries is the smallest in this ongoing series. When analyzing results of survey research, it is important to look at the answers and ask, "In comparison to what?" In this case, the 1987 comparison is not altogether favorable. The slippage since 1985, although not drastic, is clearly noticeable. Other studies we turn to in the next section point to concerns about illegal immigration, drug trafficking, and debt questions as probable causes.

U.S. National Interests: The Mexican Connection

Popularity measurements of the kind we have considered thus far are revealing, but they inevitably leave certain key countries, the Soviet Union, for example, far down the list. A variety of reasons—political, social, and cultural—leads Americans to find some countries more (or less) attractive than others. But that does not tell us much about the perceived importance of those countries to U.S. national interests.

Getting Along with Others

If, however, we pose the issue in terms of the need to "get along" with other countries, some of these culturally induced biases fall away. When one is asked how important it is to deal with another country— whether friend or foe—the key element of national self-interest is introduced into the equation:

> When it comes to pursuing our interests all around the world, how important do you think it is for the United States to try to get along well with each of the following countries: very important, fairly important, not so important, or not at all important?

Adding together those who say "very important" and "fairly important" results in the following comparative rankings for each country, as registered in surveys conducted by The Gallup Organization for Potomac Associates; also shown in column 1984(a) are responses for the "very important" category alone, with ranking shown in parentheses:[7]

Importance of "Getting Along" With Other Countries

	1978	1979	1984	1984(a)	
		(percent	mentions)		
Canada	88	93	93	78	(1)
Japan	86	89	91	71	(3)
Great Britain	n/a	n/a	91	72	(2)
France	n/a	n/a	88	57	(7)
West Germany	85	86	88	60	(6)
China	77	83	87	61	(5)
Soviet Union	86	88	85	65	(4)
Israel	81	86	83	54	(10)
MEXICO	n/a	89	83	56	(8)
Saudi Arabia	82	86	82	55	(9)
Australia	n/a	77	80	49	(11)
Egypt	78	83	78	44	(12)
Taiwan	72	77	77	37	(14)
South Korea	62	69	77	37	(14)
Philippines	n/a	n/a	76	44	(12)
India	65	70	76	35	(16)
South Africa	n/a	n/a	75	35	(16)
Brazil	66	69	72	29	(20)
Pakistan	n/a	n/a	63	25	(21)
Nigeria	n/a	60	63	24	(22)
Cuba	64	72	60	34	(18)
Iran	n/a	n/a	57	30	(19)

A look at the top ten countries on this list gives one a sense of considerable practical realism shown by Americans, with strong parallels to warmth or like/dislike measurements already noted. Geography helped to account for the premier ranking given Canada, and the relatively strong showing of Mexico as well. Strong cultural, social, and historic ties shared by large segments of the U.S. population lent special importance to our two immediate neighbors, as well as Great Britain, France, and West Germany.

This time, however, several other countries moved up sharply. China, the Soviet Union, and Saudi Arabia assumed an importance that had little to do with their popularity, or lack thereof. But even though the two major communist powers outranked Mexico, the lead was not overwhelming. With direct national interests raised, the "Mexican connection" remained strong for Americans.

Importance to U.S. Interests

These findings were buttressed by results of the 1986 CCFR study, recording views about global U.S. "vital interests" among both the general public and a leadership sample:[8]

Many people believe the United States has a vital interest in certain areas of the world and not in other areas. That is, certain countries of the world are important to the U.S. for political, economic, or security reasons. I am going to read a list of countries. For each, tell me whether you feel the U.S. does or does not have a vital interest in that country:

Does Have Vital Interest

	1982		1986	
	Public	Leaders	Public	Leaders
	(percent, ranked in order of leaders mentions in 1986)			
Japan	82	97	78	98
West Germany	76	98	77	98
Canada	82	95	78	96
MEXICO	74	98	74	96
Great Britain	80	97	83	94
China	64	87	61	89
Saudi Arabia	77	93	77	88
Israel	75	92	76	86
France	58	84	56	82
Philippines	n/a	n/a	73	81
Egypt	66	90	61	n/a
South Korea	43	66	58	80
Nicaragua	n/a	n/a	60	63
South Africa	38	54	54	63
Brazil	45	80	45	63
India	30	57	36	55
Taiwan	51	44	53	48
Iran	51	60	50	n/a
Syria	36	46	48	n/a
Italy	35	79	41	n/a
Poland	43	47	35	n/a
Nigeria	32	53	31	n/a

Not only was Mexico in the upper reaches as far as the general public was concerned, but its showing among leaders and foreign policy specialists interviewed was even more impressive. They placed Mexico close to the top of the list, tied with West Germany for first in 1982, and linked with Canada as second only to Japan and West Germany four years later.

Another 1986 study, conducted for the Overseas Development Council and InterAction by the Strategic Information Research Corporation (SIRC), also placed Mexico's perceived importance not far below that of the Soviet Union and China:[9]

Using our scale where one means not at all important and ten means very important, please tell me how important you feel each of these countries is to the U.S.:

Great Britain	7.6
Soviet Union	7.3
China	7.0
MEXICO	6.5
India	4.7
Nigeria	4.7

The age factor turned out to be of some significance here. We noted earlier that younger Americans showed less warmth toward Mexico than did their elders on various positive/negative rating scales. SIRC found that Americans over 35 were more likely to think of Mexico as "very important" than were those who were younger. One can speculate that negatives sometimes associated with Mexico—illegal immigrants, drugs, debt, and corruption, for example—weighed more heavily in the views of younger Americans than did an appreciation of its national security importance, while the latter was possibly a more influential factor for those over 35 years of age.

Geography also came to the fore, as Westerners in this study tended to rank Mexico higher than did people in other parts of the country. The growing physical presence of Mexicans in the western states was undoubtedly at play, pointing again to the potential for increasing political impact in years ahead.

Friend or Foe?

Importance to U.S. interests is one side of the coin: enemies and allies can rank equally high, depending on who they are. But a very different sorting out occurs when countries are thought of on a spectrum ranging from ally to enemy. This tends to force an amalgam of popularity and importance, with those at the two extremes the most significant. Here are results of a recent Roper Poll, with figures for "close ally/friend" and "unfriendly/enemy" combined in parentheses:[10]

Country	Close ally		Friend	Neutral	Unfriendly		Enemy
			(percent mentions)				
Great Britain	56	(85)	29	8	1	(1)	--
Canada	49	(87)	38	6	1	(1)	--
Japan	17	(66)	49	21	4	(6)	2
France	16	(54)	38	28	8	(9)	1
Israel	15	(51)	36	23	11	(14)	3
MEXICO	9	(57)	48	28	6	(8)	2
Philippines	9	(47)	39	28	11	(12)	1
South Korea	7	(39)	32	29	12	(16)	4
Egypt	3	(36)	33	34	10	(13)	3
Saudi Arabia	3	(25)	22	30	19	(26)	7
China	2	(26)	24	41	14	(19)	5
South Africa	2	(15)	13	33	29	(36)	7
Nicaragua	1	(9)	8	19	31	(49)	18
Vietnam	1	(9)	8	23	34	(55)	21
Syria	1	(8)	7	22	29	(48)	19
Iraq	1	(6)	5	15	34	(64)	30
Soviet Union	--	(4)	4	13	44	(76)	32
Iran	--	(2)	2	6	31	(83)	52

Mexico ranked sixth in this listing of nations as a "close ally." When this grouping is combined with those who think of Mexico as a "friend," it climbed ahead of France and Israel to fourth place, surpassed only by Great Britain, Canada, and Japan. By being separated out at the upper end of the scale, Mexico was distinguished as one of the key actors.

This was matched by a mid-1986 Harris Survey, which found that 20% of Americans thought of Mexico as "a close ally," with another 55% saying "friendly but not a close ally." It was also reflected in high levels of concern expressed by both general public and leadership opinion over possible peaceful communist accession to power in various countries, as recorded in the 1986 CCFR study:[11]

I am going to read a list of countries. For each, tell me how much of a threat it would be to the U.S. if the communists came to power. What if the Communist Party came to power through peaceful elections in [country x]? Do you think this would be a great threat to the U.S., somewhat of a threat to the U.S., not very much of a threat to the U.S., or no threat at all to the U.S.?

	Great threat		Somewhat of a threat		Great/Somewhat combined	
	Public	Leaders	Public	Leaders	Public	Leaders
			(percent mentions)			
MEXICO	62	74	18	20	80	94
Saudi Arabia	39	51	35	38	74	89

Philippines	37	28	35	55	52	83
France	30	41	38	38	68	79
El Salvador	27	16	43	46	70	62
South Africa	21	20	40	47	61	67

Once again, the special sense of Mexico's strategic importance comes through. A possible Mexican shift to communist rule, even under peaceful circumstances, did not sit well with those interviewed—more so among the experts than the public at large. While one can say that this is nothing more than traditional American knee-jerk anti-communism, it is worth noting that only in the case of Mexico did a majority of the public look upon such a communist victory as "a great threat" to the United States; Saudi Arabia, though second highest, trailed well behind. Among leadership opinion, Mexico was also singled out far more than any other. A bare majority mentioned Saudi Arabia, while France fell into the minority column. This can be compared to a study conducted in the early 1970s that placed Mexico ahead of England, West Germany, Brazil, and Israel, among others, as a country on whose behalf the United States "should send troops in the event (country x) is attacked by communist-backed forces."[12] It is logical to assume that Mexico's crucial strategic meaning to Americans, both the general public and their leaders, carries with it special policy implications. Let us now turn to some of those.

Some Policy Indicators and Implications

It may help to sharpen our perspective by examining some perceptions held about Mexico and its people that go beyond generalized themes touched upon thus far. What about views on specific issues, national politics, and policies? In this regard, one particularly useful study was carried out by Yankelovich Clancy Shulman for *Time* magazine, just prior to Mexican President Miguel de la Madrid Hurtado's 1986 visit to Washington. Among the relevant findings were:[13]

- 66% of those interviewed said they thought events in Mexico were either "very important" to the United States (38%) or "fairly important" (28%).
- 46% considered Mexico "a close friend" (in line with the 48% who thought of Mexico as a "friend"and 9% as an "ally," reported in the previous section).
- These positives were balanced by some negative perceptions of Mexican politics: only 8% considered Mexico to be "well governed," while a clear majority of 69% thought it "poorly governed;" close to the same majority (65%) considered Mexico to have "a lot of corruption" Among foreign policy activists interviewed in the

SIRC study, 54% believed that "the U.S. should exert political and economic pressure on Mexico to hold fair elections."

- More than three Americans in four (77%) called Mexico "poor," while only 9% responded "wealthy."
- Illegal aliens entering the United States from Mexico were seen as a major problem by almost eight in ten: 57% called the issue "very serious," while another 22% considered it "fairly serious." 38% of those interviewed said that these illegal aliens take jobs away from Americans "a lot," with another 33% saying they do so "sometimes." And 80% were of the opinion that border patrol efforts to exclude illegal immigrants should be increased. (Other surveys conducted in the same period as the *Time* study found about half the respondents wanted to reduce the flow of immigrants into the United States, primarily because the new entrants "strain U.S. resources" and "take jobs." The SIRC study recorded 35% of the opinion that immigration was the "most important issue affecting our relationship with Mexico;" 32% mentioned political stability in Mexico, and 22% referred to Mexico's debt crisis).
- In similar proportions, the movement of drugs from Mexico into the United States was seen by 60% as contributing "a great deal" to the U.S. drug problem, with another 24% calling its effects "moderate."
- Perhaps because of these considerable reservations, support for increased foreign aid to "help Mexico deal with its economic problems" was looked upon favorably by just over one in three (36%), while a slight majority (53%) came down on the negative side. This would seem to run counter to the overall feelings of warmth and friendliness toward Mexico that we have seen frequently.

It is important to remember, however, that foreign aid has regularly been among the most unpopular uses of federal tax dollars. Under the circumstances, this finding should not be interpreted as singling out Mexico as an objectionable potential aid recipient. In fact, the SIRC study found that among its selected group of policy activists, 52% agreed with the proposition that "because Mexico is our neighbor, it should get priority over other needy countries for help from the U.S." Invoking geography and *relative* aid levels put Mexico into more favorable perspective.

Current massive U.S. trade deficits have generated support in some quarters for legislation that would limit the flood of foreign imports into the United States. According to a June, 1987 Roper Poll, however, Mexico was not a prime target:

Levels of Trade

	Too Much	About Right	Not Enough	Don't Know
		(percent mentions)		
Japan	55	27	8	10
South Africa	33	21	17	29
Soviet Union	28	26	23	31
China	19	34	24	23
MEXICO	18	37	22	23
Canada	8	48	24	20

Japan was seen overwhelmingly as the principal trade threat among the countries listed. South Africa and the Soviet Union were fairly closely linked in second place—largely on ideological grounds, it must be assumed, since neither ranks as a major U.S. trading partner. The general sense of "good neighborliness" that has emerged in many of our findings again prevailed: Mexico and Canada were most favorably (or least unfavorably) viewed. This was the case even though we run deficits with both—the one with Canada being even larger than that with Japan, when viewed on a per capita basis.

Where do these various indicators of the views that Americans hold about Mexico, its peoples, and its policies leave us? As noted at the outset, the picture presented is complex, filled with pluses and minuses, and a number of contradictions.

An underlying factor not discussed thus far is the ambivalent portrayal of Mexico and Mexican life that frequently pervades American literature, film, and some reporting and other popular writing. On the one hand is the stereotyped image of the Mexican peasant, resting under his sombrero in mid-afternoon siesta. So too are comments on the *mañana* culture an easygoing and colorful lifestyle marked by lack of energy, seriousness, or initiative. On the other hand is what might be called the "bandido" syndrome, the "macho Mexican," hard-working, tough, sometimes even ruthless. These conflicting strains compete for attention, yielding what seems at times a schizoid American view of Mexico and its peoples.

Other factors shade the picture: the growth of American industrial investment in Mexico (witness the burgeoning number of assembly plants located near the U.S.-Mexico border); increased respect for previously unacknowledged managerial prowess as well as skills of the Mexican labor force; the positive appeal of Mexican culture (ranging from music to art to food); Mexico itself as a tourist haven; and broad awareness of Mexico's importance to U.S. national interests. There is, in other words, a very large reservoir of good will, recently exemplified by the immediate humanitarian response to the tragic 1986 earthquake in Mexico City.

But that reservoir is drained by concern with key problems of high public visibility and correspondingly high political salience. Three top the list: illegal immigration from Mexico; Mexico as the principal channel for illicit drug traffic into the United States; and Mexico's external debt, which threatens the economic interrelationship between the two countries. Behind these lies uncertainty over Mexico's political stability, undermined by what is perceived as widespread corruption. These reservations can, as we have just seen, lead to majority backing for putting political and economic pressure on Mexico to hold "fair elections." This is a situation unlike the acid rain issue with Canada, for example. However serious that problem may be, it has had far less public and even political impact on bilateral relations than the principal points of contention between the United States and Mexico.

It is only fair to ask whether this nexus of concerns and fears, when combined with the unease registered over the hypothetical possibility of Mexico "going communist," might translate under the right (or wrong) set of circumstances into a consensus in favor of outright interventionism. Events in Panama in the late winter of 1987–1988 provided a useful case in point: political instability and concern over alleged involvement by military strongman General Manuel Antonio Noriega in drug trafficking resulted in calls for a more active U.S. policy designed to bring about Noriega's ouster. Some observers saw in those urgings an omen of what could emerge in light of worries about Mexico. Should national concern over the issue of drugs moving across the Rio Grande reach crisis proportions, fueled in a collision of stresses by possible economic and political flux south of the border, then voices of jingoism in Washington could flourish.

On balance, however, the most important aspect of American public and leadership opinion that emerges from all the measurements we have examined is the broadly shared recognition of Mexico's importance to U.S. national interests. In the absence of dramatic political and/or economic decline in Mexico, widespread support for interventionism along the lines just raised seems highly unlikely. Leadership in both countries can draw on this. American presidents generally receive broad backing in negotiations with the Soviet "enemy," as long as their actions are seen to be in defense of U.S. interests. This can be even more the case in dealing with problems and issues of contention between Mexico and the United States, where combined American support and respect for Mexico is high.

At the same time, there should be no false illusions. From a perspective north of the border, there are genuine and serious problems at hand, working in both directions. They must be addressed, and steps to ease if not totally resolve them need to be found. If not, the potential for unanticipated lurches in U.S. policy cannot be ruled out, facilitated by the freedom of action accorded the president by the support most Americans give him in dealing with Mexico. As Mexican leaders press for attention and seek a more prominent place on Washington's agenda, this is a potential "wild card" they should keep in mind.

Notes

1. "U.S.-Mexican Relations," Department of State *Gist*, December 1987.

2. For purposes of simplicity, the term "Americans" is used in this chapter to refer only to citizens of the United States.

3. *The Gallup Report International*, vol. II, no. 3, June 1984.

4. *Gallup, op. cit.*, vol. II, no. 1, February 1984.

5. John E. Rielly, editor, *American Public and U.S. Foreign Policy 1987*, The Chicago Council on Foreign Relations, Chicago, 1987.

6. *The Yomiuri Shimbun*, December 13, 1987.

7. William Watts, *Changing American Perceptions of Asia*, Potomac Associates, Washington, D.C., 1985; *Gallup, op. cit.*, vol. II, no. 3, June 1984.

8. Rielly, *op. cit.*

9. Christine E. Contee, *What Americans Think: Views on Development and U.S.-Third World Relations*, A Public Opinion Project of InterAction and the Overseas Development Council.

10. The Roper Poll, August 1987.

11. Rielly, *op. cit.*

12. Albert H. Cantril and Charles W. Roll, Jr., *Hopes and Fears of the American People*, Potomac Associates, Washington, D.C., 1971.

13. *Time*, August 25, 1986.

11

The Illicit U.S.-Mexico Drug Market: Failure of Policy and an Alternative

Samuel I. del Villar

It is drug users who finance organized crime through their drug purchases, and it is they who must accept responsibility for the broad range of costs with the drug industry.

The President's Commission on Organized Crime[1]

The illegal drug market is one of the most disruptive single issues between Mexico and the United States. It corrupts everything it touches and undermines the moral foundations of society in both countries. Public policies for dealing with this catastrophe internationally have been modeled since the beginning of the century on U.S. initiatives. Not only have these policies failed to solve the problem of an ever richer illicit drug market; they are even counterproductive.

With 47 bilateral drug-related agreements with the United States; the oldest, widest, and most effective eradication campaign; and the largest foreign U.S. Drug Enforcement Administration (DEA) operation in its territory; Mexico has followed U.S. antidrug policies much more closely than any other country.[2] For 40 years it has increasingly committed its law enforcement and national security resources to eradicate and interdict drugs bound for the U.S. market. But to no avail. The cumulative failure of U.S. antidrug policy has created enormous problems and imposed unbearable burdens on Mexico's national security. An effective antidrug policy alternative is a matter of survival for both Mexico and the United States.

The Failure

The policy failure is manifest in the current statistics on America's drug habit. The policy is counterproductive because it fails to acknowledge this habit. The drug demand in the United States leads inevitably to a stimulation of supply in Mexico. And the costs to Mexico are immense. Each of these facets of failure are discussed briefly in this section.

A Growing Mass Drug Culture, "America's Habit"

The failure of the U.S. antidrug policy is not readily discernible from reports of official antidrug programs. To the contrary, one may draw the erroneous conclusion that antidrug policy has been a success. Recent data provide examples:[3]

- Total U.S. federal drug budget authority increased from US$1.4 billion in 1981 to US$3.8 billion in 1987.
- Budget authority for interdicting drugs at the border increased from US$400 million in 1981 to US$1.3 billion in 1987.
- Cocaine and marijuana seizures under the "Alliance" program increased from 510 kilograms and 30 metric tons, respectively, during January–May 1986, to 1,310 kilograms and 65 metric tons during January–May 1987.
- The number of countries with "U.S. eradication agreements" increased from 2 in 1981 (Burma and Mexico), to 14 in 1986 (Belize, Bolivia, Brazil, Burma, Colombia, Costa Rica, Ecuador, Guatemala, Jamaica, Mexico, Pakistan, Panama, Peru, and Thailand).
- Cocaine and heroin bound for the United States and destroyed in the field increased from 0.8 and 4.4 metric tons, respectively, in 1981, to 10.0 and 15.2 metric tons in 1986.

These impressive data obscure the failure of U.S. antidrug policy, which may be illustrated by the more relevant estimate of the House Select Committee on Narcotic Abuse and Control on the U.S. expenditure on illicit drugs: US$110 billion yearly.[4] This figure represents roughly 3% of the U.S. gross national product (GNP), twice the amount that Americans pay for oil, one-half the total U.S. military expenditure, and three-quarters of Mexico's GNP. It indicates that there are massive demands for illegal drugs in the United States, a huge business organization to supply them, and vast illegal resources for expanding the market and corrupting law enforcement. Worse, this figure substantiates that tens of millions of Americans choose to make illegal drugs part of their lives, regardless of antidrug government reports.

With 23 million regular marijuana smokers in the United States, 10 million Americans who consume cocaine regularly, half a million

who consume crack, 1.5 million who are addicted to heroin, and between 1.5 to 2.5 million who consume other illicit drugs, drug consumption has reached epidemic proportions in the United States.[5] On balance, the failure of antidrug policy may be ascertained not only by the growth of the U.S. illicit drug market during the 1970s and 1980s, but also by the incidence of drug taking among the young. In the context of cumulative "wars on drugs," the conclusions of the Department of Health and Human Services' National Institute on Drug Abuse (NIDA) 1985 survey among high school seniors, college students, and young adults are cause for dismay:

> the rather steady decline of the past four years in total use of drugs appears to have halted . . . the already high proportion of young people who by senior year have tried . . . *any illicit drug* (61 percent in 1985) grows substantially larger up through the mid-twenties (where it reached 75 percent to 80 percent in 1985). . . . There is a similar rise in the proportion using *any illicit drug other than marijuana* (40 percent among seniors in 1985 vs. 50 percent to 55 percent among those in their mid-twenties). Lifetime prevalence for *marijuana* reaches about 70 percent to 75 percent by the mid-twenties (vs. 54 percent among 1985 seniors) and for *cocaine* nearly 40 percent (vs. 17 percent among seniors and 3 percent in 1972). Clearly, this nation's high school students and other young adults still show a level of involvement with illicit drugs which is greater than can be found in any other industrialized nation in the world. Even by historical standards in this country, those rates stay extremely high.[6]

Illicit drugs have created a mass culture in the United States—a culture which, especially because of its criminal character, undermines the fundamental values and creativity of American Society. It is *"America's Habit"* as noted in the heading of the report of the President's Commission on Organized Crime,[7] not an isolated social disease restricted to ghetto residents, hippies, or jet setters. According to NIDA as long ago as 1982, for young people in the United States trying marijuana is, apparently, a part of normal maturing.[8] Nowadays cocaine is also becoming a significant part of high school and college life, a habit engaged in not only by the fashionable, but by blue and white collar workers as well. Drug and alcohol abuse cost the U.S. economy about US$60 billion in lost productivity in 1983.[9]

Drug testing has become a major issue in relations between U.S. college administrators and students, and between employers and employees. Disputes have broken out in the realms of government, business, education, and even sports over new regulations to prevent drug abuse. Confidence in the honesty of the banking system has

eroded as indications of drug-money laundering have increased. Street
security is imperiled by drug-related crime, and unusual drug-related
gang violence is hitting cities all over the United States.

Counterproductivity of U.S. Antidrug Policy

The U.S. antidrug policy is counterproductive mainly because it
fails to acknowledge that the driving force behind the drug market
is U.S. consumer demand for drugs, even though it was acknowledged
by the President's Commission already quoted. Suppliers may do the
utmost to sell their product; but if consumers do not buy there is no
market. Regulators may render the market illicit and deem its supply—
especially foreign—a crime; but if consumer preferences are not
altered, a high-priced black market is established, and the resulting
wealth goes into the pockets of the criminals who control it. If demand
is so strong that price hikes have little effect on consumption; that
consumers are prepared to assault, steal, or even murder to pay for
drugs; and that drug suppliers can corrupt regulators and enforcers;
then supply-based regulation will continue to lead to ever-increasing
social chaos administered by criminals and protected by public policy.

Police and the military are not viable instruments for changing
massive cultural patterns in a free society, as was proven by the
American experience with (alcohol) Prohibition during the 1920s.
Drug abuse, like the use of tobacco and alcohol, is based on individual
choice, despite the harm that the individual may inflict on himself
and on those near him. If the individual is not freely persuaded of
the wrongfulness of drug abuse, government coercion will not change
his behavior in a society such as America, which is based essentially
on individual freedom of choice.

Mandatory drug testing—a coercive invasion of individual privacy
to reduce the demand of drugs—has been advocated by the Reagan
administration for federal employees, and by an ever-increasing number
of business and educational organizations. However, the emergence
of a market for drug-free urine, and the court battles challenging
the constitutionality of mandatory drug testing, indicate once more
the ineffectiveness of demand-based coercion in a free society, however
mild it may be.

Federalism imposes additional constitutional barriers in the United
States in the way of a coherent national antidrug coercive policy.
Concurrent jurisdictions of the U.S. Congress and state legislatures
to define the legal treatment for the drug market, and the "fragmentation of police organization"[10] in autonomous federal, state, and
municipal police services to enforce ensuing antidrug legislation, render

impossible the articulation of common legal and administrative standards to launch a minimally effective war on drugs within U.S. territory. Furthermore, a dozen or so state legislatures have decriminalized possession of marijuana for personal consumption; and the 20,000 or so autonomous local sheriffs, constables, marshals, or police forces in the United States are, on balance, highly reluctant to arrest or even to harass the tens of millions of American drug consumers. Prosecutors are even more reluctant to press criminal charges and courts to convict (and thus jam even more into the already critically overcrowded U.S. prisons).

Given these constraints, there is in fact a generalized benign neglect of U.S. laws against drug consumption. While, on balance, U.S. antidrug policy tolerates domestic drug consumption and, to a large extent, domestic marijuana production, it resorts to a most coercive approach to deal with foreign supply and foreign suppliers, through its border interdiction and international narcotics control programs.

The discriminatory exercise of coercion has led to a vicious cycle in the economics of international illicit drugs. As foreign eradication and interdiction of narcotics bound for the United States are intensified relative to domestic tolerance of consumption, the illicit market is enhanced. Organized crime—the relevant supplier to the market— is strengthened, and the law enforcement that should fight it is further undermined by corruption.

The approach of discriminatory coercion may limit foreign supply for a while. But it also raises prices in the face of tolerated U.S. consumption which is even legally protected in some jurisdictions, leads to fatter profits for organized crime, and provides greater incentives for pushers to expand their list of customers, especially among the young. High prices and profits, in turn, attract additional supply, induce greater spending on government corruption everywhere, and provide the basis for scale economies that give comparative advantage to large criminal organizations. Consumption expands when prices decrease as a result of additional supplies and of scale economies. Because of political prejudice against acknowledging the domestic origin of the problem in the United States, its government responds emotionally and irrationally to higher consumption levels and to public opinion, reflecting the failure, indeed counterproductiveness, of its own antidrug policy. It imposes additional levels of coercion on foreign supply, foreign suppliers, and their governments, thus starting a new phase in the escalating vicious spiral.

If the asymmetry in the exercise of coercion worked against U.S. consumers (who start and support the drug market cycles), rather than against the foreign peasants (who react to them), coercion would be much more effective. However, that has proven to be constitutionally impossible in the United States. Instead, antidrug policy has resorted to coercion against scapegoat alien peasants, utilizing the security and enforcement apparatus of their own governments.

The Export of Corruption

The explosion of drug demand in the United States inevitably led to an explosion of its supply in Mexico. With its 2,000-mile border neighboring the largest and wealthiest drug consumer in the world, Mexico has felt the U.S. drug boom and the American inability to control it as has no other country. There is a generalized prejudice in the United States that narcodollars are, on balance, beneficial to Mexico. In fact they are the most potent and corrosive U.S.-financed source of corruption, with high income-concentration effects and a negligible impact on the income of most Mexicans.

According to estimates of the Office of Technology Assessment (OTA) of the U.S. Congress, U.S. consumers paid in 1985, through U.S.-based traffickers, US$2.6 billion in gross income to Mexico-based smugglers,[11] of which only around US$200 million would have gone to Mexico-based agricultural producers according to expert analysis on value added ratios in the drug industry.[12] In contrast, according to the same type of analysis, U.S.-based traffickers would have received more than US$30 billion a year from wholesaling, transporting, distributing, and retailing the same drugs that earned US$200 million for Mexico-based agricultural producers, and US$2.6 billion to Mexico-based smugglers.[13]

Mexico first became a major drug producer and supplier in the 1940s, induced by the U.S. Government to develop a supply of morphine and hemp for the American market.[14] This request was the seedbed for the drug exports and third-country drugs exported to the United States through Mexico; however, these account for only a fraction of the U.S. market. According to official U.S. data, in 1986 Mexico produced 30% of the marijuana and 41% of the heroin supplied in the United States.[15] Shares on this market are highly volatile depending on eradication policies with respect to other sources and on their impact on relative prices. For instance, in 1983 it was officially reported that Mexican marijuana commanded a smaller U.S. market share (9%) than U.S.-produced marijuana (14%), and a much smaller share than Colombian marijuana (57%). In 1984 Mexican heroin accounted for 32% of the U.S. market, compared to a market share for South West Asian heroin of 51% (in 1986 Mexico's reported share dropped to 40%).[16] The rational base for establishing the actual volume of the

PART FOUR

Conclusion

market and of market shares is, in fact, quite shaky.[17] Unofficial estimates have put U.S.-produced marijuana at higher than 50% of U.S. demand,[18] and it has been pointed out that marijuana is America's largest cash crop, and its most valuable.[19]

On the other hand, whereas Mexico does not produce coca leaves or the cocaine and crack manufactured from them, U.S. interdiction operations in Florida and in the Caribbean have made Mexico's territory and airways an optional corridor for South American cocaine bound for the United States.

Given the natural comparative advantage that Mexico has for supplying drugs to the United States—the length of the border; the ineffectiveness of U.S. domestic antidrug policies; the propitious economic environment for drug exports stemming from Mexico's per capita income (one-eighth of U.S. per capita income), from Mexico's foreign indebtedness and its servicing, and from traumatic devaluations of the Mexican *peso* vis-à-vis the U.S. dollar (from 12.50 in August 1976 to 2,300 in May 1988)—Mexico's share of the gigantic drug market of its close neighbor would have been much larger had the Mexican government not intervened strongly to reduce that share. And this reduction has ultimately been to the benefit of U.S. and other American and Asian producers; it has not reduced drug demand. For decades the Mexican government has conducted a continuous massive effort to eradicate and to interdict drugs bound for the United States.[20] This effort—which has been termed a success story both by qualified scholarly analysis [21] and by the assessment of U.S. government officials who have been privy to it [22]—has not only checked increases in Mexican supply in response to the booming U.S. demand, but also has drastically reduced supply, while the U.S. government has been extremely ineffective in preventing the expansion of demand.

According to official U.S. data, the share of Mexican heroin in the U.S. market declined from 90% in the mid-1970s to 30% in the mid-1980s. This led Secretary of State George Shultz to congratulate the Mexican government, noting that "heroin production in Mexico, which reached 7.5 tons a year, was reduced to 1.4 tons in 1984."[23] A 1986 State Department report stated that marijuana production in Mexico was reduced by almost half between 1983 and 1984–85.[24]

The achievements of Mexico's Permanent Campaign Against Narcotics Trafficking nevertheless have ultimately proved futile in light of the protection of drug consumption in the United States and the production shift to countries such as Turkey and Colombia. It is significant that the OTA estimates that U.S.-originated illicit marijuana and heroin revenues to Colombia- and South East Asia-based smugglers are significantly higher than the respective revenues to Mexico-based smugglers,[25] and that U.S.-based producers have developed the most damaging and lucrative sort of marijuana, *sin semilla*—to a large extent due to the eradication, spraying, and interdiction of Mexican-produced marijuana. The antagonistic atmosphere prevailing at the time in U.S.-Mexican relations led to disagreement between the two governments with regard to the success of Mexico's eradication programs in 1985 and 1986; but, as stated in a July 1987 U.S. official report, "things are back on track now, seizures of cocaine are up, marijuana eradication is up, cooperation between Attorneys General has improved, the program to verify eradication statistics shows over 95 percent accuracy."[26] However, the political environment is highly volatile, given the ultimate futility of such reports in dealing with the core of the problem. A recent and thorough assessment concludes the following:

> The U.S. narcotics supply reduction strategy has been an unsuccessful policy. It is very likely that the new administration in the United States elected for 1989–92 (coinciding with a new one in Mexico) will raise the issue through a renewed strategy to fight drug trafficking. The U.S. government will turn again to Mexico for renewed cooperation. At the time the problem for Mexico will be more severe since the South West of the United States will replace South Florida as the critical area of drug trafficking.[27]

If renewal is based on such cumulative failure, chaos is the likely outcome, for the costs of current antidrug policy have become literally unpayable for Mexico.

Unbearable Costs and No Benefits

The high costs of the illicit drug market for Mexico do not stem from domestic demand.[28] Furthermore, since marijuana, heroin, and cocaine are fundamentally high-priced export goods tied to the U.S. dollar, the drastic reduction in disposable income that Mexicans have endured during the 1980s and the spectacular devaluation of the Mexican *peso* have been major checks on the expansion of domestic drug consumption.

The U.S. International Narcotics Control Program (INCP) spends US$15.1 million in Mexico a year eradicating and interdicting drugs bound for the United States, basically in spraying herbicide (the use of which is forbidden in the United States) over marijuana fields. This is trivial in comparison with Mexico's allocation of roughly one-third of its military budget (in March 1987 the Secretary of Defense estimated a daily expenditure of half a million dollars), and more than 60% of its federal Attorney General's budget for the same purpose.[29]

As suggested above, the economic benefits that drug exports bring to Mexico are minimal compared with the profits that the U.S. economy draws from the drug business. Drug-related foreign exchange earnings to Mexico are also reduced by the high import content of drug trafficking (planes, equipment, guns) and by the consumption and investment patterns of Mexico-based smugglers, who are fond of expensive U.S. goods, properties, and business—especially in the border towns. The spread of high caliber U.S.-exported guns in Mexico's countryside to supply private armies of dealers and their clientele has become an expensive item in the Mexican balance of payments. It is also a major cause of the rise in crime, and presents an enormous challenge to law enforcement.

The political costs of that pattern of collaboration with the U.S. INCP are even higher than the financial ones. The coercive, punitive, and futile character of U.S. antidrug policy, and the ensuing burdens for Mexico, were carried to an extreme under the Anti-Drug Abuse Act of 1986.[30] Among other things, it orders the President of the United States to:

> deny to any or all of the products of [every major drug producing country and every major drug transit country] tariff treatment under any . . . law providing preferential tariff treatment, [to] apply to any or all of the products of that country a duty at a rate not to exceed 50 percent ad valorem, [or] to take any combination of such actions, [unless] the President determines and so certifies to the Congress . . . that during the previous year . . . the actions of the Government [of said country] have resulted in the maximum reductions in illicit drug production, [and provided that] the Congress does not enact a joint resolution of disapproval.[31]

Mexico has already allocated the core and the bulk of its federal law enforcement and national security resources to eradicating and interdicting drugs bound for the United States under the theory that, in the words of a high Mexican official, "no other country in the world than Mexico does so much for the youth of North America."[32] Even assuming the soundness of such a theory, the primary institutional responsibility of Mexico's national government is to protect the territory, life, property, safety, and national security of Mexican nationals. It is not to protect the health of U.S. nationals, which is the responsibility of their own government. This responsibility has been distorted by the INCP. Current cooperation with its terms has resulted in extremely heavy costs to the Mexican political and legal process, and the alienation of people in the countryside by the massive destruction of agricultural property and detention of peasants that enforcing "the maximum reductions in illicit drug production" (congressional wording) has required. Moreover, traffickers are increasingly viewed in the countryside as modern Robin Hoods, who finance hospitals, schools, and churches in a time of crisis, and who defy an unpopular U.S.-made "law and order" that protects rich American consumers and producers, and punishes underprivileged Mexican peasants.

❦ Mexico's costly efforts to collaborate with the United States in eradicating drugs have produced illusory benefits. The impact of the U.S.-inspired eradication program on the marketplace has been to increase prices, to give comparative advantage to large-scale criminal organizations, to shelter U.S. and other foreign sources of marijuana production, and to fatten profits and enhance the corrupting influence of organized crime.

Yet various Mexican administrations have concluded that they could not refuse to cooperate under those terms, given the extraordinary coercion that the U.S. government has used. The 1986 drug bill and the political attitude behind it raised arbitrary coercion to unparalleled levels, in fact, "legally" threatening the disruption of Mexico-U.S. trade. However, coercion to impose a futile antidrug policy is not new. "It was an exercise in international extortion, pure and simple and effective, designed to bend Mexico to our will. We figured Mexico could hold out for a month; in fact, they caved in after two weeks, and we got what we wanted." Such is the assessment of Gordon Liddy,[33] the Watergate operative and one of the designers and enforcers of the first Operation Intercept, launched against Mexico's border traffic in October 1969 to impose "chemical crop destruction" (which the courts have ruled illegal in the United States). Since then, coercion has been the essence of the INCP, including measures that the U.S. government is not prepared to make public "because of the sensitivity of much of this information. [Such a disclosure would be] tantamount to a statement of the degree to which the U.S. government applies 'leverage' to another government," according to a State Department report to Congress.[34]

Since the first Operation Intercept coerced the Mexican government into committing massive law enforcement and national security resources to the "Permanent Campaign Against Drug Trafficking," massive spraying of herbicides, and massive detentions of Mexican peasants and destruction of their property, the international political payoff has been most counterproductive for Mexico and for its government.

When U.S. antidrug policies backfire in the face of increased U.S. demand and ensuing profits for traffickers for increasing supply, as happened during President Reagan's seven years of renewed and lost "War on Drugs," Mexico becomes a favorite scapegoat. In the aftermath of the torture and slaying of DEA agent Enrique Camarena Salazar in February 1985, for example, presumably as a result of his undercover activities in Mexico, the Reagan administration implemented a new phase of Operation Intercept to punish Mexico as a country. It overlooked the fact that such a disgraceful incident, and its accompanying "Mexico Bashing" campaign, were ultimately the result of the Mexican government's acceptance of the DEA's largest foreign undercover apparatus under its sovereign jurisdiction.

Although the economic, political, and international costs of Mexico's cooperation with the INCP have been very high, the highest cost has been moral, through the wide exposure of law enforcement and national security forces to the principle stated by Mexico's Attorney General, Sergio García Ramirez, that drug-trafficking goes hand in hand with corruption.[35]

The Alternative

There is an alternative. It is a difficult one, involving political leadership, the mutual acknowledgment of common interests between the United States and Mexico, differentiating marijuana from other drugs, and being prepared to reallocate the antidrug resources now being spent to more productive uses. But it has the promise of being successful.

Political Leadership

A change for the better is always difficult to achieve, especially if it requires a change in deeply rooted and long-standing misconceptions, government structures, and policies, as is the case with the illicit drug market between the United States and Mexico. But such changes are at the core of human evolution, and history shows that they can be achieved.

The nearest historical analogy to the long-lasting U.S. "wars on drugs" is the U.S. Vietnam War. Theoretically this war could have been won in military terms by the United States if it had used the ultimate power of its technological capabilities to destroy its ideological enemies in South East Asia. If the U.S. government was not prepared to destroy with nuclear bombs Vietnamese peasants who thought differently, it is absolutely unthinkable that it is prepared to destroy—

or even put in jail—the 50 million or so American regular drug consumers whose free choice is in fact the real enemy of the war on drugs because they think differently from a transitory majority in the Congress of the United States. To the extent that those millions of Americans are more important to the U.S. government than millions of Vietnamese, its supply-side war on drugs was lost from the beginning, more surely than the Vietnam War.

For a long while this truth has been concealed in the American, the international, and the Mexican political process by the theory that the real enemies of the war on drugs are foreign-produced vegetation and the underprivileged peasants who cultivate it. The winners have been organized crime and its political clientele, which profit in terms of a monopoly position and resulting high prices both from the dollar votes of tens of millions of U.S. consumers and from the harassment of Mexican peasants.

The first *sine qua non* for overturning the trends in the war on drugs and defeating its winners is political leadership in the United States and in Mexico which is truthful and strong enough to clarify those misconceptions, and to mobilize the political process toward realistic antidrug approaches.

Acknowledgment of Common National Interests

The primary common national interest that Mexico and the United States share in antidrug policy is checking, curtailing, and eventually destroying the power that narcodollar-financed organized crime has acquired for subverting the rule of law in both countries. Neither Mexico nor the United States has a national interest in the futile exercise of massive coercion of Mexican marijuana producing peasants, which is advocated by the current antidrug policy at the same time that a dozen or so U.S. state legislatures have decriminalized marijuana consumption, the bulk of the U.S. enforcement apparatus is reluctant even to disturb its consumption, and it appears to be constitutionally impossible to penalize U.S. consumers—much less do it in the way that Mexican producers are penalized. Quite the contrary, the costs of such an irrational and unfair policy have become unbearable for the national security of Mexico and of the United States, in terms of political alienation of the Mexican countryside, misallocation of security and enforcement resources, the monopoly positions and financial strength of large criminal organizations, and their power to corrupt and subvert.

Distinguishing Among Drugs

Marijuana, cocaine, and heroin consumption and production generate entirely different social and cultural effects, as do their legal status and enforcement thereof. Marijuana is not physically, mentally, or socially more harmful than alcohol, and is easily produced everywhere in Mexico and in the United States. That is why its production and consumption is much more widespread, legalized and/or tolerated in the United States than is the consumption of cocaine and heroin. On the other hand, opium poppy production, the agricultural base for heroin, is essentially restricted to a mountainous and underpopulated Northwestern region of Mexico bordering only 3 of its 31 states. This fact makes law enforcement against its production and trafficking much more manageable, provided that resources are reallocated from the antimarijuana campaigns and that the United States opens a legal market alternative for Mexican-produced morphine, as it did under its agreement with Turkey.[36]

The Question of Marijuana Legalization

The question of legalizing marijuana seems to be politically entangled in the United States with much deeper ethical and cultural questions: Is the option for drug consumption, or even for drug abuse, primarily a moral issue pertaining to the individual's free choice, and right, in a constitutional government protective of individual freedom to dispose of his personal mental and physical health? Or is it primarily a public policy issue pertaining to the power of the government to impose the standards that individuals should follow with regard to their personal mental and physical health? Where should the boundaries between personal freedom and government power with regard to the drug market be placed? As suggested above, the answers that have emerged from the American political, legal, and administrative processes are confusing and contradictory, and so far have acted to the benefit of organized crime and to the great detriment of Mexico and many other countries.

The findings of the 1972 U.S. National Commission on Marijuana and Drug Abuse seemed to advocate legalization on the basis that it "is a rather unexciting compound of negligible immediate toxicity at the doses usually consumed in this country."[37] However, the 1986 President's Commission on Organized Crime came out "emphatic in its position that legalization of drug use is not a viable option" in the case of marijuana, on indications of its higher toxicity than tobacco, which are "inherently destructive to mind and body," although acknowledging "some merit" to the argument "that because of the clear connection between illegal drug trafficking and organized crime, making drugs legal would remove the enormous profits in the illicit drug industry *a priori.*"[38]

A wide variety of state jurisdictions in the United States have decriminalized marijuana possession for personal consumption, the bulk of the U.S. police and judicial system neglect anticonsumption laws, and tens of million of U.S. consumers cast their drug-dollar votes freely. In contrast, the U.S. Congress enacted in 1986 the theoretically toughest antidrug legislation actively urged by President Reagan, and appropriated record levels of antidrug enforcement resources for fiscal 1987—although they were drastically cut in the President's budget for fiscal 1988.[39]

Let us hope that clarification of this basic moral and political confusion in the United States will allow the fundamental creative values of American culture to prevail over the illicit drug values that threaten it, and along with it Mexican culture as well.

From Antidrug Waste to Productivity

A fundamental reallocation of antidrug resources, from wastage to productivity, is required. Two basic criteria should inspire the change: (1) at the overall level, from emphasis on the supply side to emphasis (primarily through prevention and treatment) on the demand side, which is the market's driving force; and (2) at the enforcement level, from emphasis on eradication and interdiction of vegetation and punishment of the peasants who grow it, to emphasis on investigation and immobilization of the criminal organizations that are the core of the market.

Current trends in the United States are not encouraging, however. The U.S. 1988 Presidential overall antidrug budget was cut by nearly one billion dollars (20%) from the 1987 federal budget authority; resources for prevention and treatment were reduced from US$800 million to US$565 million; interdiction and eradication still commanded nearly US$1.2 billion, the big chunk (38.7%) of the antidrug effort.[40] In the case of Mexico there is an even more urgent need to reallocate more than 60% of the Attorney General Office's budget and roughly a third of the Army's budget from eradicating drugs bound for the United States to domestic anticrime enforcement, and immobilization of criminal organizations (in the case of police and prosecutorial resources) and to appropriate military responsibilities (in the case of the armed forces).

"We Should Not Preach What We Do Not Practice"

The accumulation of drug "cooperation" agreements between Mexico and the United States indicates that a stable and effective pattern of bilateral cooperation has not been reached. In fact those agreements do not constitute the basis of a genuine binational cooperative effort to further the basic common interest of the two countries in conducting an effective antidrug policy. Rather, they constitute a fig leaf for the coercive character of a U.S.-imposed and futile antidrug policy. It is manifestly unacceptable for a sovereign nation, as is required in the U.S. 1986 antidrug bill, to submit its police and military forces to the scrutiny, "certification," and "approval" of the president and congress of the United States. To do so would not be cooperation; it would be outright subordination.

A basic symmetry should underlie cooperative efforts between Mexico and the United States. If the U.S. government cannot or will not conduct a permanent marijuana eradication campaign throughout its territory, of spraying herbicides over private properties, of massively jailing its consumers and its producers, then the Mexican government should not do so. Mexican peasant producers may not be as wealthy as U.S. consumers and producers; but they are equal as human beings, and have the same rights. Their equal treatment, and analogous standards north and south of the border, should be a fundamental premise of any antidrug cooperative effort between the two countries. In the same fashion, an effective shift in policy emphasis towards immobilizing criminal organizations—suggested above—would only work under a symmetrical cooperative effort on both sides of the border, since their targets have organizational bases on both sides. However, the Mexican legal setting has to be set up to investigate and prosecute criminal conspiracies, and the prevailing professional conditions on the Mexican investigative and prosecutorial services have to be significantly enhanced in order to meet the required standards of effectiveness.

The alternative conceptual basis on which to sustain effective Mexican-U.S. cooperation was provided by Secretary of State, George Shultz, in his major statement with regard to the U.S. international narcotics control policy: *"We should not preach what we do not practice."*[41] The U.S. government should not preach an indiscriminate international war on drugs at the same time, for instance, as unpenalized and avowed marijuana users are nominated to the Supreme Court or even to the Presidency of the United States; or as some branches of its government command, deal, and even ask for financial and other support of alleged drug barons, and other branches seek their criminal prosecution—as was disclosed in the Noriega case.[42]

Notes

1. President's Commission on Organized Crime, Report to the President and the Attorney General, *AMERICA'S HABIT: Drug Abuse, Drug Trafficking, and Organized Crime*, U.S. Government Printing Office, Washington, D.C., 1986, p. 5.

2. It is illustrative that a list of bilateral agreements of the U.S. government compiled by the Library of Congress up to January 1, 1985 shows that the Mexican government has signed 47 (46 since 1973, without including amendments and additions), compared with 3 by the United Kingdom, and 2 each by Afghanistan, Belize, Costa Rica, Cuba, France, West Germany, Japan, Malaysia and Venezuela. These are the only countries that have more than one bilateral agreement with the United States on the matter. Samuel I. del Villar *Control Perspectives over the Illicit Drug Market, U.S.-Mexico*, Working Documents, Bilateral Commission on the Future of United States-Mexican Relations, Mexico City, 1987.

3. National Drug Policy Board, *Federal Drug Program, Overview and Progress Report*, July 23, 1987, mimeographed.

4. President's Commission on Organized Crime, *op. cit.* Other estimates reported are of US$27 billion and US$50–75 billion.

5. Mark A.R. Kleiman and Christopher E. Putala, *State and Local Drug Law Enforcement: Issues and Practices*, Program in Criminal Justice Policy and Management, John F. Kennedy School of Government, Harvard University, March 1987, mimeographed.

6. National Institute on Drug Abuse, *Drugs Among High School Students, College Students, and Other Young Adults, National Trends Through 1985*, U.S. Government Printing Office, Washington, D.C., 1986, pp. 13, 16, and 20. Although reports from the 1986 NIDA survey appear to indicate that the ratio of cocaine use among high school seniors declined from its 1985 level, it was still higher than its 1984 level, a fact which does not alter NIDA's core 1985 findings with regard to historic trends.

7. President's Commission on Organized Crime, *op. cit.*

8. National Institute on Drug Abuse, *National Survey on Drug Abuse: 1982*, U.S. Government Printing Office, Washington, D.C., 1982.

9. President's Commission on Organized Crime, *op. cit.*

10. Delmar Karlen in collaboration with Geoffrey Sawer and Edward M. Wise, *Anglo-American Criminal Justice*, Clarendon Press, Oxford, 1976, p. 10.

11. Congress of the United States, Office of Technology Assessment (OTA), *The Border War on Drugs*, OTA-0-336, U.S. Government Printing Office, Washington, D.C., March 1987.

12. It is assumed that agricultural producers get 0.71% of the street value of marijuana in the United States, and 0.034% of the street value of heroin in the United States. Those ratios are the average value added ratios for agricultural production in this industry proposed by two of the foremost U.S. experts. See Peter Reuter and Mark Kleiman, "Risk and Prices: An Economic Analysis of Drug Enforcement," *Crime and Justice*, July 1986.

13. It is assumed, following the Reuter and Kleiman average ratios, that Mexico-based smugglers get 7.9% and 4.6% of the U.S. street value of marijuana and heroin, respectively. According to those ratios, OTA's estimate of US$50 billion of drug traffic revenues severely underestimates revenues received by U.S.-based traffickers. OTA, *op. cit.*

14. James Van Wert "El Control de Narcóticos en México. Una década de institucionalización y un asunto diplomático," in Gabriel Székely, editor, *México Estados Unidos 1985*, El Colegio de México, Mexico City, 1986.

15. National Narcotics Intelligence Consumers Committee (NNICC), *The Supply of Illicit Drugs to the United States from Foreign and Domestic Source: 1985–1986 (With Near Term Projections)*, Washington, D.C., June 1987.

16. NNICC *Reports* 1983 and 1984.

17. Miguel Ruiz de Cabanas, "The Supply of Illicit Drugs to the United States: The Changing Role of Mexico," Working Documents, Bilateral Commission on the Future of United States-Mexican Relations, August 1987.

18. National Organization for the Reform of Marijuana Laws (NORML) report, in *Facts on File*, Washington, D.C., May 17, 1985, pp. 360–361.

19. Jon B. Gettman *Marijuana in America–1986*, NORML, 1987, mimeographed.

20. Samuel I. del Villar, *Control Perspectives.*

21. Peter Reter, *Eternal Hope: America's International Narcotics Effort* Rand Corporation, Washington, D.C., February 1987.

22. Mathea Falco, *Historical Record: U.S. Narcotics Control Collaboration with Turkey, Mexico and Colombia*, Working Documents, Bilateral Commission on the Future of United States-Mexican Relations, August 1987.

23. George Shultz, "The Campaign Against Drugs: The International Dimensions," speech to the Miami Chamber of Commerce, December 14, 1984, *Current Policy*, No. 611.

24. Department of State, Bureau of International Narcotics Matters, *International Narcotics Strategy Report, 1986*, Washington, D.C., February 1, 1987.

25. OTA, *op. cit.*

26. National Drug Policy Board, *op. cit.*

27. Javier Trevino Cantu, "U.S. Narcotics Policy and U.S. Mexican Relations: An Assessment," John F. Kennedy School of Government, Harvard University, Cambridge, MA, April 1987, mimeographed.

28. Samuel I. del Villar, *Control Perspectives, Part One: The Relevant Market.*

29. Samuel I. del Villar, *Control Perspectives*, The Reply of the Law.

30. Public Law 99–570 (H.R. 5484) of October 27, 1986.

31. Public Law 99–570 (H.R. 5484) of October 27, 1986.

32. Statement of Mexico's Deputy Attorney General, Luis Porte Petit. Joel Brinkley, "Mexico and the Narcotics Traffic: A Growing Strain in U.S. Relations," *New York Times*, October 20, 1986.

33. G. Gordon Liddy, *Agency of Flair*, St. Martin's Press, New York, 1980. Quoted by Ted Galen Carpenter, in *The U.S. Campaign Against International Narcotics Trafficking: A Cure Worse than the Disease*, Cato Policy Analysis Institute, Washington, D.C., December 1985, mimeographed.

34. Bureau of International Narcotics Matters, Department of State, *International Narcotics Control Strategy Report to Committee on Foreign Relations, Committee on Foreign Affairs*, Washington, D.C., February 1, 1986, mimeographed.

35. Joel Brinkley, *op. cit.*

36. Falco, *op. cit.*

37. President's Commission on Organized Crime, *op. cit.*, p. 54.

38. *Ibid.*, pp. 50, 54–58, 330–332.

39. National Drug Policy Board, *op. cit.*

40. National Drug Policy Board, *op. cit.*

41. Shultz, *op. cit.*

42. Frontline, "Guns, Drugs, and the C.I.A.," Public Broadcasting Service, Washington, D.C., May 18, 1988.

12

Narcotics in
U.S.-Mexican Relations

Gregory F. Treverton

Traffic in illegal narcotics is a major issue between Mexico and the United States; from time to time it is *the* major issue, overshadowing even debt or migration. The bare statistics suggest why. Narcotics use in the United States is staggering in its proportions: 62 million Americans admit having used marijuana and another 22 million report cocaine use. Mexico, a drug control success story in the 1970s, has again become the primary source of heroin and marijuana for the U.S. market, and an estimated third of the cocaine reaching the United States goes through Mexico.

In these circumstances, the U.S. Anti-Drug Abuse Act of 1986 contained a number of sanctions pointed directly at Mexico: the president was compelled to withhold US$1 million in drug aid to Mexico until he reported on Mexican progress in bringing Drug Enforcement Administration (DEA) official Enrique Camarena's killers to justice; and the Act suggested that the president "should consider" additional sanctions against Mexico—a travel advisory and other cuts in aid and multilateral bank loan or trade benefits.

In looking toward the new administrations in Mexico and the United States, this chapter asks two broad questions: How much strain will the narcotics issue provoke between the two nations? And might other policies do at least as well in dealing with drugs while reducing the spillover of strain on other issues important to the two nations. In seeking answers, I examine the shape of the problem and its recent history.

The Shape of the American Problem

The "narcotics problem" is in reality two clusters of problems. One is the social consequences of drug abuse, itself intertwined with others of society's problems; the other is the crime and corruption that ensue because the drugs are *illegal,* enabling huge profits to be made in illicitly meeting demand. Thus far, the focus of attention in the United States has been on abuse, although American cities are no strangers to drug-related crime, and their police forces and courts no strangers to corruption.

For Mexico more than for the United States, it is the corruption ensuing from illegality that is the scourge of narcotics. Unlike some of the drug-producing countries further south, Mexico does not have much of a domestic drug abuse problem; what it has is more glue and concrete-sniffing in the vast urban slums than a cocaine or marijuana problem.

The U.S. public is preoccupied with drug abuse: in a 1986 poll that asked which two or three issues people were most concerned about, 26% cited drugs, compared with 27% for unemployment, and 7% for U.S. relations with the Soviet Union.[1] However, attention to the issue has waxed and waned. In 1986, after the death of basketball star Len Bias from a cocaine overdose, Congress passed the 1986 Act, an impressive declaration of intent to try to cut into the huge U.S. *demand* for illicit drugs. Cocaine seemed to be losing its image from the 1970s as a clean, safe, even glamorous drug—the choice of rock stars, athletes, and actors.

Now, though, the issue is much less in the public eye. The president quietly cut back his own recommended funding for the war on drugs. Although the ritual denunciations of drug abuse as the ruination of young people continue, politicians have moved on to other issues. In the words of an editorialist for the *New York Times,* it is not that the United States lost the war on drugs, it is rather that "we never really decided to get into it."[2]

Behind this seesaw in attention, it is increasingly clear—to most students of the problem if not yet to the general public or elected officials—that the whole range of efforts to restrict the *supply* of drugs in the United States is failing. Between 1980 and 1985, federal support for drug enforcement increased by more than US$700 million, while money for education, prevention, and treatment has been reduced by 40 percent; by 1985 the former totalled US$1.65 billion, the latter US$400 million.

While highly publicized campaigns to interdict drugs being imported into the United States—such as the South Florida Task Force, record huge seizures—drugs, especially cocaine, are more and more plentiful in the United States today. Indeed, wholesale cocaine prices in the United States continue to decline, from nearly US$50,000 per kilo four years ago to under US$20,000 in some places today. As President himself said at the height of the drug scare: "All the confiscation enforcement in the world will not cure this plague."[3]

f the kingpins of the Colombian cocaine cartel are in jail, one of them extradited to the United States, but their arrests have made not one whit of difference to the cartel's operations. Traffickers at lower levels in the organization are replaced faster than they can be arrested, lured in by the huge amount of money to be made.[4] As arrests and seizures grow, so does the amount and purity of the cocaine in the United States. Only its price falls. As the U.S. State Department's 1986 report puts it, coca production still "vastly exceeds cocaine consumption," and the disparity is even more striking in the case of heroin: the world produces some 2500–plus tons of opium, while the United States consumes only 3–4% of that amount.[5] Put more graphically, the U.S. heroin demand could be supplied from a few square miles of opium poppies.

Within the United States, marijuana is now the second largest cash crop, after corn, even though domestic eradications went up tenfold between 1984 and 1986.[6] Moreover, domestic marijuana is much stronger—up to ten times stronger—than the Mexican product that dominated the U.S. market two decades ago. What is true of domestic eradication is even truer of eradications in Latin America. Operation Blast Furnace in Bolivia in 1986, a massive ten-week eradication effort, had virtually no effect on drug supplies or prices in the United States. Traffickers simply had too much cocaine stockpiled.

On the demand side, drug abuse peaked in the late 1970s with two exceptions: cocaine use and drug use in general among those over the age of 26, thus past the previous prime age for drug consumption. The special concern now is cocaine, and especially the potent and cheap form of smoking it called "crack." Heroin remains a tragedy of inner cities in the United States, but the number of addicts (about 500,000) has remained roughly constant for a decade.

Cocaine has become the drug most often cited in hospital emergency room cases—25,000 cases and 1,000 deaths reported in 1986. Moreover, the demographics of cocaine use differ from previous drugs, which have been used predominantly by 18–24 year-olds. That cohort has been declining as a share of total U.S. population while cocaine use has been increasing, confirming suspicions that cocaine is the drug of choice for those now beyond previous prime ages for drug abuse.

Only in the last year is there any evidence that cocaine may have joined the post-1980 pattern of generally declining drug use among adolescents. Daily marijuana use among high school seniors, for instance, had fallen to just over 3% in 1987 from its peak of 11% in 1978. Cocaine is now the second most used illicit drug after marijuana.

Only in 1987 was the pattern of steady increase in use broken: in 1987, 15% of high school seniors had tried it, 10% had used in the previous year, and 4% in the previous month; for 1986 the numbers were 17%, 13%, and 6%, respectively.

Crack also has been on the rise, surely until 1987. The proportion of high school seniors who smoked cocaine remained constant between 1979 and 1983; between 1983 and 1986 it more than doubled, from 2.5% to 6%, and most of that smoking was crack. In 1987 there was perhaps a levelling-off in crack use. Survey evidence for other drugs, such as marijuana, indicates that use goes down as more people perceive the drug to be dangerous. Not so for cocaine, use of which so far has increased along with the public perception of its danger.

As the United States moves to address demand, antismoking and antimarijuana campaigns provide some hope, but understanding of what works remains weak. Like daily marijuana use, daily cigarette smoking among teenagers dropped by a third between 1977 and 1981, although there has been almost no decline since, despite intensive antismoking campaigns. In both cases, the declines seem to have reflected a growing awareness of the drugs' dangers, not simply that they were harder to obtain. Between 1978 and 1986, the percentage of high school seniors who reported they had used marijuana in the previous month declined from 37% to 23%; but the percentage saying regular marijuana smoking carried "great risk" doubled from 35% to 71%. Over the same period, however, the percentage reporting that marijuana was "fairly" or "very easy" to get remained essentially constant (88% to 85%).[7]

The sequence of antimarijuana campaigns demonstrates the limited understanding of what works. First efforts, running back to the 1930s, threatened dreadful consequences from one marijuana cigarette, and so undercut the credibility of their own message. Learning the lessons of these "scare campaigns," next efforts provided realistic information about the dangers of substance use. The decline in teenage cigarette smoking through 1981 seems to have reflected changed attitudes about its dangers, perhaps changes as early as age 10 or 11.

On the other hand, more information also may have the paradoxical effect of increasing interest in drugs, and information alone seems not enough to change attitudes.[8] By the same token, appeals from "cured" public figures are also ambiguous since part of the appeal is the fact of drug use and recovery. Drug use is not "deglamorized" in the process; one survey of 9–12 year olds found that 36% regarded drug users as popular.

The most recent approaches seek to bring together the lessons of previous experience, addressing substance abuse as learned behavior that results from a combination of environmental and personal factors. Programs thus range from a focus on peer pressure to developing personal competence, hence esteem. There have been some successes so far with regard to cigarette smoking; one study found these programs especially hopeful among those students at most risk of smoking (those whose parents, friends, or role models smoked).[9] Yet the uncertainties about what works remain, a comment in part on the sorry state of research in the United States and elsewhere on how to contain demand as well as how to treat drug abuse.

Analysis and Attitude

Looking at the shape of the U.S. drug problem suggests three broad conclusions relevant to Mexican-U.S. relations. First, the entire range of "police" actions against drugs—from enforcement against traffickers to seizures to crop eradication in producing countries— will have little effect on narcotics supplies in the United States. Even if it were possible to seal U.S. borders to drugs, that would not win the drug war; it would only shift it to so-called "designer drugs" made domestically from chemicals not foreign crops. Already the war against imports has been more successful against marijuana than cocaine, for obvious reasons: the former is both much bulkier and less lucrative than the latter, so stepped-up seizure has given traffickers an incentive to switch to cocaine. As a result, by some estimates the United States may produce up to half its marijuana domestically (four times the official figure).

In particular, short-term disruptions of drug supplies do not have much long-term effect. For instance, although massive drug eradications succeeded in Mexico in the 1970s, as they did also in Turkey and Bolivia, those policies did not long succeed in reducing the overall supply of illegal drugs to the United States. Drug traffickers were, and are, able to shift their supply base from one country to the next (and if necessary, from one region to the next), until U.S. drug enforcement programs subside in the chosen area.

Second, as a result, the emphasis in U.S. antidrug strategies ought to shift toward demand, as to some extent it already has. Third, however, cutting into demand is a task for the long run, one for which past experience provides some pointers but no guarantees. At a minimum, the timelag between action and effect will be frustratingly large: as with cigarette smoking, the message will take some time to reach home, still more to affect the behavior of those who received it.

Suffice it to say, however, that these conclusions do not drive the U.S. politics of the war on drugs. Understanding of the issue—in Congress for instance—remains low. The *Times* editorial cited earlier is representative of that lack of understanding: it sounded a clarion call for "stopping foreign drugs flowing into our country . . . at the source, not at our border or in the streets of American cities." Even inside the U.S. executive, "pulling up those coca plants" is a kind of crusade, almost independent of its effect.

Certainly, the conclusion that supply-side policies do not work is counterintuitive. It just seems logical that it ought to be easier to cut drugs off "at the source" than to influence the behavior of millions of potential users. Then, when it turns out that drugs cannot be stopped at the source, it is tempting for Congress to respond in frustration by punishing supplier countries. For instance, the 1986 Act required the president to certify that countries are "fully cooperating" in the war on drugs.

Aid is denied to any country not thus certified, and U.S. representatives are required to vote against multilateral bank loans to that country. Separately, the Act denied sugar quotas and imposed up to 50 percent tariffs on the exports of countries whose programs the president did not determine to be adequate; those determinations, moreover, can be overridden by joint congressional resolutions.

Mexico was certified in both 1987 and 1988, but both times the decision was controversial. In 1986 the president denied certification only to Iran, Afghanistan, and Syria—none of which received U.S. assistance in any case. In 1988 he added Panama to the blacklist, although the decision had no practical effect because aid already had been suspended in the effort to oust strongman General Manuel Antonio Noriega. When in 1987 members of Congress proposed to override the president's certification of Mexico, as well as Panama and the Bahamas, they were unsuccessful, and the Senate instead opted to compel the president to reexamine the certification.

In 1988 there were again calls for a congressional override, again unsuccessful. But the episodes underscored how much U.S.-Mexican relations are hostage to passions over the drug issue.

The Role of Mexico

As Samuel del Villar spells out in Chapter 11, Mexico has cooperated, if not always eagerly, with the United States over drugs for longer and more broadly than any other nation. It had signed some 40-odd cooperation agreements with Washington by 1985. More important, in deciding on the *campaña permanente* (permanent campaign) in the

1970s, Mexico made drug eradication a major army mission. About a fifth of the 125,000-man army is involved and about a third of the nation's defense budget. More than half the Mexican Attorney General's budget of US$36 million in 1987 went to such operations, with the United States contributing some US$15 million. Indeed, Mexico's deputy attorney general asserted in 1986 that "no other country in the world than Mexico does so much for the youth of North America."[10]

Between the mid-1970s and 1983, these eradication efforts produced a nosedive in Mexico's share of marijuana supplies to the United States, from 70% to 10%; and its share of U.S. heroin supplies tumbled from 87% to 34%. While eradication remains major business for the Mexican government, Mexico has again become the primary source of heroin and marijuana for the U.S. market, and the transit point for perhaps a third of the cocaine that reaches the United States (Mexico does not grow coca leaf).

Part of the reason surely is Mexico's economic crisis, which encourages small farmers to return to cultivating lucrative drug crops even as it strains government resources for attacking the problem. Although the total income to peasant farmers growing marijuana is relatively small, probably less than a billion U.S. dollars a year, it may still be significant by comparison to current poverty and alternative crops. By one estimate, of each U.S. dollar a marijuana consumer pays, 91–93 cents remain in the United States; for cocaine, the number is 97–99 cents. The producers in Latin America thus get a tiny proportion.[11]

Increasing corruption, especially given the scale of army involvement, is also a culprit for increasing Mexican involvement in drug trafficking; Mexico created a special police force, the Federal Judicial Police, to prosecute the war on drugs while restraining corruption. And U.S. interdiction efforts in the southeastern United States, while inadequate to bite much into total drug supplies, did manage to push traffic westward, through Mexico to the Mexican-U.S. border that is largely invisible, a fact testified to by the thousands of illegal migrants that cross it every night.

Although the Andean countries have become genuinely alarmed by narcotics abuse in their own countries, drug abuse in Mexico is not yet seen as a major social problem. And although traffickers have corrupted Mexican institutions, nowhere do they pose a direct threat to government control, as they did in the 1970s in the "critical triangle" of Sinaloa, Durango, and Chihuahua. By moving against drugs there, the central government also regained control where traffickers, perhaps mixed with antigovernment guerrillas, had become a law unto themselves.

The del Villar discussion (Chapter 11) testifies to Mexican attitudes, including among analysts who can hardly be described as reflexively anti-American: Mexico spends too much on the drug war and gains too little. It is periodically coerced into doing still more to help the United States. And when those efforts fail, predictably, to cut into drug abuse in the United States, Mexico is a convenient scapegoat. As a Mexican student of the problem has put it: "Mexico has a drug problem. It is called the United States."

Mexico responds to American pressure more out of need than any shared perception of the problem. In 1969, U.S. Operation Intercept brought cross-border traffic to a standstill and induced Mexico to mount the permanent campaign. The torture murder of Camarena in 1985 was a specific spur to the 1986 legislation and associated Mexico-bashing. In the wake of the 1988 certification debate, Mexico announced a new cabinet-level task force on drugs.

The "made-in-America" label that the drug war wears may be counterproductive to the war itself; it surely grates on a Mexican nationalism that is framed in large measure against a history of American dominance. Imagine how Americans would react to DEA agents from another country carrying weapons and conducting independent investigations on U.S. soil, or to the use at foreign urging of herbicides—not to mention police practices—that were banned in that foreign nation.

How Much Strain?

Narcotics will be an issue between Mexico and the United States during the new administrations of the two countries. The question is how serious the strain will be.

The most that can be said so far is that U.S. policy has moved somewhat in the direction that makes sense—toward a focus on demand. That seems likely to continue under any president; the major contenders have not given much prominence to specific antidrug programs but have placed the issue high in the litany of problems to which their administrations will attend. However, neither the candidates nor the broad American body politic has embraced the counterpart logic to more attention to demand—less preoccupation with supply.

Absent that embrace, the United States will, as in the past, expect more of Mexico than of other drug-producing countries: Mexico will loom large as a supplier of the U.S. drug market and will seem to have more economic and political capability to control its territory and wage the war on drugs than Bolivia or Peru.

However, the simple fact that the United States has large interests in Mexico apart from drugs—interests discussed throughout this book—operates as a check on letting the drug issue drive the entire relationship. By contrast, the Andean drug-producing countries are ones in which tangible U.S. interests apart from narcotics are weak. That makes it especially tempting for Congress and others to vent frustration on those nations, while it means that there are few countervailing interests within officialdom.

Mexico and the United States probably are too important to each other to permit the drug issue to reach a flashpoint, but the mix is explosive—drug production plus easy trafficking routes plus illegal immigration plus the U.S. perception that Mexico, as a relatively strong government, ought to be able to do better. A nasty accident is entirely possible despite the best efforts of both new administrations: suppose more celebrated drug deaths in the United States coincided with fresh murders of U.S. agents and an intense bout of concern over illegal immigrants. Pressure to "close the border" or otherwise punish Mexico might then become irresistible even as doing so remained unwise or impossible.

In the United States, there appear to be cycles of attention to the issue. Mexico has been the recipient of sharp U.S. pressure over drugs in 1939, 1948, 1961, 1969, 1975, and 1985—roughly once during each American administration. Specific events, like the Camarena murder, serve as catalysts: during February and March 1985 the *New York Times* ran a total of 24 news stories on Mexico, 16 of which were about the Camarena case; during the same period the only Mexican news on network television was Camarena news.

Mexican Choices, American Reactions

For its part, the Salinas administration will face three, perhaps four, broad alternatives in drug policy. The first would be continuing previous practice, cooperating with the U.S. antidrug strategy not because it wants to but because, having much larger fish to fry with the United States, it seeks to keep strain over drugs from getting out of hand. This has been the de la Madrid policy; on the surface it would seem the logical line for Salinas.

A second would be to all but abandon the antidrug effort as too costly, of too little value to Mexico, and too "American" to boot. In other Latin American countries signs are already appearing that the drug trade is becoming "politically institutionalized," almost "normal," or "legitimate." This development seems to reflect the simple intractability of the problem and the fact that, for countries in economic crisis, the jobs and profits provided by the narcotics business are not only a fact, they are also a help in a desperate situation.

But there are also signs of a backlash against drug-control policies that have become identified with U.S. pressure, all the more so if strong U.S. pressure is not followed by sustained assistance. Earlier this year, Colombia's attorney general, appointed after his predecessor was gunned down by traffickers, talked publicly of, in effect, suing the drug trade for peace, pardoning traffickers, and perhaps legalizing the traffic in exchange for some guarantees. Four years earlier the Colombian president had met with representatives of the Medellín cartel, eventually refusing the cartel's offer to pay off US$10 billion in Colombian foreign debt in return for amnesty.

Such a Mexican course seems improbable, but it might ensue if the new Mexican administration sought to move in a more nationalist direction to solidify its political coalition, or if domestic events pressed it in that direction. If it did, its hand would be much stronger than Colombia's, but the elements of an implicit deal might be similar: a relatively free hand for cocaine traffickers provided they kept the drug out of Mexico, coupled with reduced eradication of marijuana crops, especially those grown by small farmers. Needless to say, in pursuing this course Mexico would run the risk of a serious reaction from the United States.

A third alternative, also improbable, might result if the trafficking organizations, including the Medellín cocaine cartel, again approached the concentration of power they had in the 1970s. Then, destroying them would be more likely than cutting an implicit deal with them, and Mexico might become then a strong, if unintentional, supporter of American drug policies.

The fourth alternative lies between these two extremes. It would mean, as del Villar suggests, retargeting the effort in a way that better suited Mexican interests—for instance, away from eradicating marijuana and toward efforts to disrupt trafficking networks, especially for heroin. It would reflect judgments that eradicating marijuana is too costly and too inviting of corruption; that cocaine transiting is not yet a serious problem; and that resources would be better spent concentrated on heroin. Marijuana growing would be tolerated so long as the farmers did not move into serious trafficking.

Would Mexico be able to implement such a policy? How would the United States respond if it could? Answers can only be speculative; framing sharper answers is the purpose of project I and several Harvard colleagues are engaged in with a group at El Colegio de México led by Professor del Villar. Much would turn on whether Mexico could offer up a stream of traffickers; if it could, the bursts of good publicity would buy some freedom from American pressure. Since the general political pressure on Mexico, in Congress for instance, is to "do something about drugs," prosecuted traffickers would serve as well as dead marijuana plants, perhaps better.

Beyond that broad political judgment, a host of fine-grain assessments have to be made. For Mexico to attack the trafficking networks, it would need American help, principally from DEA but also from other elements of the balkanized U.S. antidrug machinery. Could it count on that help if it were less involved in eradication? How would Americans react when more Mexican marijuana began appearing on American streets? And so on.

These questions direct attention to the course of politics and governmental action in the United States with regard to the drug issue. So far, for all the noise, American politicians have been eager to denounce the evils of narcotics—and to bash the drug-producing countries—but not to spend much money on the problem. That ambivalence has been matched by the conflicting stakes of American government agencies: contrast DEA with, for instance, the general distaste of most of the State Department for the drug issue lest it disrupt other, more traditional diplomatic business (one recent ambassador to Mexico, John Gavin, was a prominent exception, but he was a political appointee, not a careerist); or of the Defense Department, which has resisted patrolling the border for drug purposes as not *its* mission.

If this year's relative good news about cocaine use becomes a trend, however modest, the temperature of the issue in the United States will drop. It may become clearer that there are no definitive battles in the war on drugs, that demand is key and the lead times are long. That perspective is not likely to take hold completely, and so temptations to lash out in frustration at Mexico and other drug producers will remain. But they should be more manageable.

Over the longer term, the cast of the issue should change. It has not yet; there are at most hints. For instance, as marijuana consumption has levelled off, tolerance for it—now the lesser of the drug evils—seems to have increased somewhat. Personal possession of marijuana has been decriminalized in 10 U.S. states and is legal in Alaska. Young people reflect a different attitude toward it than other drugs: nearly a quarter of 12–17 year-olds in 1985 were estimated to have tried marijuana, while less than one-twentieth had tried cocaine.[12] There has been no change over time in the percentage that has tried heroin (1%–2%). Yet despite decriminalization, there are some 400,000 marijuana-related arrests each year in the United States.

In framing policy toward alcohol a half century ago, the United States explicitly separated the problem of abuse from the crime and corruption that result from illegality; the costs of prohibition in the coin of the latter were judged too high even by comparison to reductions in both alcohol use and abuse. To be sure, legalizing any illicit drug is not an option to be addressed casually. But it seems time to ask whether the costs of prohibitionist policies with regard to drugs outstrip the benefits.

The issue is never posed this way in the United States, in part because drug use is regarded as simply wrong. Yet it is also true that the costs of current policies—violence and corruption—fall most heavily on the Latin American countries, Mexico in particular, even as they infect the United States as well.

Notes

1. John E. Rielly, editor, *American Public Opinion and U.S. Foreign Policy 1987*, Chicago Council on Foreign Relations, Chicago, 1987, p. 9.

2. *New York Times*, March 15, 1987.

3. As quoted in the *New York Times*, August 5, 1986.

4. See, for instance, the series on the Colombian cartel in the *Miami Herald*, beginning November 29, 1987.

5. *International Narcotics Control Strategy Report*, Washington, D.C., March 1987, p. 31. Everyone involved in the narcotics problem is keenly aware of the unreliability of statistics, the gathering of which is hard in principle (given that the trade is illegal), hard in fact, plus political and dangerous to boot. Readers should thus surround any numbers with large bounds indicating the uncertainties involved.

6. National Drug Policy Board, *Federal Drug Enforcement Progress Report, 1986*, Washington, D.C., 1987, p. 104.

7. High School Senior Surveys.

8. For a survey of findings on these issues, see *Preventing Adolescent Drug Abuse: Intervention Strategies*, National Institute for Drug Abuse Monograph 47, Washington, D.C. 1985.

9. B.R. Flay and others, "Are Social-Psychological Smoking Prevention Programs Effective?: The Waterloo Study," *Journal of Behavior Medicine*, 8, 1, 1985, p. 37–59.

10. As quoted in the *New York Times*, October 20, 1986.

11. Peter Reuter and Mark Kleiman, "Risks and Prices: An Economic Analysis of Drug Enforcement," *Crimes and Justice*, July 1986, p. 293.

12. National Institute for Drug Abuse, *National Household Survey on Drug Abuse*, Washington, D.C., 1985.

13

Interdependence and U.S. Policy Toward Mexico in the 1980s

Bruce Michael Bagley

In mid-1988, seven and a half years after President Reagan took office with the explicit objective of restoring American leadership in Latin America, U.S. relations with the region are in shambles. U.S.-Mexican relations provide a revealing case study of what has gone awry. This chapter analyzes the evolution of U.S.-Mexican relations during the 1980s in an effort to explain why bilateral relations between Washington and Mexico City have deteriorated so dramatically during the Reagan administration, and to clarify the key points of tension that the next U.S. president will inherit when he takes office in January 1989.

The Waning of the "Special" Relationship: 1945–1980

From 1945 through the early 1970s, U.S.-Mexican relations were essentially stable and relatively free of conflict. Indeed, the so-called "special relationship" or tacit alliance between the two nations was taken for granted by Washington; and U.S. policymakers, as a rule, devoted scant time, energy, or resources to Mexican affairs.[1] There were, of course, continuing points of friction throughout this period. Illegal Mexican immigration to the United States, for example, cropped up sporadically as an issue on the bilateral agenda. Mexico's refusal to go along with the U.S.-inspired economic embargo of the Castro regime or to sever diplomatic ties with Cuba in the early 1960s provoked considerable exasperation in Washington. Mexico's unwillingness to enter into a bilateral trade agreement and its consistent refusal to join the General Agreement on Tariffs and Trade (GATT) were perennial irritants as well. Despite such frictions, however, the basic elements of the relationship—most importantly, tacit Mexican recognition of its position as a subordinate power within the sphere of influence of its dominant or hegemonic neighbor to the north—went largely unchallenged. Conservative President Gustavo Díaz Ordaz (1964–1970), a pro-American hardliner was especially interested in cultivating a close relationship with Washington.

In the early 1970s, Mexico's tacit acceptance of U.S. leadership in many issue areas began to change. Mexico's meteoric rise as a producer and exporter of drugs (marijuana and heroin) to the United States prompted the Nixon administration in 1969 to take unilateral action against Mexico along the border (Project Intercept). This project disrupted bilateral trade and tourism, did serious damage to the Mexican economy and, in the process, reawakened deep-seated nationalist resentments and anti-American sentiments among both Mexican political elites and the population at large. Indeed, at least symbolically, Project Intercept marked an important turning point in the evolution of U.S.-Mexican bilateral relations, for it brought many Mexican leaders to the conclusion that Mexico could not count on the United States for favorable treatment: in effect, there was nothing "special" about U.S.-Mexican relations. The anti-U.S. Third-World-oriented foreign policy rhetoric of the Echeverría administration (1970–1976), its 1973 controls on foreign capital, and its publicly stated goal of diversifying the country's economic relationships in order to reduce Mexican dependence on the United States, along with the country's economic collapse at the end of Echeverría's term, further exacerbated bilateral frictions. So did the nationalist economic position on natural gas exports and the pro-Sandinista, anti-U.S. Central American stance adopted by Echeverría's successor, President José López Portillo (1976–1982), in the late 1970s.[2]

Despite unmistakable signs of rising bilateral tensions, however, as of 1980 most U.S. policymakers still viewed Mexico as essentially friendly, cooperative, and subordinate. In the wake of the 1979 oil shock, forging closer U.S. ties with oil-rich Mexico surfaced as a priority issue for U.S. political leaders across the party and ideological spectrum. Indeed, during the 1980 presidential campaign, both Republican candidate Ronald Reagan and Democrat Jerry Brown proposed the creation of a North American Common Market (involving the United States, Canada, and Mexico).[3]

From Tacit Alliance to Mutual Distrust:
1980–1988

Such U.S. proposals implicitly assumed that Mexico's leaders would readily, even enthusiastically, embrace accelerated economic integration with the United States. In fact, President López Portillo and his advisors regarded this strategy as a trap; they feared that participation in a formal common market arrangement would deepen Mexican dependency on the United States, drastically reduce Mexican economic policy autonomy, and condemn Mexico to the role of a primary product exporter to its giant industrial neighbor to the north. Instead, López Portillo proposed a more autonomous path for Mexican economic development. He rejected Mexico's entry into GATT, refused to negotiate a new bilateral trade pact with Washington, and sought to use his country's new found hydrocarbon reserves to borrow capital from abroad and to negotiate favorable trading arrangements for Mexico, while continuing the nationalist and protectionist economic growth strategy that had been adopted by his predecessors. These economic policies, in combination with his administration's increasingly assertive foreign policy stance in Central America, generated frictions with the Carter administration during 1979–1980 and infuriated the new Reagan government during 1981 and 1982. The rapid deterioration and ultimate collapse of the Mexican economy in mid-1982, López Portillo's decision to nationalize the Mexican banking system on September 1, 1982, and his stubborn refusal to sign off on an International Monetary Fund (IMF) stabilization package during his final six months in office further inflamed tensions between Washington and Mexico City.[4]

The formal tone of bilateral relations improved noticeably during the first two years of the Miguel de la Madrid government (1982–1988), a product of the "quiet" diplomacy undertaken on both sides of the border and de la Madrid's strict compliance with the provisions of the IMF austerity program negotiated during his first weeks in office. This improvement soon proved to be rhetorical and cosmetic. In late 1984 and throughout 1985 frictions between the two countries once again rose dramatically as a result of Mexico's relapse into economic crisis; deepening disputes over debt, trade, immigration, and drug trafficking issues; and growing Reaganite resentment of Mexico's "obstructionist" and "counterproductive" Central American policies.[5]

In many ways, 1985 was a watershed in the evolution of the contemporary bilateral relations, for it ushered in a period of public acrimony and criticism unprecedented in the post-World War II period. The abduction and murder of Drug Enforcement Administration (DEA) agent Enrique Camarena in February 1985 effectively catalyzed the venting of five years of intense frustration with Mexico on the part of the Reagan administration.

As early as March 16, 1982, then-Secretary of State Alexander Haig and then-Foreign Minister Jorge Castañeda had pointedly disagreed at a meeting in New York on the issues of U.S. military aid to El Salvador and U.S. support for the Contras in Nicaragua. The National Security Council (NSC) subsequently devised plans to step up U.S. diplomatic pressure on Mexico designed to deter them from maintaining their high-profile, independent foreign policy in Central America. In a secret 1984 presidential directive, President Reagan authorized U.S. officials to "intensify diplomatic efforts with the Mexican government to reduce its material and diplomatic support for the communist guerrillas [in El Salvador] and its economic and diplomatic support for the Nicaraguan government."[6]

The use of direct economic sanctions against Mexico was reportedly proposed in 1984 by an NSC official, Constantine Menges, but ultimately "cooler heads" prevailed and the sanctions were never implemented. Proposals for sinking Mexican oil tankers delivering petroleum to Nicaraguan ports were also apparently considered at this time by members of the NSC staff.[7]

In response to Foreign Minister Bernardo Sepúlveda's blunt criticism of the Reagan administration's hard-line, anti-Sandinista policy in August 1985, a rising star within Reagan's NSC—Colonel Oliver North—authorized a leak to U.S. newspapers in which Mexico was alleged (falsely) to have agreed to a visit by a Soviet naval task force to the Mexican port of Veracruz in October 1985. Reportedly, this leak was to be the "opening salvo" in an "anti-Mexican campaign" in the U.S. media, planned and directed by the NSC; but it was called off after Mexico City suffered a devastating earthquake on September 19, 1985.[8]

The López Portillo government's August 1982 announcement that Mexico was bankrupt and could not pay its foreign debt obligations, and the subsequent inability of the de la Madrid administration to resolve the country's deepening economic turmoil, also fed growing frustration with Mexico in Washington. After some initially hopeful signs of economic recovery in 1983–1984, Mexico's severe economic crisis in late 1985 and early 1986 greatly increased the Reagan administration's sense of U.S. vulnerability vis-à-vis Mexico, and further fueled the feelings of frustration and resentment that had been initially expressed publicly by U.S. officials after the death of Camarena. The rising tide of illegal immigration from Mexico into the United States, exacerbated by Mexico's economic turmoil and the debt crisis, also heightened Washington's sensitivity to Mexico and fed the Reagan administration's conviction that Mexico should be pressured even harder to undertake major internal economic reforms.

In combination with the deepening debt crisis and soaring illegal immigration, the de la Madrid government's resort to, or at least tolerance of, fraudulent electoral practices and political repression to maintain PRI control of state and local governments, especially in the northern sections of the country in 1985 and 1986, heightened concern in U.S. policymaking circles over the PRI's ability to preserve the country's traditional political stability, and thereby, safeguard vital American economic, political, and strategic interests in Mexico. These fears, in turn, focused the Reagan administration's attention on the newly discovered "defects" of the PRI-dominated Mexican political system, and further strengthened convictions in Washington regarding the need to pressure the de la Madrid government more vigorously for internal political reforms and democratization.

Against this backdrop of rising Reagan administration concern with potential economic and political instability in Mexico and the negative consequences for U.S. security interests that might flow from it, the 1985 revelation that DEA agent Camarena had been kidnapped, tortured, and murdered in Mexico by drug-traffickers, "with the assistance of former and present Mexican police officials," precipitated virulent denunciations of Mexico in Washington.[9] Subsequent revelations of widespread drug-related corruption in the upper echelons of the Mexican Interior Ministry and Judicial Police, and the Mexicans' alleged foot-dragging in pursuing Camarena's killers, added to the intensity of this reaction.[10]

Virtually overnight, the Reagan administration shifted from the established pattern of low-profile U.S. diplomatic pressures to a high-profile strategy of public criticisms of Mexico's antiquated, dysfunctional, and corrupt regime. The factors that had set off the alarm bells in Washington were subsequently synthesized in a 72-page CIA report entitled, "Mexico: Growing Challenge to Current Stability." The CIA analysis specifically highlighted the Mexican military's inability to guarantee the power of the PRI or to "quell widespread intense disorders in major Mexican urban areas," especially if combined with unrest and sabotage in the nation's rural areas.[11]

After Camarena: Intensifying U.S. Pressures

Although the Mexico City earthquake derailed some existing NSC plans to pressure the Mexican government on Central America, it did not put an end to U.S. pressures altogether. Reagan's Ambassador to Mexico John Gavin, openly and repeatedly criticized the de la Madrid administration's handling of the earthquake disaster, the government's failure to move more swiftly against those responsible for Camarena's murder, and the slow pace of economic and political reform in the country. He also engaged in conversations with prominent

Panista opposition leaders, much to the dismay of the de la Madrid government and the PRI leadership.

In May 1986, right-wing Republican Senator Jesse Helms scheduled the first of a series of Senate Foreign Relations Committee (Western Hemisphere Subcommittee) hearings on Mexico, at which Assistant Secretary of State Elliot Abrams, U.S. Customs Commissioner William von Raab, and other senior Reagan administration officials publicly voiced harsh U.S. criticisms of Mexican electoral fraud, corruption, and drug-trafficking. Von Raab, for example, denounced "ingrained corruption in the Mexican law enforcement establishment . . . [which is] massive . . . all the way up and down the ladder." In a subsequent hearing in June, Helms himself denounced Mexico's 1982 presidential elections as fraudulent and went so far as to suggest that President de la Madrid should resign.[12] This series of public denunciations has been characterized by at least one observer as "the worst official U.S. criticism of Mexico since 1927, when the Administration of President Calvin Coolidge assailed Mexico for assisting anti-American forces in Nicaragua led by guerrilla leader Augusto Cesar Sandino."[13] Others point to the public diplomatic acrimony that followed President Lazaro Cardenas' 1938 expropriation of U.S. oil companies as perhaps the most appropriate parallel.

Congressional concern with Mexico in 1986 was by no means confined to Jesse Helms and the far right of the Republican Party. The new "Simpson-Rodino" immigration law passed in late 1986 was specifically designed to deter the "silent invasion" of illegal Mexican immigrants into the United States. A number of Democrats also singled out Mexico as a target for protectionist trade legislation during 1986. Senate Resolution 437—a nonbinding sense of the Senate motion—introduced in August 1986 by Senators Dennis Deconcini (D-Arizona) and Pete Wilson (R-California) expressly condemned the fraudulent 1986 elections in the State of Chihuahua and requested President de la Madrid to annul them and to carry through on his earlier promises regarding the "moralization" and "democratization" of the Mexican political system. The anti-drug-trafficking law of 1986 was also directed in part at Mexico, and included specific recommendations to President Reagan for sanctioning Mexico if the de la Madrid government failed to cooperate fully with the U.S. War on Drugs. Finally, during the 1986 electoral campaign in the United States, Senator Wilson requested a stepped-up U.S. military presence on the Mexican border if Mexico failed to act forcefully against illegal immigration and drug-trafficking.[14]

In mid-August, President de la Madrid traveled to Washington to meet with President Reagan. Although U.S. Attorney General Edwin Meese had previously apologized to his Mexican counterpart for von

Raab's undiplomatic remarks, the Mexicans were still smarting from what they viewed as gratuitous and petulant attacks by U.S. officials who had little understanding of Mexico or its problems. The meeting itself went well and seemed to signal a return to cordiality and constructive cooperation between the two countries.[15] Unfortunately, the more positive atmosphere established during this Washington summit was seriously damaged on the final day by the revelation that another U.S. DEA agent, Victor Cortez, had been kidnapped and tortured by drug traffickers in Mexico.

Confirming the PRI's worst "paranoid" suspicions, on August 14, 1986, just a day after President de la Madrid's meeting with President Reagan in Washington, Colonel Oliver North's private Contra aid fund raiser, Carl "Spitz" Channell, approached key PAN leaders with an offer of U.S. backing in return for their help in financing the Contras. While no PAN financial support for the Contras was ultimately provided and Channell was later convicted of tax fraud, the Mexicans "concluded that the Reagan Administration had started a campaign against Mexico in reprisal for . . . positions on Central America."[16]

In the wake of the Iran-Contra revelations in late 1986 and early 1987, U.S. pressures on Mexico diminished considerably. Nonetheless, in January 1988, after an interlude of almost one year of relative diplomatic calm, tensions between the United States and Mexico once again appeared on the rise after the U.S. government obtained indictments against three former Mexican military officials for their alleged involvement in drug-trafficking. This indictment coincided with the release of a U.S. General Accounting Office report sharply critical of Mexico's drug eradication program and was accompanied by a State Department statement that no additional U.S. funds for Mexico's drug program would be requested until an evaluation of the effectiveness of the Mexican effort had been completed. In April 1988, the Senate voted overwhelmingly to "decertify" Mexico for its failure to cooperate fully with the United States, in spite of the Reagan administration's objections that such action would needlessly inflame bilateral relations and might well reduce Mexico's willingness to cooperate in the future.[17]

Explaining the Tensions

Some Mexicans argue that the principal reason for the outpouring of U.S. criticism against Mexico in recent years is attributable primarily to the Reagan administration's desire to "punish" Mexico for its independent, anti-Reagan stance in Central America. Others attribute it primarily to Reagan's conservative ideological rejection of Mexico's statist economic policies and interpret such attacks as part of a concerted

U.S. campaign to force Mexico to reorient its economy along market lines more acceptable to Washington.

While both positions undoubtedly contain elements of truth, neither completely captures the depth and breadth of current policy concern about Mexico in Washington. Over the course of the 1980s U.S. policymakers have, by force of circumstance, become increasingly cognizant of the intensifying interdependence that characterizes relations between the two countries. In the context of Mexico's serious economic and political woes, however, this realization has not been a cause for celebration in Washington. At least since 1985, Reagan officials have increasingly tended to focus on the potential risks inherent in deepening U.S.-Mexican integration rather than on the potential benefits that may derive from it.

At the economic level, the Reagan government has become convinced that the statist Mexican economy is so riddled with problems, distortions, and inefficiencies, and so dependent on U.S. concessions and bailouts, that it constitutes a serious potential threat to the economic health of the United States. Their conclusion is that the United States can no longer afford to indulge Mexican revolutionary rhetoric and nationalist sensibilities or defer to Mexican sacred cows. Rather, it must seek to defend U.S. interests by pressuring Mexico into a structural transformation of its badly debilitated economy—decentralization, privatization, elimination of subsidies, greater reliance on market mechanisms—even if such reforms prove politically disruptive to the "peace of the PRI."

At the political level, there is a widespread, bipartisan consensus in U.S. policymaking circles that the Mexican political elite is largely responsible for its own problems. Whatever virtues it may have possessed in the past, today the Mexican system is seen to be inflexible, poorly governed, corrupt, indifferent to illegal immigration, and tolerant of drug-trafficking. In short, the political regime constructed by the PRI during the last sixty years has become dysfunctional and must be reformed and democratized if it is to remain stable. U.S. national interests demand, therefore, that Washington apply pressure to the Mexican leadership in order to encourage the necessary reforms.

At the foreign policy level, the Reagan administration believes that the Mexican government has failed to understand that its pro-Sandinista, pro-Contadora policies in Central America put Mexico itself at risk. As President Reagan has repeatedly stated, he views Mexico as the final Central American "domino": If the Sandinistas, backed by their Soviet and Cuban mentors, are allowed to consolidate their revolution, Mexico would be vulnerable to external subversion from the South. Thus, despite Mexico's public opposition to Washington's

Central American policies, Reagan administration officials have felt completely justified in undertaking both covert and overt measures to undercut, derail, or otherwise neutralize Mexico's "wrongheaded" approach to the Central American conflicts and especially the Sandinista "problem" in Nicaragua.

Assessing U.S. Pressure Tactics

Have Washington's pressure tactics paid off from the Reagan administration's point of view? On the economic front, during its first five years in office the de la Madrid government undeniably set in motion new economic policies oriented toward liberalizing the nation's trade regime, creating a more favorable climate for foreign investment, introducing market mechanisms, eliminating subsidies, and reducing the role of the state in the productive sectors of the economy. For example, after years of obdurate Mexican resistance, in 1986 President de la Madrid signed off on Mexico's entry into GATT, signaling his government's determination to move away from the country's traditional protectionist development strategy. In October 1987, Presidents Reagan and de la Madrid announced that they had reached an agreement on an unprecedented bilateral trade pact designed to facilitate a substantial reduction in trade and investment barriers between the two countries. The agreement also set up a mechanism for settling trade disputes, although it does not include provisions for binding arbitration as does the more comprehensive U.S.-Canadian Free Trade Pact.[18]

Under de la Madrid, Mexico has also sold off or closed down a wide variety of unproductive state enterprises (such as the gigantic Fundidora de Monterrey steelworks). It has adopted a far more flexible attitude on foreign direct investment than in the past, as exemplified in the decision to allow IBM 100% ownership of its new personal computer plant in Mexico and in the encouragement it has given to the booming in-bond or *maquiladora* industries along the Mexican border.[19]

Mexico has also proven to be a reliable source of key raw materials imports for the United States, especially petroleum and natural gas, despite contrary indications during the López Portillo years. Finally, Mexico has for years been viewed by international bankers as an "exemplary" debtor that has consistently eschewed confrontational rhetoric and actions despite the country's severe debt service burden of approximately US$ 10 billion annually.[20]

In sum, the Reagan administration's hard-line tactics vis-à-vis Mexico in recent years appear to have resulted in major (some might say

radical) economic policy reforms quite consistent with the changes
advocated by U.S. policymakers. Thus, from Reagan's perspective,
Washington's policies toward Mexico have contributed to economic
reforms of great potential importance which, early in the next century,
could lead to the establishment of a North American Common Market
along the lines envisioned by President Reagan in 1980–1981.[21]

Of course, not even the most enthusiastic Reaganite would argue
that U.S. pressures have been the only factor involved in bringing
about these changes. The country's serious economic problems have
convinced important segments of Mexico's economic and political elites
of the need to pursue new policies and models quite independently
of any U.S. advice or pressure. Nonetheless, Reaganites both inside
and outside the government clearly believe that Washington's tactics
have led the Mexican leadership to move more rapidly on these reforms
they otherwise would have.

Mexico's positive economic showing in 1986–1987 adds some empirical weight to this upbeat evaluation. Industrial exports, for example,
grew by 35% in 1986 and by an additional 57% in the first seven
months on 1987. Boosted by these export figures and a gradual upturn
in petroleum revenues, the country registered a US$9.5 billion trade
merchandise surplus in 1987, its third highest ever, and financial
reserves rose to a substantial US$15 billion.[22]

There are, however, many observers who point out that optimistic
conclusions about the real effects of de la Madrid's economic reforms
on the still troubled Mexican economy are at best premature and
possibly seriously incorrect. Bailey and Watkins for example, note that
much of Mexico's economic improvement in 1987 was ephemeral,
achieved at the cost of lower real growth. In 1987 "real economic
growth was declining by 1.5 percent, manufacturing production was
falling by 2.1 percent, and gross fixed investment was down by close
to 10 percent. More ominously the budget deficit seemed stuck at
close to 15 percent of gross domestic product, inflation was nearing
an annual rate of 150 percent—also the highest level in recent history—
and real wages in the first half of 1987 were 9 percent lower than
in 1986 and 50 percent below their 1976 level."[23] If pessimistic
conclusions about Mexico's medium and long-term economic prospects
are, in fact, still warranted, whatever short-term successes Reagan
administration officials might claim for their overall strategy toward
Mexico (and by extension for the effectiveness of specific pressure
tactics they have used) will amount at best to a pyrrhic victory. At
worst, such tactics might ultimately catalyze intense nationalist and
anti-American sentiments in Mexico that would lead the Mexican
leadership to slow or abandon their current reform efforts, or even

to adopt unilateral economic decisions (e.g., a moratorium on debt service payments) directly at odds with U.S. preferences.

The U.S. push for domestic political reforms and more rapid democratization within Mexico have certainly not met with the same degree of success, no matter what criteria of evaluation are employed. In fact, they may have been counterproductive, fueling a negative, nationalistic backlash among the leadership of the PRI that has inhibited rather than prompted political liberalization. De la Madrid has not acted forcefully or effectively against endemic corruption within the PRI and the government, despite his campaign promises and some tentative efforts during the 1983 state and municipal elections. Electoral fraud, media manipulation, and official intimidation, directed especially against PAN candidates, the Democratic Current (Corriente Democrática) opposition movement, and elements of the conservative Catholic Church hierarchy have continued and even intensified in Mexico throughout his term in office. In addition, the PRI leadership publicly rejected calls for internal "democratization," "renovation," and "popular consultation" presented by dissidents from the Democratic Current, led by Cuauhtemoc Cardenas and Porfirio Muñoz Ledo, during its March 1987 Party Congress. In the words of PRI President Jorge de la Vega: "we will not tolerate the invoking of democracy, which we practice, to reverse our party activity," or to "undermine our cohesion and structure,"[24] Rather than yielding to these or other proposals for reform, the party leadership quickly moved to further curb internal dissent by expelling for all practical purposes the dissidents from the party ranks. "From now on, all those who do not want to respect the will of the immense majority of party members should renounce our party."[25]

At least in the short term, high profile U.S. criticism of the Mexican political system, its leadership, and its internal procedures, have not only been ineffective in stimulating internal change, they have backfired by generating a siege-like mentality among the top PRI leadership. They have also provided the Mexican elite with the opportunity to decry U.S. interventionism and to rally PRI activists and a substantial sector of public opinion around the banners of Mexican nationalism and sovereignty, thereby undermining the legitimacy of the most pro-American segments of the opposition, and reinforcing the political status quo rather than encouraging internal reform.[26]

In contrast to the economic side of the ledger, where at least some short-term results are in evidence, in the political arena the Reagan Administration's pressure tactics, at least to date, must be judged as disappointing. Moreover, as of mid-1988 there is little reason to believe that U.S. persistence in harsh public criticism of the "defects" of the

Mexican political regime will prove any more effective over the next three years than it has been over the last three. Indeed, a plausible argument can be made that such tactics could seriously damage the cause of domestic reform by further narrowing the political space for internal dissidence within the PRI and for opposition party activity outside it.

The results of covert and overt Reagan administration pressures in curtailing Mexican foreign policy independence and assertiveness in Central America and elsewhere have been mixed and are more difficult to evaluate. On the one hand, the de la Madrid government has unquestionably lowered Mexico's previous high profile in Central America, distanced itself somewhat from the Sandinistas in Nicaragua and moved to reestablish working relations with the Duarte government in El Salvador. For the Reagan White House, these policy outcomes are clearly on the plus side of the ledger. On the other hand, President de la Madrid never abandoned the Sandinistas altogether, despite U.S. pressures; his government remained active in Contadora, despite U.S. criticisms of the regional peace process; and his administration endorsed the Arias Peace Plan (Esquipulas II), despite President Reagan's open denunciation of it as "fatally flawed" and White House insistence on the need for additional funding for the Contras from the U.S. Congress. Furthermore, although Mexico is now less active and influential in Central America than it was at the outset of the de la Madrid term in office, in November 1987 the Mexican government joined with other Latin American countries (the Group of Eight) to reaffirm their collective support for peace negotiations in Central America. Moreover, the Group of Eight presented united positions on other issues beyond Central America that may well engender considerable friction in their relations with the United States in the future. For example, they demanded major concessions from the international community in the area of debt relief, despite Washington resistance to such radical steps.

In sum, Mexico has unquestionably found its relative autonomy in hemispheric affairs increasingly constrained in recent years by the combination of economic crisis, regime legitimacy problems, and U.S. pressures. But it has not been sidelined entirely, nor has it been obliged to "knuckle under" to the Reagan administration in all issue areas. In fact, the results of the Group of Eight meeting suggest that Mexico and the other participating countries—Argentina, Brazil, Uruguay, Colombia, Venezuela, Panama, and Peru—may be moving to develop collective foreign policy positions in order to limit their vulnerability to U.S. pressures and to increase their collective bargaining power in issues such as debt, trade, and external credits. Their pledge to work together to overhaul the almost moribund Organization of American States (OAS), their proposals to reform the institutional structure of the Inter-American system (e.g., the OAS, the IDB, the Rio Treaty), and their collective invitation to Cuba to rejoin the Latin diplomatic community, for example, should be seen as symbolic gestures intended to encourage greater Latin American solidarity and, thus, to enhance their collective bargaining power vis-à-vis the United States.[27]

The decision to convene a Group of Eight summit yearly and to institutionalize a "mechanism for mutual consultations" from which the United States was explicitly excluded reflect the widespread distrust and resentment toward Washington found among Latin American governments. The announcement of their collective intention to seek interest rate limits, to press for changes in IMF policies toward debtor nations, to "sever links" between IMF and commercial bank loans, and to demand the opportunity to purchase their public foreign debts at the real (discounted) market value, may presage the formation of an informal debtor's cartel down the road—an eventuality that the Reagan administration has labored long and hard to forestall. Some observers speculate that if at least some of the Group of Eight's demands are not met in 1988, the Group may collectively opt to place a limit or cap on foreign debt interest payments during their next meeting scheduled for late 1988.[28]

Despite intimations of possible confrontation between the Group of Eight countries and the United States, especially on economic issues, it is important to note that several Latin diplomats in attendance went to considerable lengths in their public statements to underscore the moderate tone of the document and to squash speculations that it was intended as a direct criticism of the United States: "It has no specific address, only the intention of addressing concerns that interest us as a whole."[29]

Even if joint action does not materialize, the possibility that the next Mexican president (who will take office on December 1, 1988) might choose to act unilaterally if Mexico's economic plight continues to worsen over 1988, cannot be dismissed out of hand. The new president is almost certain to be the PRI candidate Carlos Salinas de Gortari, the principal architect of de la Madrid's current economic strategy. In a January 1988 interview with *New York Times* correspondent Larry Rohter (the first with a non-Mexican publication since his designation as the PRI presidential candidate for the July 1988 elections), Salinas de Gortari urged the United States to adopt a more "dignified and realistic relationship with Mexico."[30] When asked "if he could envision Mexico's shifting its general conciliatory tone on repayment of its foreign debt, he replied, 'What is considered impossible today may be possible tomorrow.'" In other words, he explicitly tied future Mexican servicing of its foreign debt to the country's continued economic growth: "Mexico will pay if it can grow."[31]

Slow global economic growth or a recession in 1989 or 1990 would be the most likely circumstances in which such a decision might be taken in Mexico City. Even in the absence of any dramatic Mexican action, the potential for increasing friction between Mexico City and Washington over the debt issue during the next year or two appears very high. Moreover, it would appear all but inevitable that the tensions and frictions generated over the debt problem will spill over into and make more contentious the management of other aspects of the bilateral relationship as well.

Inconsistencies and Contradictions
in U.S. Policy Toward Mexico

Although the Reagan administration claims that its policies toward Mexico have been both coherent and effective, any minimally objective evaluation cannot avoid uncovering a number of inconsistencies and contradictions that place such claims in very serious doubt. First, Washington has pushed hard for the Mexican leadership to implement radical changes in the country's political economy that make David Stockman's relatively modest (and by his own account unsuccessful) efforts to rationalize U.S. federal economic policy pale in comparison.[32] In comparative context, the Reagan administration's expectations regarding what Mexican policymakers can and should do, and how fast it should be done, are simply unrealistic. As such, they are bound to generate disappointment and frustration in Washington and continuing tension in the bilateral relationship.

Second, despite the severe constraints within which he has had to operate, President de la Madrid has managed to telescope into the last five years dramatic changes that under other circumstances might have taken decades to introduce into Mexico. In effect, President de la Madrid has pursued economic policies essentially consistent with those advocated by the Reagan administration at considerable sacrifice to his own presidency and his party's popularity, while at the same time he has been subjected to sharp public criticism of his government from Reagan officials on the issues of drugs, electoral fraud, political corruption, and so on. The point is not that President de la Madrid or the PRI-government elite should be exempt from official U.S. criticism, but rather that such criticisms have contributed to weakening

President de la Madrid and thus his capacity to implement the very economic reform policies advocated by the United States.

Third, U.S. policymakers, both in congress and the executive, are often oblivious to, or unmoved by, the impact that American economic policies have on the Mexican economy and its prospects for long-term recovery. Skyrocketing interest rates in the United States during the early 1980s were undoubtedly an important factor in precipitating Mexico's 1982 economic collapse; the fact that they remained at historically high levels during much of the decade obviously complicated the country's efforts to stem capital flight, to service its burgeoning foreign debt, or to reactivate the economy. In the same vein, the Reagan administration's myopic refusal to recognize the severity of Mexico's (and the rest of Latin America's) debt crisis and its failure between 1982 and 1985 to assume any real leadership role in the search for solutions to the debt problem—a situation only partially rectified by the announcement of the so-called "Baker Plan" in October 1985—further exacerbated Mexico's intractable economic difficulties.[33]

Tacitly recognizing the insufficiency of its earlier policies, including the Baker Plan, on December 30, 1987, the Reagan Administration announced its support of the "Morgan" Plan for addressing the Mexican debt problem. Although this innovative mechanism may provide some help, most observers agree that it is no panacea and that much more comprehensive programs of debt relief for Mexico and other major Latin debtors will almost certainly be necessary.[34]

The U.S. Congress has also had a hand in complicating Mexico's economic recovery during the decade—whether out of ignorance, the intention to "punish," or simply a lack of concern is often hard to determine and largely irrelevant. The United States is Mexico's principal market, absorbing some 60% of all Mexico's exports. After petroleum, the two most important Mexican exports to the United States are textiles and steel; others include automobile parts, shoes, and agricultural products. All these key nonpetroleum exports are highly sensitive to U.S. trade restrictions and yet they are precisely the kinds of products that the U.S. Congress has been most likely to protect from foreign competition. As a result, Mexico has consistently been disadvantaged by congressional protectionist measures, even when such legislation is not directed primarily at Mexico but rather at third countries such as those in the Far East.

Some progress toward ameliorating these trade barriers has recently been made with the signing of a new U.S.-Mexican trade pact, particularly in the areas of steel, textile, and apparel exports. Nonetheless, in the absence of an even broader agreement along the lines of the

U.S.-Canadian pact, U.S. protectionism will remain a potential source of considerable hardship for Mexico.

The apparent inability (or unwillingness) of the U.S. government to rein in its own huge fiscal deficits, along with America's enormous trade deficits and the attendant weakness of the U.S. dollar, the instability in international currency markets, and the volatility in stock and commodity markets, do not bode well for continued economic growth in 1989. If the U.S. and world economies slow dramatically or plunge into recession, Mexico's economic problems will literally become unmanageable. Moreover, in a recessionary environment Mexico's *maquiladora* border program (in 1987 its second most important source of foreign exchange) will almost certainly become a target for hard-pressed U.S. labor and the subject of protectionist legislation in congress.[35]

Protectionist pressures may also emanate from U.S. businessmen, for example, catalyzed by rising concern about the growing use of Mexico's in-bond program by Japan and other Far East countries as a platform for exports into the U.S. market. Although presently at modest levels (1% to 2% of the approximately US$1.4 billion of *maquila* exports to the United States in 1986),[36] both Mexican and foreign experts predict that substantial increases are possible in a broad range of manufactured exports (e.g., chemicals, plastics, glass products, medical instruments, automobile parts). The potential for increased tensions and punitive protectionist legislation will grow exponentially in the event of an economic slowdown or recession north of the border.

Conclusion

The central conclusion that emerges from this short list of inconsistencies and contradictions in U.S. policy toward Mexico is that prospects for lowering tensions in the bilateral relation are slight to nonexistent. It is conceivable that formal diplomatic relations may improve, as they did during the better part of 1987. But Mexico's highly negative image, fostered by harsh official criticism in recent years, will continue to mar U.S.-Mexican relations for some time. Intense U.S. media scrutiny of Mexico's upcoming 1988 elections has the potential to add further to Mexico's growing "black legend" in the United States and abroad, especially if the PRI indulges once again in thinly veiled electoral fraud and the traditional end-of-office corruption. Debt problems, recession, economic nationalism, trade disputes, illegal immigration, drug trafficking, Central America, and a host of other frictions and problem areas will almost certainly help to keep the heat in the relationship up at maximum levels. Finally, the growing involvement of the U.S. Congress in the conduct of American foreign policy toward Mexico is likely to add to the sound and the fury of both sides of the border, no matter how legitimate such involvement may be.

The bottom line is that deepening interdependence in the 1980s has significantly expanded the range of issues that now appear on the bilateral agenda. U.S.-Mexican relations are no longer, if they ever truly were, the sole province of the executive branch foreign policy bureaucracy. Events in Mexico impact directly on a wide variety of domestic interests and actors, and, therefore, have become inextricably intertwined with domestic U.S. politics and policies.

As a result, whether they like it or not, the Mexicans now find that rather than being ignored or taken for granted by the United States as was traditionally the case, their country has become a hot issue in U.S. politics. Given the messiness of American politics and policymaking, the Mexican leadership will inevitably be discomfited and at times greatly displeased by this intensified attention. Nevertheless, heightened U.S. awareness of Mexico would appear to be one of the unavoidable costs of the growing interconnections between the two societies.

Perhaps the most important lesson to be gleaned from de la Madrid's often painful relationship with the United States during the last five years is that the root causes of the frictions and tensions between these two neighbors are structural—the result of basic conflicts of interest—rather than the conjunctural product of particular personalities or the ideological inclinations of any given president or administration. Indeed, many of the most difficult issues on the bilateral agenda are simply too complex and too deeply imbedded in domestic political struggles to be resolved by presidential initiatives alone, whether they emerge from liberals or conservatives, north or south of the border. The key challenge for both countries is not to avoid conflict altogether, an impossible task, but rather to find ways to manage more effectively the tensions and frictions that will inevitably arise as the intricate patterns of contemporary U.S.-Mexican asymmetrical interdependence become more complex in the 1990s.

Notes

1. For a review of U.S.-Mexican relations in the post-World War II period, see Josefina Zoraioa Vazquez and Lorenzo Meyer, *The United States and Mexico,* The University of Chicago Press, Chicago, 1986.

2. On U.S.-Mexican relations during the Echeverría *sexenio,* see Yorum Shapira, *Mexican Foreign Policy Under Echeverría,* Sage Publications, the Washington Papers, No. 56, Beverly Hills, 1976.

3. In an August 1981 report to Congress, President Reagan was forced to abandon this project (at least with regard to Mexico), "because of economic and philosophical differences." See Alfonso Chardy, "The Case of Mexico: From the Alliance, to Pressure, to Distrust," *The Miami Herald,* December 27, 1987.

4. On the conflicts between the United States and Mexico during the López Portillo *sexenio,* see Bruce M. Bagley, "The Politics of Asymmetrical Interdependence: U.S.-Mexican Relations in the 1980s," in H. Michael Erisnor, editor, *The Caribbean Challenge: U.S. Policy in a Volatile Region,* Westview Press, Boulder, 1984.

5. Bruce M. Bagley, *Mexico in Crisis: The Parameters of Accommodation,* Foreign Policy Briefs, Foreign Policy Institute, SAIS Johns Hopkins University, Washington, D.C., 1986.

6. Chardy, *op. cit.,* p. 14A.

7. *Ibid.*

8. *Ibid.*

9. See William Branigin, "Mexican Antidrug Campaign Failing to Stem Flow in U.S.," in *Washington Post,* August 1987, p. A11.

10. After initially responding defensively to the uproar in Washington over the murder, during the next two years Mexican officials did move to "clean house." By mid-1987, 67 people had been jailed in connection with the killing. In addition, the Mexican government had fired more than 500 agents of the Federal Security Directorate, an intelligence agency under the Interior Ministry, and 300 members of the Federal Judicial Police, and both institutions were reorganized. In Sinaloa, where the smuggling ring was headquartered, F. Labastido, who assumed the governorship in January 1987, dismissed the Chief of State Police, fired more than 100 state policemen, and had the local military commander reassigned. Branigin, *ibid,* p. A11.

11. J. Anderson and D. Van Atta, "CIA: Disorder Could Overwhelm Mexico," *Washington Post,* June 5, 1987, p. E5.

12. The von Raab quote is from Chardy, *op. cit.,* p. 14A. For a Mexican view of these hearings, see J. Gonzalez et al., "El Impacto de las audiencias Helms en la relación bilateral," *Carta de Política Exterior Mexicana,* vol. VI, no. 2, April-June, 1986.

13. Chardy, *op. cit.,* p. 14A.

14. Wayne A. Cornelius, "Mexico/EU: Las Fuentes del Pleito," *Nexos,* no. 118, October 1987.

15. Juan Gonzalez, "El Viaje de de la Madrid a Washington," *Carta de Política Exterior Mexicana,* vol. VI, no. 3, July-September, 1986.

16. Chardy, *op. cit.,* p. 14.

17. Larry Rohter, "Tension in Drug Trade," *New York Times,* January 17, 1988.

18. Clyde H. Farnsworth, "Mexico easing U.S. Trade Policies," *New York Times,* January 11, 1988.

19. As of year end 1987, there were almost 1,000 *maquiladora* plants along the U.S.-Mexican border. American firms have invested some US$ 2 billion in these operations over the last decade. They currently employ 310,000 Mexicans. The U.S. Department of Commerce has estimated that by 1995 the *maquiladora* program could employ over one million Mexican workers and U.S. imports of *maquila* products could reach US$25 billion annually. (See Jim Kolbe, "Factories on the Border: Made in Mexico, Good for the USA," *New York Times*, December 13, 1987.

20. Larry Rohter, "Mexico's Hard Economic Struggle," *New York Times*, December 16, 1987.

21. Clyde H. Farnsworth, *op. cit.*

22. Norman A. Bailey and Alfred Watkins, *New York Times*, December 29, 1987.

23. *Ibid.*, p. 24y.

24. William Branigin, "Mexico's Party Curtails Dissent," *Washington Post*, March 9, 1987, p. A16.

25. *Ibid.*

26. On the problems of internal political and party reform, see Susan Kaufman Purcell, "The Prospects for Political Change in Mexico," Paper prepared for a Conference on "U.S. Interest in Mexico: Agenda for the Next Decade," August 21–22, 1986, Washington, D.C.; John Bailey, "What Explains the Decline of the PRI and Will it Continue?" in Roderic A. Camp, editor, *Mexico's Political Stability: The Next Five Years*, Westview Press, Boulder, 1986.

27. Andres Oppenheimer, "Eight Latin Presidents Vow to Try to Modify the OAS," *Miami Herald*, November 30, 1987.

28. *Ibid.*

29. Larry Rohter, "Latin Chiefs Urge Overhaul of Debt and of OAS Too," *New York Times*, November 30, 1987, p. 9y.

30. Larry Rohter, "Mexican Candidate Ties Debt Service to Economy," *New York Times*, January 18, 1988, p. 6y.

31. *Ibid.*

32. The Stockman analogy is drawn from a presentation made by Wayne Cornelius on "The Changing Terms of U.S.-Mexican Relations," at the 1987–1988 Conference of the SSRC-MacArthur Foundation Fellows in International Peace and Security at the Hotel Hacienda Cocoyoc, Morelos, Mexico, January 9–13, 1988.

33. Albert Fishlow, "Coming to Terms with the Latin Debt," *New York Times*, January 4, 1988.

34. For details of the Morgan Plan, see Peter Truell and Alan Murray, "Debt Breakthrough: Loan Plan May Help Mexico, Some Banks; But It's No Panacea," *Wall Street Journal*, December 30, 1987.

35. For a preview of the types of antimaquila arguments likely to be advanced, see John LaFalce, "*Maquiladora's* Cost American Jobs," *New York Times*, December 13, 1987.

36. Larry Rohter, "Mexican Non-Oil Exports Jump," *New York Times*, February 23, 1987.

14

Nondependence as an Alternative Foreign Policy for Mexico

José Juan de Olloqui

Mexico has inherited the legacy of several great civilizations. Two of the three main prehispanic cultures flourished on its soil; for more than two centuries it was the most important colony of the Spanish Empire; and when it gained independence, Simon Bolivar recognized its status as first among equals by suggesting that the center of his confederation of states (amphictyony) be located in Mexico.

Mexico's progress to greatness has been interrupted, however, by civil wars, foreign invasions, the loss of more than half its territory, and other calamities. In spite of these setbacks it is today one of the 13 most important countries of the 159 members of the United Nations (considering factors such as population, territory, and gross domestic product). Sixty years of political stability, a growing infrastructure, a relatively diversified economy, qualified technicians, and pride in its heritage, allow Mexico to face the future with confidence and to view the present crisis with a historical perspective which makes it seem minor in comparison to problems confronted successfully in the past.

Taking into account all these factors and its historical experience, Mexico feels that it has the legitimate right to exercise the full range of its political and economic options and that in order to do so it should adopt a policy of nondependence. However, proximity to the largest market in the world weighs heavily and has made Mexico gravitate toward it. The remoteness and weakness of Latin American markets, in contrast, have made it difficult, though not impossible, to create a structure which would enable it to benefit more from regional support. Although Mexico will continue to work toward Latin American integration, we cannot hope to solve our trade problems through this mechanism in the short term.

Consequently, we should consider the ways in which the future existence of a U.S.-Canadian common market might affect Mexico. Due to the proximity and importance of this process we cannot ignore it, even though we should try to take maximum advantage of other alternatives in the coming years. Such alternatives include: integrating Mexico into the trade flows of the Pacific Basin; increasing Mexican trade with Europe by taking advantage of our access to the North Atlantic; and expanding as much as possible Mexico's relations with the socialist countries, utilizing the most appropriate mechanisms of their centralized economies.

Mexico cannot afford to ignore the dynamic process of a United States-Canadian common market, only to be forced to react when faced with its consequences. Mexico must anticipate events and design a strategy best suited to its interests, which should be based on the following principles:

1. Mexico will never acquiesce to being a satellite or a dependent country. It will never sacrifice its freedom, dignity, or sovereignty.
2. It would be unthinkable to condemn Mexico to a state of permanent underdevelopment, or even to slow development, through an unsustainable idea of self-sufficiency bordering on autarky or in order to sustain the theoretical purity of certain foreign policy ideas. I believe foreign policy should be designed first and foremost according to national interest.
3. Although nothing must be placed above Mexico's national interest, in a well-designed foreign policy pursuit of these interests need not collide with basic principles.
4. Economic strength is normally accompanied by increased autonomy and an expanded range of options.
5. The challenge Mexico faces is to reconcile the apparently contradictory goals of autonomy of choice and action, on the one hand, and the achievement of the fastest possible economic development in the shortest possible time, on the other.

The main purpose of Mexico's foreign policy should be to establish the necessary conditions for the country to attain the greatness for which it is destined. Greatness will have been achieved, by my definition, when Mexico becomes:

- a country of which Mexicans and their descendants can be proud
- a country that provides social justice to its people because without it freedom and progress have no meaning

- a country that is prosperous, where Mexicans not only satisfy their basic needs but also have ample opportunities for personal and social advancement
- a country that is strong, capable of insuring its sovereignty
- a country that is respected for its adherence to principle, foreign policy success, and stature in the international community.

I have discussed the actual design of a foreign policy for Mexico elsewhere.[1] The purpose of this chapter is to establish the basis upon which Mexico can obtain a more beneficial relationship with the United States, taking advantage of our proximity while, at the same time, maintaining a policy of nondependence in our relations with it.

I begin by analyzing the meaning of dependence and interdependence and attempt to clarify my definition of nondependence. I go on to discuss the unequal relationship between Mexico and the United States and indicate some of the steps that should be taken in order to strengthen Mexico's position. Third, I review recent trends in both countries and how they create more strain in the bilateral relationship. Finally, I mention some of the basic elements on which a healthy and friendly relationship between the two countries should be based.

Before proceeding, I should emphasize my view that, in striving to achieve "conceptual integrity," Mexico should never get into a situation in which pursuit of conceptual integrity leads us to act against the national interest, much less sacrifice concrete objectives or benefits for the Mexican nation.

Analytic Framework

Most writings on U.S.-Mexican relations make frequent reference to the concepts of dependence and interdependence. In each case, the significance of the terms is biased by the ideology or political interests of the user. As a result, the two concepts have so many different connotations that they have almost lost all meaning.[2]

Precisely because of these conceptual problems, it is necessary to dwell for a moment on these overused terms in order to clarify the significance I attach to them in this chapter. I believe that dependence is a situation in which the economy of a country or countries is conditioned by the development and economic growth of other countries. Interdependence, in contrast, is characterized by the existence of such a closely linked bilateral or multilateral relationship that the development of the countries involved is mutually conditioned.

In both cases, there is an international division of labor based on comparative advantage that in a sense generates increased benefits.

However, in the case of a relationship of dependence, there is a situation of subordination that tends to perpetuate itself due to the unequal strength of the countries. An interdependent relationship, on the contrary, can only exist between equals; thus the distribution of benefits is equitable and the potential for both the interdependent countries to reap mutual benefits is increased.

In the case of dependence, decision-making is influenced greatly by external factors, whereas in an interdependent relationship there is a mutual influence on both foreign and domestic policies with no government exercising complete control over the other. Either dependence or interdependence results in the economies of the countries involved becoming very sensitive to changes in the international environment; and economic impulses are transmitted faster and more strongly.

In summary, dependence and interdependence are similar in that they both result from a growing network of closer bonds among nations. They differ in that, whereas interdependence is a relationship of equals, dependency exists between unequal countries. Interdependence, strictly speaking, means mutual dependence, and dependence means subjection or subordination. Some authors prefer the term asymmetric interdependence to dependence. I view this as a contradiction in terms, but its intuitive meaning is closer to the truth.[3]

Nations on the periphery of the industrialized economies cannot be considered part of the process of growing interdependence, as several authors have pointed out, because these nations were incorporated into the international economy in a subordinate role.[4] Therefore, it would be unrealistic to refer to a relationship of interdependence between Mexico and the United States. In fact the disparity between the two countries is not likely to disappear in the near future, and the gap between the levels of development in the two countries has widened in the last decade.

It should also be stressed that, although there is a close interrelation between economic dependence or interdependence and the limits of political autonomy, the interrelation and limits are not simple. In fact they frequently affect both countries in such complex ways that the results are difficult to predict, especially if we take into consideration other country-specific factors (such as, in the case of Mexico, our strong nationalism, our vigorous cultural identity, and the prestige of our foreign policy, among others).

There are several areas where Mexico is autonomous, and even in those areas where it is not it has more than one option. Additionally, the ties with the United States are in themselves a source of leverage. Most of the policies the United States could adopt that would go against Mexican interests, for example, could have repercussions within the United States and could provoke internal opposition. A recent example of this is the Simpson-Rodino Act. The law is being enforced with great flexibility due to the negative reactions of parts of the agricultural, industrial, and service sectors in the United States. At a more general level, it is in the best interest of the United States to have a friendly, prosperous, and stable neighbor, all of which limits its room for possible negative actions against Mexico.

Mexico's relative autonomy and the repercussions in the United States generated by the close interrelation of the two economies constitute, in my opinion, sufficient grounds for Mexico to opt for a third alternative, which I call "the politics of nondependence." I mean by this that Mexico should take the present political and economic reality into account, and design its policies with the objective of widening the range of options for action.

The politics of nondependence does not pursue autarky. A state of autarky is not only impossible but, as in the case of Burma after World War II, translates into economic backwardness and greater vulnerability in the long term.

From the point of view of Mexico, the search for nondependence consists of being able to exercise a greater number of political options and at the same time increase as much as possible the benefits derived from Mexico's geographical proximity to the United States. In other words, in its relationship with the United States, Mexico should strive to have the best of all worlds: on the one hand, the autonomy to make decisions based on its national interest and, on the other, the ability to increase the benefits which its proximity to the United States brings.[5]

To adopt a policy of nondependence Mexico must avoid the defeatist attitude that nothing can make a difference. For many years Mexico viewed the United States through a glass tinted by the theories of dependency elaborated during the 1950s and 1960s to explain the inequalities between the industrialized and the underdeveloped countries—inequalities which were, according to such theories, perpetuated by the international economic order. While very useful to explain certain aspects of the problems faced by the less developed countries, dependency theories are distorted in that they imply the absence of autonomy and decision-making power on the part of the dependent countries, as well as little control of their situation.[6] Dependency thought, to a certain extent, created a sense of helplessness that had a perverse effect on the relationship between Mexico and the United States by denying Mexico two important possibilities: Mexico's capacity to induce and negotiate improvements in its relations with the United States, and Mexico's own economic potential to develop.

An attempt on the part of Mexico to adopt a policy of nondependence may seem pretentious or even doomed to failure. This is a misconception. Numerous countries in the international community have, in fact, been able to adopt independent policies and defend the autonomy of their economic policies, in spite of being tightly linked to others in a position of dependence or close interdependence. An economic example is provided by Canada which, in spite of its tight economic relationship with the United States, has maintained relations with the People's Republic of China and Cuba, even during periods when the United States had trade embargoes against them.

An example in the area of defense matters is provided by France, which has maintained its autonomy notwithstanding its dependence on the North Atlantic Treaty Organization (NATO) for its effective protection. Another example is Finland which, despite the fact that it has a security treaty with the Soviet Union, has been able to define its policy of neutrality and widen the margins of its economic independence. Yet another example is Ireland. In spite of its close and unequal relationship with Great Britain, Ireland has managed to have an independent posture in such important matters as its neutrality during World War II and its opposition to the European Economic Community's economic sanctions against Argentina during the Malvinas War.

Quite obviously a policy of nondependence will not overlook the gradual and progressive strengthening of Mexico's economic base. Brazil and Algeria, for example, have wide margins of action precisely because of the structure of their economies and their access to multiple markets. Equally obviously, such a policy will not include an excessively active foreign policy unless it is accompanied by a solid internal base. Indonesia under Sukarno, Egypt under Nasser, and Ghana under Nkrumah provide instructive examples.[7]

In this context, it is worthwhile mentioning that the search for nondependence should not be understood as a policy of confrontation with United States. It is simply an attempt to defend Mexico's interests, increase its autonomy, and make an effort to close the development gap between the two countries.

Within this framework, we should analyze Mexican-U.S. relations without the limitations imposed by preconceived notions of dependency or interdependence. Mexico and the United States have several common interests and objectives while, at the same time, each is independent and autonomous. This should never be forgotten. The two countries have different historical backgrounds which have led them through different roads to growth and development. This constitutes yet another reason why we can be neither dependent nor interdependent on each other, but must be nondependent.

The Unequal Relationship Between Mexico and the United States

Several of the problems that affect the relationship between Mexico and the United States have become chronic and will not be completely solved until the basic structure of inequality which created them disappears. In other words, those problems will exist as long as there is a gap in the level of development between the two countries. There are several areas, however, in which the two countries can collaborate in creating a mutually beneficial relationship and relaxing present tensions.

In strictly economic terms, being a neighbor to the most important market in the world is an opportunity as well as a challenge for Mexico. It can also be a nightmare, however, insofar as it tends to leave Mexico excessively exposed to the fluctuations of the North American economy and protectionist trends in the United States, the effects of which are potentially disastrous for the Mexican economy. The United States is an important source of capital and technology for Mexico and it can also absorb some of Mexico's excess labor force and exports. In exchange, Mexico can provide some raw materials which, although available in other parts of the world, have the advantage of being cheaper and more accessible due to the proximity of the two countries.[8] At the same time, as Mexico's economy recovers, it may continue to be an important buyer of U.S. products. Even in the present crisis, it is worth remembering, Mexico is the third largest purchaser of U.S. goods.

The U.S. and Mexican economies are so intertwined, with so many factors linking them at different levels, that the whole relationship resembles a spider web. Some have considered it to be a symbiotic relationship that imposes constraints on both countries. However one may wish to see it, the relationship certainly entails a number of mutual interests which are always present whatever the negotiating process or policy decision.

In order to increase its autonomy under these circumstances, Mexico should, on the one hand, optimize its relationship with the United States and, on the other, diversify its economic relations with others. Optimizing its relationship with the United States means that Mexico should take advantage of the opportunities offered by the North American market without creating dependence on it. These two objectives are apparently contradictory because the more Mexico's trade is focused towards the United States, the more dependent the Mexican economy becomes. The dilemma can be solved by concentrating not on maximizing trade but on optimizing trade, in the sense of finding the right balance between increased trade with the United States and reduced dependence on it. Several factors have to be considered in order to identify this balance.

Special consideration should be given to the fact that if Mexico orients export production toward the U.S. market, it may be producing items that it will not be able to sell in other parts of the world, thereby propitiating even more dependence. Certainly not all exports can be produced to fit different markets, although in fact the process is being applied to oil exports.

Diversification is absolutely essential in a policy of nondependence in order to decrease the Mexican economy's vulnerability to the fluctuations of the North American economy. Mexico has access to many markets that have not yet been explored, and is in a privileged geographical location for trade and maritime transportation. The Pacific Basin, Western Europe, Latin America, and the socialist countries are particularly promising possibilities for increased trade in the medium to long term.

Another element is strengthening the internal market coupled with a greater capacity for self-sufficiency in order to avoid a trade deficit, especially in a period when there is an acute need for foreign currency due to Mexico's financial obligations.

In summary, for Mexico to improve its position in order to adopt policies of nondependence it should strengthen its internal market, increase its access to foreign markets, optimize its trade relationship with the United States, and take advantage of its geographical location to diversify its economic relations with other countries.

Recent Trends

During the past few years there has been a clear deterioration of the bilateral relationship, which can best be explained in the context of recent events. Both Mexico and the United States face difficult economic situations and have been affected by the problems and uncertainties of the international market. Without a doubt, these factors have altered the basis of understanding on which the relationship between the two countries functioned in the past.

The United States faces tremendous challenges and feels threatened by international competition, not only at the military level but at the economic one as well. It is no longer the undisputed leader of the world economy, having lost ground in both trade and finance. It cannot act as the "world banker" as it did in the past and has, therefore, lost a certain flexibility in managing the international economy according to its own interests.[9] The recent fall in the stock markets and the decline of the U.S. dollar are clear evidence of the weakening of the United States vis-à-vis the other industrialized countries.

These difficulties have made the United States extremely sensitive to the attitudes and policies of other countries and less tolerant of dissent, all of which has been reflected in the Mexican-U.S. bilateral relationship. The United States seems to have harsher reactions to policies that were previously accepted, a phenomenon that can be explained in part by the insecurity of a nation that has become conscious of its loss of power and the erosion of its hegemony. Other factors are also very important, among them the personality of the incumbent American president.

While the United States is particularly sensitive to matters relating to its national security, Mexico tends to react vigorously to anything that may be perceived as an intent to interfere in its internal affairs or to dominate it.

As Zbigniew Brzezinski has pointed out, Mexico and Poland are countries with justified grudges against their neighboring powers. In the past both were larger and more powerful, had more sophisticated cultures, and a more transcendent set of values than currently. Now they are at a disadvantage due largely to the military aggressions and the loss of territory they have suffered at the hands of their neighbors.[10]

Additionally, Mexican sensitivity vis-à-vis the United States is increased by the economic crisis originated largely by international instability and the policies of the industrialized countries, particularly the United States.

During the early 1980s, for example, the U.S. fiscal deficit and its tight monetary policy caused international interests rates to rise, which tripled the burden of servicing Mexico's foreign debt. This, coupled with the fall in the price of raw materials, brought about a crisis that halted Mexican economic growth throughout this decade. At the same time, as always when U.S. trade policy becomes more restrictive, Mexico is one of the countries to suffer the most.

In this connection I should underline the fact that Mexico has been excessively responsible in its attitude toward servicing its foreign debt; but it cannot continue to subject its citizens to decreasing living standards in order to do so. Mexico needs to grow at least 2%–3% over the rate of growth of its population if it is to continue servicing its foreign debt without causing undue sacrifice in order to do so.

In this context, there has been a radical change for the worse in the U.S perception of Mexico. From World War II until the late 1970s, Mexico was perceived in a generally favorable manner by North Americans. The way Mexico featured in comparison to other developing countries due to its political stability and sustained economic growth received the basic approval of the United States. In fact, Mexico was considered an example of what third world countries could achieve.

Due to this basically positive perception, the relationship between the two countries, though distant, was less strained than today. The United States tolerated foreign policy differences, including some of Mexico's independent positions (such as its opposition to the embargo against Cuba during the early 1960s). Although communications between the two countries were never as smooth flowing as would have been ideal, the generally positive perception of Mexico held by North Americans allowed room for negotiations.

Mexico's present economic crisis once again brought the country to the attention of the U.S. media after years of relative neglect. Numerous reports and articles about Mexico were published. These could have fostered a better understanding of the problems in both countries had they been written in a different spirit. But, quite to the contrary, news coverage tended to concentrate exclusively on the negative aspects of the Mexican situation.

There is a natural tendency in the media to highlight problems, since after all, good news is rarely news at all; but U.S. news reports have suddenly chosen to see Mexico as a place full of corruption, violence, and trafficking in drugs. It is as if the only news about the United States published in Mexico dealt with the U.S. drug addiction, the crimes of the underworld, and the large number of Reagan administration officials who have been involved in legal problems.

This negative perception has obviously influenced the way U.S. public opinion sees Mexico. It has also influenced government authorities, congress, businessmen, and even some Mexicans. It has hardened U.S. negotiating positions toward Mexico and has led to increased tensions between the two countries. On the Mexican side, it has created great resentment, and an atmosphere of distrust and misunderstanding that makes it even more difficult to communicate and augments the tensions inherent in the bilateral relationship.

Great confusion prevails in the United States about Mexico and its real possibilities, policies, and objectives. Certain groups have even ventured the opinion that Mexico is on the edge of a revolution. Although the U.S. media has been to a large degree responsible for these misperceptions, perhaps Mexico should share part of the responsibility due to its inability to communicate effectively with its northern neighbor.

A Look to the Future

In this context of increasing tensions in Mexican-U.S. relations, the 1980s have witnessed an increasing number of issues on the bilateral agenda that generate conflict. To the traditional problems of undocumented workers and trade, we have now to add the problems of Mexico's foreign debt, drug trafficking, and Mexico's position on certain international issues, particularly the conflict in Central America. Even some matters that are strictly internal to Mexico, such as the election process, are now points of disagreement.

In order not to muddle progress in our relations with an increasing number of problems, it seems indispensable to establish two basic premises on which a better relationship should be based:

1. We should recognize and respect the different interests derived from different historical experiences and economic development. Our interests need not necessarily coincide.
2. In order to foster a relationship conducive to mutual benefits in the long term, we should identify and develop areas of agreement or common interests, without overlooking the asymmetry between the two countries.

From the point of view of Mexico, it should be added that the United States should not pressure, much less intervene in Mexico's political life. Such action provokes a nationalist reaction that is frequently counterproductive to U.S. objectives and further translates into anti-yankee sentiment.

Respect of each country for the position of the other demands better communications. To be successful, any attempt to improve relations between Mexico and the United States must be based on better communication and more sophisticated mutual perceptions. These factors, subjective though they may be, are fundamental in the development of a better relationship. If communication fails or perceptions are distorted, serious problems may arise which can be expected to further strain the relationship; with good communication, in contrast, problems are simplified and solutions reached more easily.

My tenure as Ambassador to the United States led me to realize just how important communication is and what both countries can do to improve it.

The style that characterizes Mexican political discourse has contributed to make communication more difficult, since it tends to be baroque and full of hidden meaning, whereas the U.S. style is more direct. If Mexicans want to be understood, we must be prepared to use a style in accordance with the audience we address.

The United States is fundamentally a pragmatic country that bases its policies on concrete interests. Mexican foreign policy, on the other hand, seems to be oriented more toward the defense of principles than of its own interests. The two nations, therefore, speak different languages. If Mexico could make a more substantive effort to emphasize a straightforward connection between its principles and its interests when communicating with its neighbor, a better understanding might be fostered.

As far as the second basic premise on which the relationship between the two countries should be based, it should be noted that the strategies that both countries have adopted to confront their problems in the short term and to effect structural changes in their respective economies make it necessary to redefine the relationship itself. After all, Mexico is the third largest trading partner of the United States, and its most important supplier of oil; Mexicans constitute the largest group of tourists that visit the United States and 35% of Mexico's foreign debt is owed to the United States.

The quantitative importance of the bilateral exchange is such that both countries could benefit enormously from a better qualitative relationship based on mutual respect and acknowledgment of the asymmetry and differences as well as from the search for a more balanced relationship in the longer term.

In this sense, Mexico should consider carefully the implications of a North American "common market." It should study carefully from beginning to end similar examples such as the EEC and its implications for the countries that one way or another have been affected by it: the initially antagonistic position of Great Britain and the costs of such an attitude; the consideration given to countries with different degrees of development, such as Greece and Portugal; the costs and benefits of Norway's decision not to participate; as well as the alternatives of external links both bilaterally between countries and multilaterally through the European Association of Free Trade.

In any case, it would be useful for Mexico to reinforce our position with Canada for reasons of symmetry and balance with the United States. Mexico should also explore the possibility of formalizing some type of coordination of with Canada and Japan, taking into consideration that in spite of differences among them, Mexico, Canada, and Japan are the three principal trading partners of the United States.

Finally, Mexico is part of the Pacific Basin which should also give it a special position in that region.

Needless to say, the more diversified Mexico's trade and economic relations are, the stronger will be its position vis à-vis the United States and Canada. For that reason, Mexico should continue to strengthen its relationship with Western Europe in the short term since this offers Mexico an immediate alternative by reducing dependence on the North American market. It should also continue to strengthen its relations with the socialist countries and with Latin America and gain the support of the North American population of Mexican origin.

Only under these conditions—a relationship that respects differences, the support of other U.S. trading partners (mainly Canada and Japan), and the strengthening of Mexico's position within the United States with the support of the population of Mexican origin—will Mexico be able to improve its situation vis-à-vis the U.S.-Canadian common market.

Final Comments

Recognition by Mexico of the importance of our relationship with the United States does not mean that such a relationship should determine Mexican foreign policy and even less our domestic policies. Bismarck assumed a similar position: he designed Prussian policy toward England, France, Holland, and the Balkans in accordance with Prussian interests but taking always into account a possible Russian reaction.[11]

It is obvious that despite our geographical proximity, Mexico and the United States are two nations with our own needs, interests, and objectives. Our countries are at different stages of development and, therefore, have different interests. The real possibilities of improving the bilateral relationship should be accepted and respected by both parties. It does not matter if we do not agree on everything as long as we respect our mutual right to disagree.

In recent times, Mexico has implemented economic reforms that could favor a better relationship, such as the opening of its markets to international trade, the improvement of its public finances, and the privatization of unproductive State enterprises. Mexico has also cooperated more than its share in the fight against the drug traffic and in the search for a shared solution to the border problems. It seems, however, that these efforts have not been entirely recognized by the United States.

A new stage in the relationship is beginning, which could bring new opportunities for its improvement, with benefits accruing to both sides. Mexico and the United States will elect new presidents almost at the same time, which will mean new styles of government and different perspectives.

Mexico is at the threshold of a new model of development of export-induced growth. In order for Mexico to overcome its problems, it needs to find once again its path to development and economic growth. To a large extent, our success will depend on whether we can improve our access to the North American market and find new opportunities in other parts of the world.

Mexico and the United States have come a long way together. There have been moments of conflict and moments of agreement. There is still a long way to go.

Notes

1. José Juan de Olloqui, *México Fuera de México*, UNAM, Mexico City, 1980, pp. 11–22; *Consideraciones sobre dos Gestiones: Servicio Exterior y Banca*, Porrúa, Mexico, 1986, pp. XI–XXXI; "El Diseño de la Política Exterior de México: Sus Objetivos y Dos Casos Específicos," *Informe Sobre las Relaciones Mexico-Estados Unidos*, vol. 1, no. 2, Centro de Estudios Económicos y Sociales del Tercer Mundo, Mexico, February-June 1982, pp. 185–295.

2. For a discussion of the concept of interdependence and its semantic evolution see Carlos Rico, "Las Relaciones Mexicano-Norteamericanas y los Significados de Interdependence," *Foro Internacional*, no. 74, October-December 1978, vol. XIX, no. 2, p. 258.

3. de Olloqui, *op. cit.*, pp. XII–XIII.

4. Mario Ojeda, "Mexico and United States Relations: Interdependence or Mexico's Dependence," Carlos Vasquez and Manuel Garcia y Griego, editors, *Mexican-U.S. Relations, Conflict and Convergence*, University of California, Los Angeles, 1983.

5. José Juan de Olloqui, "Mexico frente a la Política de Estados Unidos en América Latina," *México y sus Vecinos: Estados Unidos, Guatemala y Belice*, PRI Foreign Affairs Commission, Cuaderno 8 de la Política Exterior, Mexico, 1983.

6. Some of the most important representatives of this theory are Fernando Cardos, Theotonio Dos Santos, Raul Prebisch, Oswaldo Sunkel, and Helio Jaguaribe.

7. de Olloqui, *Consideraciones*.

8. *Ibid.*

9. See Robert Triffin, "Correcting the World Monetary Scandal," in *Challenge*, January-February, 1986; "The International Accounts of the United

States and their impact upon the rest of the world," *Banca Nazionale de Lavoro Quarterly Review,* no. 152, March 1985, pp. 15–30.

10. See Zbignew Brzezinski, *Game Plan, How to Conduct the U.S.- Soviet Context,* Atlantic Monthly Press, Boston and New York, 1986, pp. 85 ss.

11. de Olloqui, *México Fuera de México,* p. 14.

Index